ITERATE
AND
OPTIMIZE

Optimize your creative business for profit

SEAN PLATT
JOHNNY B. TRUANT
WITH DAVID WRIGHT

ITERATE AND OPTIMIZE

By Sean Platt &
Johnny B. Truant

For Robin and Cindy, who stuck with us
while things were less than optimized.

"Write. Publish. Repeat" Conversations

The Smarter Artist, #1 Amazon Bestselling Authors, Podcasters, ...

 (12)

Write. Publish. Repeat. Conversations is a 30—plus-part instructional video series (retail price $49) in which the authors elaborate on the cutting-edge insights learned in self-publishing since releasing the book version of their #1 best-selling guide, *Write. Publish. Repeat.* in 2013.

Visit the link below to get the *Write. Publish. Repeat. Conversations* course for FREE!

SterlingAndStone.net/repeaters

ITERATE
AND
OPTIMIZE

Is This the Right Book for You?

Hi there. I'm Johnny, and I'll be the written *voice* in these pages. You're holding a book that I co-wrote with my partners, Sean and Dave. (Their contributions are equally strong, though I'm the mouthpiece.) But contrary to what you might expect, **the first thing we'd like to do as you hold our book is to suggest that *Iterate and Optimize* might not be right for you.**

Because here's the thing: We set out to write a book that would apply to all creative entrepreneurs. "Doesn't matter if you're a writer or a musician or a moviemaker! What's in these pages will equally apply to all of you!"

Well, that's not how things turned out.

This book is all about the changes we made to our small indie publishing business, Sterling & Stone, over the course of two years to turn it into a much larger (but still fairly small) indie publishing business. It's about how we added new book imprints and genres and product lines. It's about how we ratcheted the term *solo authorpreneur* up until it grew into *little empire*. How we strategized bigger, optimized our writing systems to tell better stories, hired people to help us grow, diversified our work into multiple media (audio, paperback, hardback, foreign rights, surely combining those soon into Frankensteins like foreign audio), how we built our tribe, bought better advertising, and leveraged social media. How we diversified into software and app development and are now turning our eyes toward scriptwriting, TV, and film. It's even about how we created a series from scratch with the specific purpose of engineering a hit that would (and did, and continues to) generate a lot of money in book sales.

We will mention places where non-authors can apply what we do (and I still think there's a lot of that; everyone should build a community and can benefit from a high-converting email autoresponder series, for instance), but who are we kidding? **This is a publishing book … and one for entrepreneurially minded authors, at that.**

Throughout this book, there are places where we'll point out ways that non-writer creative entrepreneurs can apply what we're teaching. We've also interviewed a bunch of creative entrepreneurs from non-writing disciplines — as this book's case studies — to round out our otherwise writerly focus. But for the most part, the provided examples are those of Sterling & Stone: our own company. *That's* the business we know. *Those* are the specific, brass-tacks examples we have for how to take your business to the next level.

Because that's where we're coming from; the approach we've taken with *Iterate and Optimize* narrows this book's audience. The only way we could have kept this book *for everybody* would have been to dilute the hell out of it. To remove all of our specific examples. To make this book not just applicable to any creative entrepreneur but to any writer and publisher as well.

We think that by reading about what we've done to vastly improve our business's growth and profits, you'll learn a ton that you can apply in your own publishing business, even if you're working solo. But on the other hand, chances are there are things in this book that won't apply to you. At all.

If you aren't going to run a five-figure crowdfunding campaign, the bit about our Kickstarter optimizations won't be relevant to your business.

If you don't plan to launch a podcast network, your eyes may glaze over when you get to the section about Sterling & Stone FM.

We considered pulling out anything we thought wouldn't apply specifically to indie publishers. Then, beyond that, we considered pulling out anything that wouldn't apply to *the average* indie publisher. If we had, we could have created a middle-of-the-road book that might have applied almost entirely to you, dear reader. But we didn't. We figured there was still a lot of value in the more niche book you're holding … even if it meant appealing to a smaller readership.

So yes, it's possible this is the wrong book for you — and if you feel strongly that it is, we'd rather you return it now than end up disappointed. Accordingly, we hereby promise there's a bunch of stuff in these pages that you'll never have any use for. Only read on if you want to see what we've done and take what applies … then leave the rest. Or, as *we'd* do with a book like this: *Read it all for inspiration whether it applies or not, just to see how another successful company does business.* The concepts, if not the specifics, are universal.

Similarly, **if you're brand new to publishing and haven't yet read this book's predecessor *Write. Publish. Repeat.*, you'll definitely want to close this book and read that one instead — or at least first.** After you've read *WPR*, you can decide if you want to know more about how we do what we do and how you might apply it to yourself — and then, if the answer is yes, you can read *Iterate and Optimize.*

So that's the deal. We haven't stripped this book down. We haven't removed stuff that's highly specific to Sterling & Stone but might not be applicable to certain readers. Amy, our Studio Manager, called this "a manual for how to build a company exactly like ours," and while that's a bit tongue-in-cheek, it's still far more accurate than to claim this as a how-to guide for everyone.

So, are you still with us after all that?

Awesome! We promise to give you all of what we've promised above … plus a whole lot more than you'll ever need.

(SARCASTIC SIDE NOTE: This means that by proceeding, you've waiving your right to say, "Man, these guys won't shut up about their specific business!" Because hey, that's what this book *is*!)

Welcome to the advanced course. We promise to overdeliver.

So with that out of the way, let's Iterate and Optimize together.

it·er·ate

ˈi-tə-ˌrāt/

verb

To do shit better each time around

op·ti·mize

ˈäp-tə-ˌmīz/

verb

To get more from the shit you've already got

Why "Iterate and Optimize"?

You've found this book in a store or on a digital storefront. You almost certainly know who we are, because as mentioned in the introduction, our book *Write. Publish. Repeat.* is a necessary prerequisite for this one. But maybe you don't listen to the *Self-Publishing Podcast*, which forms the cornerstone of our public presence. If that's so, it means you haven't heard us talking endlessly about *iterating* and *optimizing* — two words our listeners are probably sick of by now.

So I'll bet you're wondering why we chose the title we did, because it's kind of a strange one.

The reason — as with most things at our company, Sterling & Stone — comes down to story.

Some companies write mission statements. We do that. Some hold crazy team-building retreats where they climb rock walls and ride zip lines. We haven't done that yet, though I'm sure it's coming. But beyond those things, we like to choose a *word of the year*. Each year, we decide on a term that represents where we most want to go, then spend the year actualizing that word with our day-to-day decisions.

In 2013, our word was **Produce.** (That's the verb, not the section in the supermarket.) And so, in 2013, we spent most of our time *producing* new work. We wrote stories until our fingers about fell off. We didn't pay attention to much of anything else, including marketing and sales. Nothing was coherent or coordinated. It was a deluge of words and pages. By year's end, Sean and I alone had published over 1.5 million words, in addition to those that came from the Sean/Dave pairing.

We'd made livings as full-time fiction authors in 2013, but we'd done a lot wrong. We wanted to do better in 2014, but the thought of going back through our existing catalog to make it more harmonious was daunting — and worse, doing so would have forced us to turn our backs on production, thus murdering our young company's momentum. We had to keep producing, but to do it without looking in the rearview mirror.

We decided to spend the year learning to do better on *future* projects rather than revamping old ones. And so 2014's word became **Iterate**: *to do the right things over and over as you move forward* (and, in the Sterling & Stone definition, to do them a bit better each time, incrementally stacking successes).

We didn't go back to improve the descriptions for our already-published books during the *iterate* year. We simply wrote better descriptions for our new books, getting a little better with each go-round.

We didn't try to make our existing catalog more coherent. Instead, we focused on writing books that fit more logically into what we already had, building coherence bit by bit as we went along.

We couldn't make the writing of past books flow more smoothly, but we could improve our collaborative (and solo-writing) processes going forward. So our pre-planning (a process we call *beats*) improved dramatically during 2014. We learned how to write better stories faster … again, advancing only an inch at a time.

Iterating kept us improving while maintaining our momentum — in our opinion, two essential things for any young business just finding its feet.

By 2015, Sterling & Stone was starting to do quite well. We were still young and immature as a company, but no longer starving artists. We needed leverage more than anything. We needed to maintain our momentum yet again — while using what we'd already done to earn us even better results and get that back catalog from 2013 and earlier working harder rather than just sitting there.

So in 2015, we decided our word would be **Optimize**. That meant getting more juice from the same squeeze: making our existing books more compelling for readers, increasing conversion, finding ways to broaden our audience, getting more traffic, and generally improving everything we were doing so we could get more out of it.

It was a large and daunting task that made a world of difference.

We commissioned around one hundred new book covers in 2015. We rewrote our product descriptions. We tweaked our keywords, shuffled series, created pen names, and planned coherent, line-spanning promotions. We talked to experts and paid for consultation. We delved into Facebook (advertising and simply using it), which was something we'd been ignoring. We hired an audio producer to improve our current podcasts, then launched seven new ones. In the past, we'd launched podcasts without fanfare, just so we could ship like madmen. But in 2015 we did so more elegantly, and those new podcasts all hit iTunes's coveted New and Noteworthy list and broadened our audience with every new show.

So why is this book called *Iterate and Optimize*?

At the end of 2013, we wrote a best-selling indie publishing guide that you have (unless you've ignored our twice-stated advice) already read. It had a three-word title — *Write. Publish. Repeat.* — that could have been condensed to that year's single word: *Produce*. WPR was all about *producing* and writing your ass off — a shoot first, aim later approach to success through brute force, because sheer prolificness couldn't *help* but get followers of this advice in front of readers.

This book, by contrast, is about what we've done in the two years that followed that time of Writing, Publishing, and Repeating — or, perhaps for you, about *what comes next.* After you've made a lot of whatever you intend to sell (books and other book-related stuff, for most of you), what can you do to sell it better?

Iterate and Optimize is about two main things: incrementally improving what you do in ways that add up while continuing to produce (*iterating*) and getting more out of what you already have (*optimizing*). It's about being more elegant and effective — getting more done with less effort, selling more of your assets, increasing revenue, and growing faster than you ever have.

So let's get to it.

P.S: I know people will ask, so here's the answer: 2016's word is **Parlay.** Producing, iterating, and optimizing has made Sterling & Stone quite profitable and has birthed a lot of non-monetary wins: strategic partnerships with big players, a network of popular podcasts, a first-of-its-kind story-planning app, and much more. So the way we see it, when you're winning, you should leverage those wins — not gambling to *win big or go broke trying*, but sensibly and logically using the ground you've gained, thus *parlaying* those wins into bigger victories.

(Maybe 2017's word will be **Relax.** But I kind of doubt it.)

Who We Are and Why You'd Ever Care

This book has three authors: Sean Platt, Johnny B. Truant, and David Wright. (To keep things readable, all "I's" and "me's" refer to Johnny, the guy who wrote the first draft, speaking on all our behalf.) Together, we're the founders of Sterling & Stone: a story studio whose primary business is publishing books, podcasting, telling stories in their many forms, speaking, and supporting artists and creative entrepreneurs through education and software. But our primary foci will change over time because we never stop evolving — which just so happens to be the point of this book.

You almost certainly already know who we are because you're one weird duck if you've read this far not knowing us at all despite several warnings to bone up on our other stuff first. But we'll introduce ourselves briefly anyway because the introduction has changed since 2013 ... and because this time, we've added the *why you'd care* element. Which matters.

As of this writing, Sterling & Stone has between six and seven million published words distributed across eight publishing imprints (or product lines, if you prefer that way of thinking). Several of our series are best sellers while others are still relatively undiscovered. Most of our written work is fiction, but we do have a single nonfiction imprint — the one that contains this book — called *The Smarter Artist.* We host a popular flagship podcast called the *Self-Publishing Podcast* plus a suite of others in our Sterling & Stone FM Network. We've recently sent a groundbreaking app into development and are soon moving into author website services. We speak professionally and have begun writing screenplays, though those parts of our business are, as of now, relatively under-optimized (that's what iterative improvement is for!). We also run a mastermind of high-grossing, well-connected creative entrepreneurs and will hold our first large, live conference in March of 2016, with ambitious plans to scale it larger in subsequent years.

Whew. Almost done. And I promise there's a point coming.

The last thing I'll mention before getting to the *why you'd care* part of this introduction: We've successfully run two rather large crowdfunding campaigns on Kickstarter, both for things nobody would think it sensible for authors to do.

The first, called *Fiction Unboxed,* was a *writing performance* (Sean's daughter called it a "concert for writing") that our podcast audience requested so they could peek inside our prolific writing process. We fully funded that campaign in eleven hours, set some records, then fulfilled the project by writing a full-length book from scratch — in thirty days, while everyone watched. The second crowdfunding campaign was for a story-planning app called StoryShop, which bears the tagline *Better Stories Faster.* That one is in the development phase as of this writing, so its own story is still being written.

Now: Why would you, reading this book, ever care about anything I just said?

Well, you might not. It's possible you think we're braggarts who like to talk about ourselves. (If you do, you're in good company. We've certainly heard that before.) But I'm articulating the scope of our business for a simple, specific reason:

We want you to understand that although we have got a lot going on, we didn't build our Rome in a day. We're three guys who started from nothing then iteratively improved (and optimized) what we were doing every single day.

Let's turn back the clock.

In early 2012, I (Johnny) had no published books, no earnings from storytelling, no podcasts, no friends in the business, and no idea that I'd one day make an excellent living as a fiction author even though I'd dreamed of it since I was a kid. Sean and Dave were doing well with their first-of-its-kind serial, *Yesterday's Gone,* but even *YG* was barely a year old. Sean still had a lucrative *real job* writing copy and was bankrolling their fledgling fiction business.

There are eight of us at Sterling & Stone today. Only the three partners are full-time, and we still have many staff holes left to plug (not to mention wrangling the systems we do have), but we've come a long way from just being three guys who were winging it. In early 2012, the company only existed on paper, and in a totally different form. Today, we do a lot of diverse and (we think) awesome stuff. We make good money. But not long ago, none of this existed.

Little by little, we built our careers from scratch. By continuing to take the same basic steps, we expect to grow much larger in the coming years (in evolutionary leaps if not literal size) than we are today. If you're where we used to be and follow some of the same strategies we followed, you can do the same.

We live by a few rules. Might as well get familiar with them now:

• Persistence is more important than perfection. If at first you don't succeed, it doesn't matter as long as you always try, try again.

• Small improvements, made consistently, add up.

• You cannot fail unless you quit. What most people call *failures* are merely unsuccessful experiments. Failures are bumps on the road as long your story remains a work in progress.

• You can always do better with what you already have — and often, it's much smarter to find ways to do so than to invest time and money trying something entirely new as your next *one sure thing*.

• And most importantly, **being *good* doesn't matter nearly as much as being *slightly better than yesterday*.**

The rest of this book will explore the ways in which we turned tiny, non-intimidating steps into big wins — and how you can, too.

How This Book Is Organized

We've arranged this book in four primary sections:

In Part I, we'll ask you to do some inventory taking and self-assessment, necessary to lay a solid foundation for improving your creative business. Not to be too simplistic, but here's the most obvious of the Part I considerations: *Do you ac-*

tually have anything to iterate and optimize? In the extreme case ("No, I'm still a bricklayer and do nothing creative; can you guys tell me how to improve my storytelling profits?"), you should maybe stop reading this book and actually create something. But most of you will be somewhere in the middle — between zero and where you ultimately want to be. In that case, taking stock, assessing yourself and your goals, and creating a game plan is an essential first step. We'll cover those pieces in Part I.

In Part II, we'll lead by example, telling you about everything that Sterling & Stone iterated and optimized in our business in the two years following our period of mad production. This is the biggest section. Most of it will be in-the-trenches relevant for writers and indie authors. But as promised in the first introduction, there will *for sure* be stuff in here that doesn't reflect your experience (or even your ambitions) even if you're a full-time publisher. One of the most consistent questions people ask us is of the form, "How do you do XYZ at Sterling & Stone"? This book is our answer, given in as much detail as we could stand. It's very comprehensive. So if you run across sections that don't interest you, feel free to skip them. But we think there are still nuggets (reasoning, big-picture strategy) in *every* section for readers like the three of us tend to be: those who are interested in business for the sake of business, since many things are universal, regardless of the product or service being rendered.

We'll also tell you how we marketed and advertised our catalogue (useful to anyone who sells stuff); how we improved our structure, flow, and organization (useful to anyone who works with others and/or could benefit from improving their structure, flow, and organization); and how we formed new strategic partnerships. We'll talk about how we improved our podcasting enough to consistently attract iTunes's New and Noteworthy attention and used that platform to accelerate many of the things we were already doing (i.e., podcasting as a time saver versus our old, less effective, time-intensive ways of working and broadcasting every week "just to have a podcast").

In this section, we'll also discuss social media, crowdfunding, building product funnels, growing our email list, pre-optimizing a book series as a way to ignite our *other* series, what we learned about how people buy (this section could be called "Let's Be Honest: If Your Book Cover is Great, Your Book Will Still Sell Even if It's Shit, at Least until the Reviews Come In"), how we hired new team members and shuffled them to fit into the jobs they did best, and many, *many* more business lessons we learned so you can get smarter faster than we did.

Then, in Part III, we'll give you some steps you can take right now to iterate and optimize your way to a better and/ or more profitable creative business. Don't tell Dave because he hates everyone and thinks that nothing good ever comes from anything and that nobody ever really improves, but we also think of this as the motivational section. Because while it's possible that you'll read Part II and get fired up to start improving your business in ways siphoned out and adapted from our examples, you may get overwhelmed. We do a ton of stuff, and there's a lot of nitty gritty — and even though we warned you it'd be comprehensive, some of you eager beavers will try to microanalyze it all. So Part III, by contrast, is more grounding. It encourages you to forget *us* and all we do. It's about some things *you* can do *right now*, wherever you are.

Finally, in Part IV, we'll introduce you to successful Smart Artists who've iterated and optimized their own businesses and the lessons they've learned by doing so. You can call these "Case Studies" if you're boring, but we prefer to think of them as "Success Stories from the *Self-Publishing Podcast* SuperFriends."

The interviews we did in the back of *Write. Publish. Repeat.* were popular with readers, so we wanted to do them again. You'll see some familiar, book-world names here if you've read *WPR's* interviews — C.J. Lyons and Joanna Penn — as well as some new authors and non-authors alike, like Julie Huss, Tucker Max, Danny Iny, Tara Jacobson, and Steve Kamb.

We're mixing and matching new with previously featured items for two main reasons. One is so you can see how the people you may have first met in *Write. Publish. Repeat.* have evolved their ways of working since. The second is that we've simply met some new, amazing people since *WPR*, and we think you should know them, too. And then there's the myopia reason, too. If you only study authors and publishers to learn about your authoring and publishing business, you'll end up thinking too narrowly, believing that the way things are done now is the way they should, for the most part, always be done. Adding these non-writers breaks that paradigm and lets you see other options. Business tends to be business, so we wanted to include companies and individuals that approach their creative issues in different ways than you may have seen.

As with any nonfiction book, you can certainly skip around and go directly to the sections you want to read most — especially if you encounter a section that you don't feel applies to you. But the way we'd do it (and this is just a suggestion, so feel free to ignore it) is to read this book all the way through. It does tell a story, after all.

Let's begin.

PART I:
KNOW THYSELF (AND THINE OUTCOMES)

Pause the Cassette Now

When I was in my teens, my mom had all sorts of self-improvement audio programs that kicked around in the footwells of our family cars. A few were sort of wishy-washy and even New Age, but many of those programs were about business and money — things, in other words, that a young and entrepreneurial Johnny was very interested in.

Denis Waitley could tell me about *The Psychology of Winning*? Hey, I liked winning.

Zig Ziglar promised to *See You at the Top*? Cool; that's where I wanted to go.

I could learn about *Ultimate Power* from Anthony Robbins? That was tempting …

And, wait: Robert Allen could tell me how to have *Multiple Streams of Income*? SIGN ME THE HELL UP!

But there were always sections in those audiobooks where the narrator asked me to "pause the cassette now" (yes, *cassette*) and do something. Like making a list of my strengths, weaknesses, aspirations, or goals. Those parts were annoying. I just wanted to get to the later parts where they told me how to make money. Or possibly *How to Win Friends and Influence People*. So I hung in there and let the tapes play through the pauses allotted for me to act.

"I know you're not pausing the tape, so seriously … pause it now," Tony Robbins would tell me.

But I was sixteen. So fuck that. He couldn't tell me what to do.

Well, this chapter is a lot like the sections I hated in all those audio programs. It's no longer 1992; if you're listening to the audio here you can just skip forward a few tracks instead of waiting me out like I did to Tony. If you're reading, it's even easier to pass over this chapter and get to *the good stuff*.

Don't do that. Seriously.

We're going to ask you three questions in the following sections:

Who are you?
What are your strengths and weaknesses?
What do you want?

And you, like sixteen-year-old me, might think you can answer those questions so easily that there's no point in my asking them. You're you; you're good at X but not good at Y (which you can farm out or ignore); you want to sell the film rights to your book … or whatever.

But take it from a guy who did it wrong: *You want to take the time to know, plan, and set the stage before screwing up in a way that won't feel like folly until it's too late.* You want to think it out from all angles, which is what we'll help you do in the following pages.

I thought I was a kid who liked academics because I mistook default trajectory for intentional momentum. I graduated college *summa cum laude* and began a PhD in molecular genetics because that's what someone like me was supposed to do. That mistake cost me two years and a few months of panic attacks before I got my head straight and started over, moving down the creative entrepreneur's path I'm so happy to be on now.

I thought I wanted to make money. I did, but it turned out that income was secondary to variety, happiness, and fun. (Ask my wife about this. During our leanest years, I turned down all sorts of sane, profitable ventures because they bored me. Robin *LOVED* the way I walked away from money and security over and over again … but to her credit she *did* like it when I wasn't in a deep depression.) That mistake cost me a lot, too. Specifically, it cost me more panic attacks and a bankruptcy. Ironically, I got into financial trouble because I *thought* I wanted monetary success more than I actually did.

I won't keep beating this dead horse (or dead unicorn, except that we all know they're immortal and only get angrier when you beat them). You get the idea: at any stage, it's easy to assume we all know our starting points and our aspirations so well that we needn't bother asking, but that's rarely true.

We get hypnotized by life. We go on autopilot. We start to think we're after something just because we were chasing it yesterday — which, of course, happened because we wanted it the day before.

The path of iteration and optimization is like following a route on your personal map. But our GPS can get busted through the process of living life. And as anyone on a trip will tell you, trying to reach a destination if you're unsure (or flat-out wrong) about the starting point is a great way to get lost or drive into a ditch.

One of the things we say most often on the *Self-Publishing Podcast* when people ask us about a tactic or strategy is, "Know your outcome." For instance, we like our books to be available on as many platforms as possible. But if we have certain specific outcomes in mind, *going wide* onto all platforms might be the worst thing we could do.

Know your outcome.

Know your starting point as well as you possibly can.

Truly *know thyself*, and you'll get to where you want to go much faster.

Skip the following sections (like I skipped Tony's prodding) at your own risk.

CHAPTER ONE:
Who Are You?

I recently met someone who could write twenty-two thousand words in a day (good words, not crap) but didn't think that was anything special. She was down on her writing, not realizing it was a superpower.

One of the smartest, most creatively minded people I know doesn't think he's very intelligent.

Dave shits on much of his own work, including his own *Walking Dave* podcast. And yet fans love him to pieces, and his podcast is arguably the most popular in our new network.

All the time, I meet people who are clearly one thing (talented, smart) but have been conditioned to believe they are something else. I already told you my story in the introduction: I graduated first in my high school class, so clearly I thought I must be an intellectual whose life should be spent in a lab, counting fruit flies. (Literally.)

Most of the time, it's not our fault that we misunderstand who we are. Sometimes, we simply drift down the river of *supposed to* on our own. But sometimes, parents have identities for us that we don't carry for ourselves. Obvious examples abound:

gay people told they're straight, kids shoved toward being football stars because Dad's life deserves a second round, legacies groomed to take over a family business they want nothing to do with. My own father, who makes his living as a painter (art, not houses), was shoehorned into a career as an executive because he was told — and then came to believe — that doing so was more "respectable" and "proper" than the flighty life of an artist.

Here's a fun example: My mom doesn't like it when I swear, and I find myself wanting to keep her away from ventures like the *Self-Publishing Podcast*. I discourage her from reading most of my books and try to hide anything with a sex scene.

Why? I'm almost forty motherfucking years old.

But in my head, I'm still a kid. In my head, I'm still living by rules and expectations that are long dead, long obsolete. And hell, I'm one of the lucky ones. My mom flinched when I quit grad school, but she didn't judge or protest. My dad is half anarchist and was behind me when I wanted to leave college years before. Both have always encouraged me to follow my muse and passions in life. But like I said, I was lucky.

I don't want to turn this section into a personal development seminar, so I'll move on from all of this uncomfortable growing-up stuff. But before I do, let me say a few last things.

An artist-entrepreneur must be driven. So ask yourself: *Are you?* Do you give up easily, or do you forge boldly ahead even if it seems like you're failing? There's no right answer; stubborn refusal to back down and quit is the reason Sean and I both made it in this business — but that same dogged bullheadedness dragged our families through hell along the way. I had a bankruptcy, as I mentioned. Sean lost his house. Both of our wives have had many sleepless nights filled with panic because of who and how we are. We're proud of what we've done. But we're not thrilled that we did those things to our loved ones.

You need to be selectively arrogant to be an artist-entrepreneur. You might think you're shy, but it's still egotistic (or perhaps simply proud) to feel that your work is deserving of public attention. It might be hard for you to put a book or movie out into the world, but if you manage to do it, you're arrogant in the way I mean. You're saying that someone should pay for — or at least pay attention to — that thing you've created. Even a book released for free carries a bit of me-first bravado because you're asking readers to spend something more precious than money: their time.

Before you begin considering ways to iterate and optimize your work, you'll want to run through a self-assessment that can help you see your creative business with fresh eyes. Identify yourself multiple ways, and grow from your responses. Your first answer might only be rehashing what you've come to believe about yourself, and it might not be true. *Keep asking.* Keep wondering if you're telling the truth or regurgitating learned bullshit.

You might say: *I'm great at writing thrillers, but I could never write a romance. I don't have the depth of emotion to pull it off.* But is that true? Or is it what circumstances have led you to believe?

Let's stick with a theme, sliding from romance to erotica. What if you really want to sex it up but tell yourself that nice people don't talk or write that way? What if you feel ashamed — because of parents, friends, church, whatever? *That kind of writing is for dirty girls, but I'm a good girl,* you might tell yourself. And in this case, I'd ask you to challenge a double-layer assumption. The first is that answer's truth: Are you *sure* you're a good girl? But the real question is deeper: Who told you what's *dirty* and what's *good*, and why do you believe it? In cases like that, your judgments aren't usually your own. If you want to write erotica but think it's dirty, I'll bet almost anything you didn't decide it was dirty alone. Someone told you that, and you believed it.

So: Who are you?

Are you a determined person? A positive person? A loud or a quiet person? Would you rather have artistic freedom or financial security? Are both an absolute must? Are you a fast writer? An intuitive creator? Do you trust your instincts or rely on convention? I recently heard an interview with filmmaker Robert Rodriguez wherein he explained the "brilliant style and voice" people attributed to his first film, *El Mariachi*: In truth, he cut the movie like he did because the film he used was too expensive for more than one take per scene. Are you that kind of filmmaker, or does the idea of doing things *wrong* paralyze you? Are you bold or timid?

Whatever you believe about most of the questions above, your knee-jerk answer is probably wrong. If you think you're too timid to buck convention, that's probably because you haven't learned to be bold. If you think you're not instinctual, that's probably because you've always preferred to follow a plan. And if you think you're not brave, that might just be because nobody's pointed out that bravery is supposed to accompany fear, not happen amid unbridled optimism.

The point isn't to say that you can be whatever you want, that you can talk yourself into the ideal artist-entrepreneur personality through sheer will. The point is to question your assumptions. Keep asking until you get genuine answers rather than regurgitating what your high school guidance counselor told you about yourself and what you'd probably be.

In the end, you're going to reach conclusions about who you truly are right now. Your job is to uncover the truth, not to change things right away. Because remember, we're trying to find the starting point on the map so that we can begin.

So: Are you more introverted or extroverted? If you're somewhat of an introvert, that's something you need to know. Every *Smarter Artist* must speak to fans and customers, but introverts may choose to do it through better author's notes and solid email communication rather than in-person networking and videos that make them uncomfortable.

Are you verbal or quiet? It's a big joke among us that Sean never stops talking. The fact that he knows that about himself completely changed our company's direction and the format of our website. Originally, Sterling & Stone was writing blog posts.

But because Sean and I are highly verbal, we changed our blog into a podcast network. That way, we could talk instead of writing, and save the written word for our stories.

Are you a niche person or a squirrel? Among our trio, Dave is the former, and Sean and I are the latter. His writing all rests in a similar tone, with slight variations inside a single genre. Dave writes horror, dark sci-fi, dark fantasy — basically anything dark where hope is lost and children end up in jeopardy. But whereas Dave wants only to paint in shades of gray, Sean and I want to use every color of the rainbow. The two of us write in wildly different genres, from sci-fi to action to westerns to literary mind-benders to young adult fantasy. There are even a few genres so divergent from our core work that we had to slip those books into pen names: irreverent comedy written under the name Max Power and a few romances that were published under Lexi Maxxwell. Sean loves writing for children and does so under the name Guy Incognito.

I could go on and on, but this is the sort of personal inventory you'll want to take — then acknowledge as worth heeding. If Dave forced himself to write outside of horror and darkness, he'd be uncomfortable. But on the flip side, if Sean and I forced ourselves to stick to *any* single genre, we'd be miserable. You have to be happy and have fun, or your art will show the inverse. You must operate with full knowledge of *who you are* rather than *who you've been told you're supposed to be.*

If you believe you're not creative even though you clearly are, and if you believe succeeding is somehow taking something away from someone else (and hence you should do it in secret, if at all), it's probably because the people around you believe those things — about you, themselves, the world, whatever. If those people remain your only peers, you're going to have a hell of a time trying to grow.

It's true what they say: you really are the company you keep.

If this is you, we'd like to gently suggest that one of the first things you iterate and optimize is the group you choose to spend your time with. You don't need to turn your back on negative family members and old friends — though there are definitely cases where it might be best if you do. Remember, this is iterative. Find one peer that will help you to improve your game, even if it's an arm's-length online relationship in a forum or social media, then seek to improve that connection and look for more solid peers. Do that slowly until your station is better, taking your time, always evaluating whether or not you want to keep people full of negativity and limiting beliefs in your inner circle.

Eventually, you want the best people around you. People who are like you, who believe what you believe or want to believe. People with similar goals, maybe who have already achieved what you want to. People who uplift you, inspire you, make you laugh. People who make you want to *do* and *be better*.

This is something Sean and I believe in enough to have formalized. Sean has been a paid member of various mastermind groups throughout his professional life, and we've recently assembled our own brain trust: a small group called the Stone Table that meets twice each year and in a private group year-round.

Find better, more positive, upward-thinking, and possibility-minded peers. Improvement will then feel closer to effortless, guaranteed.

CHAPTER TWO:
What Are Your Strengths and Weaknesses?

If you hired a tennis coach to help improve your game, the first thing the coach would want to know was how well you played right now: how good your forehand, backhand, and overhead were, how well you volleyed, how precise you were with shot placement, which opponents you'd played, and how you'd fared against them. The coach would ask you questions. She'd drill you and make two lists while watching you play, in her head if not literally, detailing the things you did well on one hand and things you were weak at on the other.

In this section, we're asking you to make two similar lists for yourself and your business, even if that business is just you working alone. It's important to gauge your strengths against your weaknesses.

You can proceed without this information. After all, if you write books, you could probably stand to optimize your covers regardless of whether you're a fast or slow writer, whether you're persistent or tend toward lethargy, whether you have a single book in your catalog or a hundred. So yes, you could keep right on reading this book and optimize the hell out of everything in the exact same way Sterling & Stone did without bothering to make your personal balance sheet.

But consider what would happen if your tennis coach did things the same way. She wouldn't watch you play tennis. She wouldn't drill you. She wouldn't ask you any questions. Instead, she'd just say, "Let's practice learning how to hold a racket." Or maybe, "It's time to get you up against Roger Federer." It'd be a guess. Like the idea to optimize book covers, maybe her advice would work out regardless of your skill level. But good luck if you're a casual player and she slots you into Wimbledon on Day One.

Taking anything from this book without honestly assessing your current strengths and weaknesses would be equally foolhardy. You don't need to optimize your advertising if you only have one or a few books. Doing so is a waste of time and money. Podcasts are a large part of our strategy because articulating ourselves verbally is one of our strengths, and an awesome team that handles the production and setup of those podcasts is one of our assets. Without those particular assets and strengths, creating a podcast is a different beast.

Similarly, there are surely strengths, assets, and connections you have that we don't. We're shit at Facebook, but have friends (see Julie Huss's interview in Part IV) for whom Facebook is a strength — and therefore a *must* for their businesses.

You need these twin lists, and you need them written down or at least firmly in mind because you will want to play to your strengths and work around, hire out, or improve upon your weaknesses. Improving your weaknesses is usually our last choice among the three but the first for many creatives. Most artistic entrepreneurs feel the need to do everything themselves, including muscling through things they're awful at. *Not good at book cover design? Well, I'd better learn to do it.* But that's rarely the best approach. Your job is sticking to what you do best. Improve weaknesses in your core craft, but patch those in other areas by outsourcing when you can. *Hire* a cover designer. You don't need to be a jack of all trades.

What are your strengths? What are your weaknesses?

Make a list. Seriously. This may seem corny, but it's shocking, once you get on a roll, to see how long those two lists will grow, and you should detail as much as you can.

In the case of strengths, you need to truly internalize all you have going for you. Art of all sorts tends to be a lonely affair, and it's easy to feel like you're a hack with nothing going on without proof to the contrary.

In the case of weaknesses, you need to see what you'll eventually want to outsource, partner for, or adapt in some way. Some of those deficiencies will point to areas requiring improvement. For writers, you may need more time at the keyboard to improve your prose or more time pre-planning to sharpen your ideas. Other weaknesses are outside of your sweet spot, but acknowledging them will help you remember what needs attention — even though it probably shouldn't come from you in the long term. Sean, Dave, and I are awful at audio production, video production, formatting, financials and legal, dashboard management, book cover design, project management, and dozens of other things. That's why we have partners who handle those things for us.

You'll need to do some of the things you're not great at on your own in the beginning. That's fine. You can iterate your way into hiring those jobs out, but go ahead and acknowledge what they are now.

Related to strengths and weaknesses, make a list of your current assets and liabilities as well. Not in an accounting, dollars-and-cents way, but as relative to your business needs.

For assets: How many finished books (or other creative works) do you have? How many are in production? Are those works related to one another in ways that compound their value — three books, for instance, that all share a series? Do you have decent equipment? For us, this means software, computers, monitors, microphones, mic stands, etc. In other words, do you have the tools you need to do your best possible job?

On the flip side, what's missing and therefore standing in your way? Stephen King tells a story about writing his first stuff on a typewriter with a missing E key. We'd call that a liability in need of fixing the moment income allowed. I've had my current desk for nearly half my life. It still holds a monitor fine, but I sit at this damned thing all day, and sitting too much will kill you. I want a standing desk — one that adjusts from sitting to standing position whenever I need to change my state. It's not a big liability, but it's on my list for sure.

Take a full, honest inventory of your creative business: strengths, weaknesses, assets, and liabilities. List it all. Are you a fast typist or a slow one? Are you great at first drafts but crap at editing? Do you know you need your books in print because you meet people in person all the time but have yet to figure that out? Are you an author using Microsoft Word and know that Scrivener is better (it is, by a lot) but still need to get it? Do you have that standing desk I want, which will help keep you healthier? Do you have a supportive environment? A quiet office or a loud one? Do you have time to work in the early mornings or on a train commute that's ideal for banging out words? If you get distracted by sound, do you have headphones or earplugs? It sounds trifling, but one of my strengths is the ability to write first-draft words while listening to loud music. One of my assets is a comfortable pair of Sony MDR-7506 headphones. The combination gives me the superpower of being able to write no matter how loud it is in my house because I can kill the noise.

What's your superpower? What's your Kryptonite? You need to know these things before moving forward. Once you do, you can get to the most important of the *know thyself* triad: knowing what you truly want.

But it's not as simple as you think, so be careful.

CHAPTER THREE:
What Do You Want?

It may seem obvious that you should *know what you want,* but for most people it isn't. Despite this being a vital step on the path to success, many people never stop to so much as consider it.

We don't mean goals. Goals are specific accomplishments. But for many people, goals tend to be blanket must-have statements without rhyme or reason to fuel them. "My goal is to make a million dollars," someone will say. But *why?* And why a million rather than some other number? The answers are often arbitrary, amounting to: "Because it sounds good." Maybe $100,000 would pay off your mortgage (a significant, meaningful milestone that frees up money every single month), but a million sounds like a much cooler goal.

We're not saying you shouldn't have goals. On the contrary; goals are great, and we constantly make them. We're simply saying you shouldn't make *empty* goals, and that when you make a goal, you should stop and consider the reason you want it.

Here are some other goals that writers tend to set, if they set any at all:

Many writers say, "I want to be a *New York Times* best seller." And yes, okay, I've had that goal from the start even though Sean's never cared.

Why exactly do you want to hit the *New York Times* Best Seller List? Is it so you can tell your mom and make her proud? Is it so you can attend your next high school reunion with your chin held high? Is it so people will stop acting like your writing is a silly hobby and take it seriously for a change? Or is it something more sensible from a business perspective: Say, so you can put the accolade on your book cover and in your product description as social proof and hence sell more books?

Now, some months are easier to hit the list than others, due to competition and general buying trends. Supposedly, January is easy, and September is hard. So let's pretend it's May. You have a book on pre-order for September but think you can hit the list in January. So you postpone the launch by four months.

Is this idea good or bad? Well, it depends on the *reason* behind your goal.

If you have a Hollywood agent waiting in the wings and a good reason to believe she can land you a movie deal if you pull off an *NYT* best-selling book, it might be worth postponing your launch.

But if your only reason to hit the *NYT* Best Seller List is *so you can say you hit the list*, you're making a silly choice. All those readers waiting for your release might not appreciate being put off for the sake of your ego.

I've already mentioned my dad. He worked as a stiff suit in corporate America for decades before quitting to be an artist. He hated every second of office work, glad-handing, networking, and kissing the boss's ass. He only did it so he could make a lot of money, buy himself some free time, and use that free time to play his guitar and paint.

Then one day it dawned on him: He could cut out all those middle steps. Instead of making money to buy free time, he could simply stop working. He wouldn't make a lot of money if selling paintings was his sole source of income, but who gave a shit? He didn't want money. *He wanted to paint.*

It's like that scene in the movie *Office Space* where Peter tells his neighbor Lawrence that if he had a million dollars, he'd "do nothing." Lawrence says, "You don't need a million dollars to do nothing, man. Take a look at my cousin. He's broke and don't do shit."

What do you *truly* want out of your art and your business? Be specific. Keep asking yourself *why* you want those things until you're certain you agree.

Do you want to make a million dollars?

Do you want to make enough money to sustainably replace your current income and quit your day job?

Do you merely want the freedom of artistic expression and don't particularly care about money, like my dad?

Do you want the excitement and joy of building a boundary-pushing business?

Do you want to get good reviews from important sources and win literary awards?

I'm asking without judgment. If you want to win haughty awards because the praise of certain folks feels good enough to please you, that's great. The key is being honest with yourself.

Sterling & Stone has a specific method of operation: *We make stuff and talk about it.* We want to change the face of indie publishing, do stuff that's never been done, and push our creative pursuits hard and fast enough that our results surprise even us. I personally have a clear aim in life that is as nebulous as it is specific: *to do cool shit with cool people.* The company's purposes and outcomes as a whole are more focused but not much. We want to do new things. We want to push boundaries. We want to explore things in our own ways, free of constraints and other people's rules — which is why we'll always be indies rather than working for someone else.

Whenever we wonder which direction to take the company, we look at our purposes and outcomes. We look at what we want, and the way forward is simple.

In the first year of Realm & Sands (Sean's and my primary imprint within S&S), we wrote in about a dozen different genres, building series loyalty in none. Everyone told us we were stupid. Conventional wisdom says that if you want to succeed as an author, you should write a series of books in a single genre so that readers know what to expect and come to anticipate it. You do things that way, and each release will be bigger than the last. By writing in different genres instead of accumulating fans in one (our first books were a fantasy western, a political sci-fi serial, a kung fu thriller, a shapeshifter book, a robot story, and a trio of comedies), we were shooting ourselves in the foot. We'd never make money that way.

And those skeptics were right: We *didn't* make much money in year one. But our intended outcome wasn't profit. It was to create a broad base of varied stories so people would understand that Realm & Sands didn't like being confined to boxes right from the start. We wanted to establish R&S as an imprint that stood for a style of storytelling (we call it inquisitive fiction) rather than a genre.

To iterate and optimize, you must make sure you're iterating in the direction you truly intend to go and optimizing your systems for the results you actually want.

Knowing your purpose helps you take the pulse of your best possible audience — those fans who will help to support your ultimate vision. Realm & Sands went the long way around — and yes, it took us much longer than it could have to see profits and gain fans. But Sean and Dave's imprint at Collective Inkwell had a more obvious outcome in mind and hence found its fans more quickly. CI only wanted to write dark stuff. That was its purpose, its outcome, its goal … all those things at once. And the results came faster.

Now, a final word of caution to close this chapter: As you take inventory of who you are, what your strengths and weaknesses might be, and what you ultimately want, *be careful.* Because you may just succeed.

Project your ideal trajectory five years into the future, ten years, twenty years. Ask yourself where you'll be if and when everything goes according to plan.

You can't know what's coming, but do your best. If you're engaged now, you'll be married then. If you have a five-year-old son, he'll be fifteen in a decade. Guess at your living situation, your day-to-day routine, whether Grandma might come to live with you as she ages, what life might require outside of work, and how your interests may shift. Maybe you always wanted to spend every afternoon fishing once you could afford the time to do so. Bank on that, in your fortune telling.

Now ask yourself if the plan you have in mind for your business fully jibes with that future.

Or, to put it another way, take the next step in asking, "What do I want?" and shift to asking, "What will I want in the future?"

Your art and business is one organism. It will live and breathe with you, constantly evolving whether you like it or not. If you want to succeed as a romance author, consider that romance fans are notoriously voracious readers. If you aren't releasing something new at least four times a year, those fans might forget you and find other books to occupy their time. You'll lose momentum, and your income will drop. It's not a forgiving genre, and we've heard from many romance authors that although they're grateful, there's definitely an element of being trapped by their success. They can't take a break, or it all comes crashing down. It brings new meaning to the old expression "publish or perish."

Or consider the issue of pigeonholing. I doubt Dave will want to write women's fiction instead of dark horror any time soon, but woe unto him if he does. The reason Sean and I spent our first years unprofitable was to avoid pigeonholing ourselves

— so our fans, in the long term, would understand that we'd write whatever we damn well pleased, as long as its tone was inquisitive. You might iterate the bejesus out of your thriller writing as you read this book, then optimize those thrillers to sell a ton of copies … but realize too late that you don't want to write thrillers forever but will now need to start all over with a pen name if you want to do anything else.

As you consider what you want from your career, *just keep asking yourself if you're thinking short or long term.* The Kindle Gold Rush isn't just dead; it was stupid as shit to begin with, filled with quick-cash assholes intent on (it sometimes seemed) ruining indie publishing for the rest of us. If you're in any art to make a quick and scammy buck, you're reading the wrong book. We're people who love what we do and plan to be doing it for the rest of our lives, no matter how rough the short-term seas might get.

If you're the same — and we hope and believe you are — then do yourself a favor. Don't make stupid, shortsighted decisions today that will hurt you tomorrow. Don't sprint by tomorrow's dollars in pursuit of pennies today. Don't screw yourself in five years just because you were impatient and wanted something now that doesn't work with the future you've always wanted.

But of course, you're better than that. You're like us: in this for the long haul.

So let's start hauling, inching nearer to our final destination by the day.

PART II:
WHAT WE ITERATED AND OPTIMIZED, WHY WE DID IT, AND WHAT WE LEARNED

The Art of Incremental Growth

Hey, remember the time some guy discovered the secret of success that worked for absolutely everyone regardless of who they were or where they were in their lives and then sold that secret, and pretty soon everyone was reinventing 100 percent of what they did each day from the ground up and changing literally overnight, and the world was suddenly overflowing with people living their dreams now that they'd pulled all of the right levers that they'd somehow missed pulling for no apparent reason but had been obvious all along?

No? That never happened?

Maybe that's because it's an incredibly stupid concept. Call me pessimistic, but I don't really believe in overnight success or overnight reinvention. If we stick with writing and publishing, my hands-down favorite breakout of the past few years was *The Martian*, written by Andy Weir. Throughout 2014 and 2015, if you were paying attention, you may have noticed that book slowly but steadily taking over the world. It had originally been indie published, but then suddenly Andy got a big audiobook deal, then a big print deal, and then a damned *movie* deal with Ridley Scott and Matt Damon. And it's tempting to think, "Andy hit it big with his first novel. That could be me, too."

But if you think that, you're ignoring a few important things.

First of all, *The Martian* was Andy's first *novel*, but it wasn't his first story or creative project, by far. He'd put in his time, earned himself a very loyal audience, and written the on-blog serial that became *The Martian* without acclaim for a long time.

What changed the game was when Podium Publishing made the audiobook from the initial self-published version of the book and began ninja-marketing it all over the place. Then came the Random House deal. Then came the wham-bam rapid-fire takeoff of the audio, well before Random House had even published.

So clearly, having Podium make the audiobook was the secret, right? No need to iterate over time. Just copy that same crucial step, right?

Well, Podium makes our audiobooks, too. And those books are doing very well, but they're no *Martian* just yet. Shockingly, the same basic steps and triggers didn't create the same overnight success.

When something takes off, it's inspiring. It makes others feel that overnight success is possible. But there's also an element of luck, and of a certain hard-to-define it factor when the right projects strike the right chords in the right places at the right times. Nobody anointed Andy Weir. Nobody reached down and said, "You shall be the beneficiary of this great success, so just churn something out, and we'll make it big." He put in his time, did the hard work before getting noticed, and would have kept right on writing even if none of it had happened.

The Internet democratized our society quite a bit almost immediately, but it's made the biggest difference for people like you and me since 2010 or so, and increasingly so as time goes on. More and more, creators can put their art out into the world and find their own audiences, skirting middlemen entirely. Amazon led the way with Kindle Direct Publishing, and other platforms (Apple iBooks, Barnes & Noble NOOK, Kobo, and others) followed. Macklemore's big breakthrough happened as an indie musician, ensuring that more of the $9.99 I paid for *The*

Heist went to him instead of some gatekeeper and that nobody could have told him in the first place that he wasn't allowed to put the album in front of me because it didn't fit into a big publisher's catalog. Photographers and painters can find audiences through blogs, Flikr, Instagram, Pinterest, Facebook, and whatever new networks arise to replace the old ones by the time you may read this. These days, no one is stopping us from creating a business based on our art. But nobody's helping us, either.

And that's why *what's the magic key to change it all right now* thinking is a mistake. You can get lucky. Maybe your audiobook will become the next *Martian*, and maybe Oprah will do the Book Club thing again and make you insta-rich. Maybe someone will put your music in a TV show and make it famous. Jace Everett, the guy who wrote the *True Blood* theme, "Bad Things," is the friend of a friend; apparently, he was floored by it all. But you never know, and exposure is far from a guarantee. I've repeatedly seen my dad's paintings in the televised shows Howard Stern used to do of his radio program, but nothing ever came of any of it.

We have some good news and bad news.

Bad news first: There really is no way to engineer luck. Andy Weir deserves 100 percent of his success, but if time were rolled back with all of our memories intact, there's no way even Andy could guarantee it all would happen again. You should be prepared for discovery, but you can't count on it or force it into play. And what's worse, big indie breakout stories set unrealistic expectations for success in general. Not only are you probably not going to be the next Andy Weir; chances are you won't be one-tenth the hit in five years or ten. Without even meaning to, many people set their sights on that kind of phenomenon as a subconscious goal. And when growth is slow rather than fast, it feels like failure.

But the good news is that it's not failure at all.

We said in our book *Write. Publish. Repeat.* that success these days comes down to simple math. If you believe that ten sales of one book in a month plus ten sales of another book in the same month equals twenty sales total, then you should believe success is possible. Because you can turn those ten sales each into twelve sales each. You can publish another book and add twelve *more* sales. If the three books are part of a series, you can lower the price on the first book and promote it — and if the books are good, you'll see a spike across them all.

The *Iterate and Optimize* twist on that *Write. Publish. Repeat.* truism is that it's *iterative* math. You slowly improve one number then watch that small change percolate throughout your catalog. Little ripples become big. One change you make to the email series people get when they sign up to your mailing list ends up propagating into something totally unexpected, causing that to grow, too. Maybe you end up having your breakout hit at some point (at S&S, we refer to this coming event as "our *Toy Story*"), but it doesn't matter if you do. Math adds up.

The following section is all about the small, slow changes that we at Sterling & Stone made during 2014 and 2015 (and continue to make) to tweak the numbers in our favor. Nothing happens quickly — until you hit critical mass. But that's just more of the math doing its job. *You* should focus on the little improvements. The process of being better today than you were yesterday, even if only by an inch.

In fact, *do* go for the inch wins. Don't get greedy and grasp for feet, yards, and miles (or meters and kilometers — hello, rest of the world!). More good news is that there is no real growth ceiling for scalable businesses, which is the kind we suggest you create in the following chapters. You want systems and controllable factors that you can tweak, not random moon shots. The more scalable your business, the bigger you can get without a lot of extra effort all at once.

If you're reading this, you're an independent artist of some sort, even if your art is more about entrepreneurism than paint on canvas. And correspondingly, you're a creative entrepreneur if you're a successful artist today. I don't care if you have a traditional book deal or a Hollywood agent. At the end of the day, we're all indies, and nobody's looking out for our businesses but us.

Don't abdicate control of your trajectory to a *big hit* mentality. Don't plan only for the big wins because the smaller steps don't seem worthy of your time. Don't put all of your eggs in one basket: giving one platform too much control, relying on a single promotional venue to advertise your work, failing to build a direct connection to your fans because you think you'll be able to reach them on Facebook forever. Always be building. Always be looking at creating breadth, diversification, and scalability.

I know it might feel daunting. But if it does, breathe. Remember the title of this section and the title of this book.

Stop sweating the details. Stop worrying about how the hell you're ever going to be able to build a business that can stand on its own, that is beholden to no one gatekeeper, that can grow as big as you want it to be and reap profits accordingly.

Just focus on taking one little step today and then another tomorrow.

The next chapter begins the meat of this section, and as we said in the introduction, this part will focus on us here at Sterling & Stone. We know you don't care about us (you care about you!), so read each bit that follows with an eye to what you can learn from what we did, and apply it to yourself. The goal isn't for you to end up knowing our growth plan. It's for you to take the relevant aspects of that growth and use them in your creative business.

Each of the following chapters refers to an aspect of our company's iteration and/or optimization, starting with the coming chapter: "Our Team." If it makes more sense, you can mentally add "How We Iterated and Optimized" to the beginning of the chapter name.

So: How's your team right now? You don't need a partner or an employee to have a team. You can have like-minded friends.

Those who are in the same business, whom you can ask for help and advice.

Do you even *have* a team? You should.

If you do have a team, could it be better? Could it be tighter, more efficient, more powerful at assisting every person in the group?

Turn the page. We'll show you how we did exactly that.

CHAPTER FOUR:
Our Team

Here's a fun fact: For a while there, our main cover designer was making more money than any of the company's three partners. We found this out when we tried to hire her and stop getting one-off work on a freelance basis. We wanted her to move from cover designer to Sterling & Stone graphic artist. She could do a bunch of work on our website as well as other graphic projects. But we stopped trying when her requested salary doubled any of ours.

But that designer — the best from a handful we work with — was only one of the people who joined our team in 2015. In that same year, we also added a studio manager, a tech/admin person, a copywriter, a video/Facebook/all-purpose guy, a podcast producer, and a controller/financial dude.

If that list makes you dizzy, don't let it. We added them one at a time and bartered for most at first and have yet to take them on as formal employees — everyone's a contractor. Our company is still small, but it's a lot more complicated than we'd have imagined a year ago. And that right there shows the power of changing slowly — then leveling up at the right time.

But before we detail our team's iterative story, let's revisit the first sentence in this chapter.

We paid our cover designer more than we paid ourselves. She was making more money from our book sales than we were.

And the issue only magnified as our team grew. I think Sean told me that S&S's credit card bill last month as I write this was over $14,000. If you'd have told me last year that we'd be spending so much, I'd have thrown a fit. And right now, if you're smaller than we are, you might be looking at that number and gagging, thinking of how you'd never want those kinds of expenses.

Conversely, some of you are thinking it's a drop in the bucket. *Hell, fourteen grand? That's nothing!* But that's exactly the point. Let me enumerate a few truths, seeing as this is the first real *what we iterated and optimized* chapter and all:

1) **Although I'd have thrown a fit last year, I didn't throw one this year.** That's because despite it being a big number to us, we can afford it. That's actually kind of cool. In the past, fourteen grand would have broken us. It's pretty neat to realize we've grown to the point where it doesn't. Which leads to …

2) **Expenses are in alignment with income.** We are always top-heavy on expenses because we're still in growth mode, but we're not stupid. When you grow, you need to spend, but that's not even a kissing cousin to gambling.

3) **Expenses should almost always (or always) be made in expectation of a return on investment.** This is true even if it's spend now and profit later. Our book cover expenses are a perfect example. Those bills hurt, but we knew the books would sell better with the new covers. They did, and that gave us the return on investment we needed. Without some expectation of

a return on our costs, we are hesitant to (and sometimes refuse to) spend.

4) **The expenses grew slowly.** This time a year ago, we had very few expenses. *Very* few. It's hard to imagine we cracked $1,000 most months. We didn't leap from one extreme to the other. We didn't start with nobody and immediately take on six or seven new team members. Expected ROI on those team members or not, we weren't about to leap with both feet. Add one, see the difference in productivity and profit, and only *then* add another person or ongoing expense.

5) **We worked with people who had faith in us and the company.** Half of our new hires originally worked for barter, and others worked for way less than they would normally charge. You can only pull that off if you have deep-faith equity with your people. There's a fine line between hiring friends and people you know because they'll work cheap and are available (which is a terrible idea) and working with highly qualified people whom you meet and who like you before striking up an employment relationship (which is awesome). But if you can pull it off — and if I may be so humble, I think we did because the *Self-Publishing Podcast* has a history of giving more than it takes or requests of its listeners — you can grow a lot faster because no new expenses (or smaller expenses) hit your bottom line.

So let me tell you about our team. As we mentioned in the last chapter, you may not be looking to hire, but you should read through these because informal teams are real things, too. Informal teams can always trade services, share what works and what doesn't, and generally help each member of the informal mastermind get smarter faster.

Here's who we have at Sterling & Stone at the time of this writing:

The Partners

Dave, Sean, and I are the rather obvious core of the team, composing the triad that runs the business, the podcasts, and does most of the core writing. We work as true partners. We create stuff collaboratively (books, podcasts, etc.) and generally row our oars in the same direction to keep this ship moving.

It breaks down like this: Some books are co-written by Sean and Dave *(Yesterday's Gone, Whitespace, 12)* and some are co-written by me and Sean *(The Beam, Invasion, Dead City)*. There are a few loose ends that were written by just one of us *(Penny to a Million, Fat Vampire)* and there will be more co-written books in our future with other authors (Garrett Robinson, farther down in this section, will be the first), but for now most of the company's catalogue came out of one — or, almost always, two of us.

I'll break some of this down a bit in the "The Company Itself" chapter to follow if you're looking to build something similar for yourself, but for now I'll say the three of us are working in concert to create the fuel that drives the S&S train: *stories*. And we've found our personalities mesh well to develop our media, which right now means our Sterling & Stone podcast network.

If you find the right partner, collaborative relationships like ours can be a wonderful way to build your team. It's not easy to find people you harmonize with (Sean and I gel differently than Sean and Dave, and it's taken four years for me to finally begin meshing with Solo Dave because he scares me), but if you can, it's win-win, and nobody needs to come out of pocket. The work earns for both (or more) of you.

We have a LOT more to say about collaboration and will almost for-sure be releasing a book all about it in 2016 or 2017. So if you're interested in that, be sure you're on our list at SterlingAndStone.net/repeaters so you'll be the first to know when it's finished.

Our Studio Manager

If you're wondering what a studio manager is, so did we. Amy created her title. Sterling & Stone is a story studio, so I'm sure it means she *manages* it — and us. I'm also sure it's vague for a reason. You know, because we're such a mess without her, and she needs to clean up so much of our crap.

Amy is what we think of as a master hire, meaning she's the top-level person who coordinates everything with us then passes it on down to whoever should do the actual work. We come up with ideas. Amy makes them happen and makes sure they're done right.

You're probably not going to hire someone like this at first, but the minute you can afford it (and your business is complicated enough to benefit from such a hire), we'd urge you to seek this person out. Amy came to us; she seemed to think we were pitiable and needed her help. She was correct. But this is the kind of person you find through trial and error or a referral (if you can get one). It's hard to find your top-level person by searching for skills, because what they're good at and what they need to do is initially hard to define.

When hiring any sort of assistant or admin (virtual or in person), know that trying to find one person who can do everything is usually a fool's errand. At S&S, we need web pages built, podcasts created and posted, videos made, copy written, and an endless array of additional tasks. Most solopreneurs look for someone on Upwork (formerly Elance) who can do all of those things, but you're not likely to find that person.

Most admins do a few things well, not everything. That means you need to do one of two things: hire several admins over time, or hire an Amy to run interference.

I won't lie; this is a hard position to fill and harder to fill well. Amy is great at what she does because she's analytical and intuitive (so she knows what needs doing or will ask us until we explain), organizationally minded (she makes lists, builds systems, and ensures that nothing falls through the cracks, including verifying that stuff gets done after others say it will), detail oriented (she's always thinking of bits we forget, like the fact that we've forgotten to update book 1 in a series when book 2 comes out), and takes zero shit from anyone. This last one means she can badger people relentlessly on our behalf, reject people that need rejecting so we don't have to do it, and speak honestly and directly without shame. The downside is that she yells at us a lot too.

If you already have a task-oriented admin, consider hiring a project-based assistant like our studio manager as your next step. That person will help plug holes without requiring you to do all the grunt work — so for instance, she might suggest hiring a dedicated website admin, find a good one, then manage that person for you. Leverage becomes your best friend.

If you don't have any help yet, wait on *getting your Amy*. You might get lucky, but the world's Amys don't really want to push buttons or do a lot of grunt work. They're strategists and fill that higher level best.

Our Tech/Admin Person

I'm including this one next because there's a direct line between studio manager and tech/admin person. And I'm sorry I don't have a better name for this role, but whatever.

For most small creative entrepreneurs, this position — held at S&S by Maya, who like Carl from *Phineas and Ferb* "knows what all those buttons do" — is the first one you'll outsource. We all have websites/blogs; we all have content to share in this or that place; we all have documents in need of creation and projects that require assembling. This is who handles them.

Maya is sort of all purpose. She genuinely likes figuring things out and mastering highly intricate skills. Thus far, we've given her mostly website and podcast-posting tasks, but she'll move into compiling our ebooks, uploading books for sale on the various platforms, scheduling promotions, setting up our online meetings and broadcasts, and much more.

Amy manages Maya, and we pass instructions down through our studio manager. Amy also manages everyone else to a greater or lesser degree. Which is sort of the point. You don't want to pull a big task apart and figure out who should do which parts; you want your master helper to take your big idea and just make it happen in whatever way seems best. This is something we've had to learn. We like Maya a lot, and so it'd be natural to ask her to do X task or Y task and be done with it. But if we do that, Amy is left out of the loop — and then *we* (not Amy) need to keep it in mind, check back to see when it was done and if any loose ends were left hanging.

Outsourcing this position is simple in concept, but you'll probably go through a few stinkers before finding a good fit. I've had great results in the past with HireMyMom.com, but we've also used Upwork. For us, it was easier: Maya was one of our podcast listeners. There is no standard arrangement. You might hire someone to work two hours a week or twenty, and there's any combination of tasks they might be good or bad at. It's experimenting, trial and error, and — you guessed it — an iterative process to find and secure an excellent admin arrangement.

Because it's iterative, know it will require time to train this person to do things the way you want them done. At first, it will cost (rather than save) you time. But stick with it. Get a bit better each day. Once the fit is good, you can give that person more tasks. Then add more, and more after that. Eventually, you might hire someone to manage them and hire others to do the tasks your first admin can't. Baby steps will gradually get you where you want to go.

Our Podcast Producer

As I write this, our network, called Sterling & Stone FM, has nine podcasts. (You can find them all on iTunes at SterlingAnd-Stone.net/fm.) Recording those podcasts is actually easy, and we'll discuss it in a few chapters. But producing them? Adding all the music, bumpers, calls to action that shift and change as we need new ones? Doing the voiceovers, posting them where they belong, wrangling the feeds and podcast artwork and the metadata and … and … (Okay, I'm getting out of breath just typing this.) Well, *that's* hard.

But thanks to our podcast producer, Audra, here are the steps involved in recording an episode of the *Smarter Artist Podcast* as far as I'm concerned:

1)   Speak into my mic for a few minutes on the day's topic while my software records it.
2)   Drag the resulting raw audio file into the Dropbox folder we share with Audra.

That's it. I don't have to do anything else. That's the magic of having a producer — and it's how we can manage all the podcasts we have.

I won't go into a ton of detail here because this is a specialized position that few of you reading are likely to have, but it *is* an excellent example of iterative growth. Before Audra came on board, all of that extra bullshit fell on me — and, later, on Maya. When the *Self-Publishing Podcast* began, I set up the Google Hangouts where we all met, I made the recordings, I adjusted the audio if it needed editing, I turned the WAV files into MP3s, I tagged them with the right metadata, I uploaded them to the web host, wrote the show notes, made the posts, and tended the feeds when they got buggy. And on and on.

Whether you have or will ever have a podcast producer (or even a podcast), what we want you to get out of this section is that there's a clear pattern to taking on new things. At first, you'll just do it yourself, and it'll be a pain in the ass. Then maybe you can outsource it part of the way (even after Maya took over prepping and posting the shows, I still did half of the stuff involved and spoke my own intros and outros). Then you might be able to outsource it all the way.

Once you can outsource it all the way, the only part you need to do is the part you're best at: creating content, crafting you *art*. Then you can scale upward. Think about it: How easy is making new podcasts for us when all we need to do is have the idea and speak into our mics?

Our ... Whatever Garrett Is

I'm not even going to try and come up with a title for this one. Sean and I were very proud of ourselves at one point, having lovingly crafted a title we thought Garrett would like. We figured he could be our so-called viral engineer. Because Garrett — whose varied skills include fiction and nonfiction writing, some copywriting, video production, formatting, and generally making things get attention — is good at making noise and thinking up clever ways to make stuff go viral. He's a guerrilla, a scrapper, a clever and enthusiastic little machine. So hey, why not viral engineer? He can make us go viral. And he can engineer that shit.

Garrett didn't like it. Although he said recently that he *does* really like the not-quite-a-title of recovering fuck-up.

Garrett has been with us from almost the beginning. He, like — wow, I'm now realizing *like everybody else* — started as one of our podcast listeners. He wanted to be a screenwriter and director and figured he could backdoor his way in through writing. Then he made a lot of noise and forced us to pay attention.

Garrett's position is constantly shifting, but here are a few of the things he does for us, all of them vital: making videos (book trailers, positioning spots, crowdfunding videos), creating and running Facebook ads, professionally compiling our ebooks in a way that makes them stand apart from most other indies, compiling all of our print books (paperback and hardback), writing book descriptions and updating them on the booksellers' sites, training people to do the aforementioned tasks, and writing fiction. The last in that list is the newest and most interesting. We tried to pay Garrett for his work, but he refused. Garrett wanted ownership in our newest fiction imprint (Legendary, which publishes fantasy) instead.

Garrett is invaluable to us, but you don't need a Garrett in your business. You just need to consider what Garrett handles for us and see if any of those needs are relevant to your creative business.

If so, the same rules apply: Slowly, by inches, see what you can outsource. Garrett's example should also show some outside-the-box ways you can bring help into your company: He's our writing collaborator, and right-fit collaborators can be invaluable. He's a diehard entrepreneur, so he wouldn't accept a salary because entrepreneurs want ownership to vest their interests and provide incentive. If you don't have money to hire, maybe you can partner instead.

I probably don't need to keep saying this, but Garrett's role, like everything else, was a slow evolution. We worked with Garrett on one small task at first then added more over time. Only recently were we willing to hire him, and only *very* recently did we have any way to give him ownership in the Legendary imprint.

Start small. Grow into it.

Our Controller

Archer Caldwell — who could be our chief financial officer if we had such a thing, who might best be described as our accounting guy, but whom I still like to call our controller because it sounds so fucking boss — is both our newest hire and one of the original gangsters at S&S. Let me explain.

Not to get too woo-woo on you, but I'd like to point out before going on that sometimes things really do seem to happen for a reason. Things do seem to turn out the way they're supposed to. And so on.

Archer was beaten to the punch by Garrett. He was an aspiring author who wanted to work with us, but Garrett got there first, and we weren't ready to take on anyone else way back then. But Archer stuck around. We loved his work ethic, and we're always eager to work with people who actually want to do stuff and do it well. So when we were looking for a project management position, Archer stepped up — augmenting a rather oddly peripheral job he already had as the chief poobah and continuity librarian for our series *The Beam*. At the time, Archer just wanted to do whatever we needed. He said he was inspired. He wanted to write and to be around hardworking authors.

That position didn't work out (not his fault), and for a while we lost touch.

Then, not long ago, Archer hit us with an email with the subject line, "I miss *The Beam*." He wanted to know when Season 3 of our serial would be out so he could reprise his continuity role, and we told him. He did it. And all was well.

But then, quite by-the-way, we realized that Archer actually has a high-powered banking job. Like, his salary chased ours around the playground and put gum in its hair. And this just so happened to coincide with Sean's and my discussions that — oh, I don't know — I *wasn't officially even part of the motherfucking company I was helping to build*. Dave's, Sean's, and my agreements were all on a handshake. We'd reconcile what everyone was owed against what they'd been paid sooner or later but had no idea how to do it or when it could be done.

And that's when Archer reappeared. One meeting later, he's casually saying things like, "Oh, just do XYZ complicated shit that you'd never possibly know and sign here and here, and it'll be fixed." And then, not long after, we had a joint venture deal for our StoryShop app in the works, and our partner Seth sends us legal concerns that made our eyes bleed until we realized we could just send it off to Archer. Then Archer flapped his cape and said, "HAVE NO FEAR, GENTLE WRITERS! I'LL HANDLE IT!" And again, all was well with the world.

We knew we needed a controller (I'm going to keep using that title because it's awesome), but we had no idea *how* it would happen. The knot we'd bound ourselves in made us sweat just thinking about it. What we'd done in the area of legal and finances wasn't iteration; it was plugging our ears, closing our eyes, and yelling, "BLAH BLAH BLAH IF WE DON'T HEAR IT, IT DOESN'T EXIST."

The lesson here isn't about iterating your finances (though I suppose there is one like, "Don't let legalese stop you; build now, and reconcile later"). The lesson is about being cool to people, having faith in whom you like, and keeping your eyes open.

Everyone has assets around them, like we had Archer. Everyone knows someone who can do something that badly needs doing and might be happy to help. If there's something you need doing, look around. You can and should always start small and thank the people who help you to thrive.

The League of Extraordinary Others

This loose group of informal allies and cohorts is the last stop on our team tour, but it may be your first and only. Because not everyone even has a virtual assistant (though we think you should get one to handle your admin and tech at least), and few people need a podcast producer or a … a whatever Garrett is.

But you have friends, don't you?

At the beginning of Sterling & Stone's journey, this small group was all we had. It wasn't composed of the people it is now but was vital to our education, experience, and growth.

Consider the people around you. Your peers. Think about the people you see out there on social media, always around when you both comment on the same blog or YouTube video. Many of you in the *SPP* community have this group already.

Start small, and iterate your way to an awkward teenager of a team like ours, which is still just finding its way. This is where you begin, and what we're willing to bet you already have.

Consider:

Anyone You Hire

Think you don't have a team? Well, have you ever paid to have a book cover designed? That's outsourcing, Son! (Or Daughter.)

Have you ever had business cards printed? Had someone make hats with your logo on it? I'm not saying you should do any of those things (in fact, you shouldn't; make more art instead), but if you do, those people are part of your team.

It's like that with our cover designers, including 99Designs. com/spp (hey, podcast listeners, you bet your ass that's the /SPP link because if you go there, you have nothing to lose).

These people aren't on our payroll, and we don't have ongoing, regular payouts. But we know them, and they know us. They've developed a feel for our style and understand what we're about.

Same for our editor, Jason. He might as well be on the team; he knows us better and has been with us longer than everyone who's official, going back so far as to have been Dave's boss at a newspaper. Your connection with a solid editor becomes hand in glove. You'd better bet that's a relationship that improves over time, and one you can deepen as your workload grows.

Friends

And hey, if you don't use an editor or cover designer (stop it, by the way — you need both), you still have friends. Friends can be a great team.

The first guest we had on the *Self-Publishing Podcast* was a guy named Ed Robertson. If you've been listing to *SPP* from the beginning, you've heard Ed on the show, like, a dozen times. We joke that he's the Justin Timberlake to our *Saturday Night Live*. Ed always has great tips and tricks because he's brilliant.

We've never paid Ed money or hired him. We've never outsourced anything his way. But Ed's knowledge has aided our growth, and his help when we needed it has absolutely enhanced our business.

The same is true for everyone in Part IV of this book and many others.

Mentors or Anyone You Look Up to

If you listen to the *Self-Publishing Podcast* for long enough, you're going to hear us mention Pixar. And J.J. Abrams. And Stephen King and James Patterson. Specifically, you'll get the very clear impression that Sterling & Stone wants to be like Pixar. That the three of us want to create like J.J. and write like (or at least have the success of) Stephen and James.

Are we anywhere near as big or awesome as Pixar? As popular and successful as J.J., Stephen, or James? No, not remotely close. But all of these mentors give us big role models to look up to. Huge targets to aim toward.

Especially if you're near the start of your journey to build your creative empire, you've got people like these on your virtual *team*. You may not know or ever meet them, but they're right there in your mental boardroom — with you watching and taking notes, learning from their methods, aspiring to their achievements. Those you look up to, teaching you often as much as those who you actually interact with you in person. They help you get better.

Don't discount this piece of your community. You might be one of these people for someone else if you keep making small connections and advances over time.

Partners with Compatible Skills

Sometimes, we have a venture in mind that requires skills we don't have, but the solution isn't to hire someone to do the job in house. Instead, we form partnerships and split the profits.

The simplest version of this within our usual audience is collaborators. Collaborative writing isn't for everyone, but my world changed when I started writing with Sean. He didn't *hire* me, and I didn't hire him. Instead, we created something together and shared the benefit. Same for Sean and Dave. And same for all three of us when we started our first podcasts then formally joined forces as Sterling & Stone.

Today, we have three partners like this.

The first is Danny Cooper — an entrepreneur, like us, who runs a website setup company. When we realized that authors needed websites with unique needs, we partnered to form OutstandingAuthor.com.

The second is Seth Atwood, who runs Strange Wind Studio. Seth is our partner on the first-of-its-kind story-planning app, StoryShop (available at SterlingAndStone.net/storyshop). We wanted to make an app that would facilitate our own process and help others write "Better Stories Faster," but what were we going to do, build an app ourselves? Of course not. Instead, we found someone we already knew who was great at app development and formed a partnership.

The third partner is a bit different, as it's more of a commission-based arrangement, but I'd be remiss not to mention them here. Podium Publishing does most of our audiobooks. They're fierce entrepreneurs, whip-smart, and want to try all the crazy shit we do. Look for their big contributions in our *Indie Fiction Podcast* in early 2016 — and that's in addition to the award-winning audiobooks they've made from our humble stories already.

Look around. Opportunities to build your team or flesh it out are everywhere once you start paying attention.

CHAPTER FIVE:
The Company Itself

In corporate terms, Sterling & Stone is a tiny company. As of right now, we don't have any employees because everyone you've just read about is an independent contractor. And in fact, if we're being honest, it doesn't legally have any *partners*. Sean owns it all on paper, officially, and Dave and I just kind of trust that Sean won't run off holding a canvas bag with a big dollar sign on it and leave us hanging.

In truth, one of the reasons our company has survived so far *is* that trust. We'd never suggest you operate for long as we have — meaning, on a handshake — but the fact that we were willing to do so says a lot about the dynamic that makes our partnerships work. We weren't constantly keeping vigil, looking for ways the other two might screw us. That includes Dave. And holy shit, if you know *anything at all* about Dave, you know what a big deal that is. Dave doesn't trust anyone, ever. And yet he's been on faith with us for years.

There are a few points to this.

The first is that you should only partner with people you trust. And I'm not talking about looking that person in the eye and thinking, *Can I trust you?* I'm talking about something so deep that the question honestly never arises. Your gut knows there's no point in asking. And no, we're not naive. There was of course always the possibility that one of us might have screwed the others. It wouldn't have ruined our lives, but it sure wouldn't have made us want to keep building S&S — and interestingly, our shared love for what we're building was probably enough right there.

The second point is that the evolution of the company's structure, like anything else, has been iterative. Because like I said, this company is small by most people's standards — but large compared to most independent artists'. Most authors we know are lone wolves with a laptop. A few work in pairs, but that doesn't stop most from being intimidated by all we're doing and how far we've stretched.

And to that, I'd say, *We weren't always this way, and we didn't get here overnight.* It would have been a huge mistake to even *try* getting here overnight. If, four years ago, the three of us had sat down and said, "Okay, let's call an attorney and draft an ideal partnership arrangement and hire this person and that person," we'd never have left the ground. It would have been like my first business, where I painstakingly designed a logo and researched the perfect printer for letterhead, envelopes, and business cards — then never did any business, leaving all that stationery as scrap paper my kids still use today.

We're not lawyers, and this is the furthest thing in the world from legal advice, but if you are where we were back then and want to grow to where we are now, don't worry about dotting every I and crossing every T, at least not right now.

Make your art. Then make more art. Try and sell it if that's your goal. Inch toward formality.

Let's break down what we've iterated and optimized in our company.

Getting Our Official Shit Together

My wife has an accounting degree. She's not a CPA. She has exactly enough knowledge of what S&S does versus what's proper to see it for the train wreck it used to be. It's kind of like what it must be for a dermatologist visiting a sunny beach to watch people tan, or what a septic tank specialist must think when you flush something that ought not be flushed.

I won't go into every cell of our structure because that's both boring and private, but I will tell you the broad strokes so you can see the path we took to grow from no organization to finally getting our shit together, both legally and accounting-wise.

I started publishing fiction in 2012. Sean and Dave started in 2011. Back then, we were pretty much just guys doing our thing. I had my own Amazon dashboard (I hadn't yet published on non-Amazon platforms), and Sean and Dave had one they shared. There was no formality to the early partnership at Sean and Dave's Collective Inkwell — previously the whole of their business, now just one of Sterling & Stone's imprints. Sean collected the royalties and sent Dave a check for half. Things were simpler for me. I deposited what I received, such as it was. I was already a self-employed guy filing a self-employed tax return. This simply meant adding another few digits on the bottom line.

Because Dave is paranoid (or maybe sensible, in retrospect), Sean and Dave formed an LLC, but I'll bet you anything they did it wrong, with income coming to one of them rather than the LLC as a legal entity. Bottom line: we were doing the minimums, writing more, and figuring that it would all eventually be okay.

Things got more complicated when I joined the guys — and by more complicated, I mean all over the place. I published half (but not all) of the *Unicorn Western* series in my personal publishing dashboards. The rest went into either Sean's personal dashboard (which was ostensibly one of two Collective Inkwell dashboards; Dave kept the other under lock and key and generally ▮▮▮▮▮▮) or into a shared CI dashboard on the non-Amazon platforms.

If you're keeping track of this shell game, you'll see that we had nowhere that was actually *pure*. Not a single place to split where we could simply take (for one person) or split (for two people) the dashboard's income. Everything was polluted: either Sean/Dave and Sean/Johnny in the same place or Johnny solo and Johnny/Sean in the same place or some other monstrosity.

I hope you're now getting exactly how messed up this was, and why this is NOT an example you should emulate.

Anyway, for a while, we tried tracking sales and profits book by book to "solve" (ironic quotes intentional) the problem. And by *we*, I mean *me*. Sean ignored sales tracking. At some point, I sent him a reconciliation with a virtual shrug and said, "This might be about right." Sean didn't check it. He just sent me money. We always figured we'd understand it some day in the future.

Year-end came. Taxes were a mess. We triple checked to make sure we did everything legally, but I also know we did it 1) inefficiently and 2) with Sean taking it right up the butt from the tax man. It was stupid.

Our next attempt to reconcile came when the company started to make decent money. Now, to be clear, we had no idea where this money was coming from. We knew about X percent was coming from Collective Inkwell sales (to be split between Sean and Dave), Y percent was coming from Realm & Sands (Sean and me), and Z percent was coming from *Smarter Artist* projects like *Write. Publish. Repeat.* and our first Kickstarter campaign. The latter wasn't even to be split evenly because Sean and I did more work on the projects. How much more? "About this much," we said. Nothing was written down. Heads nodded between the three of us. More virtual handshakes were made, nothing official.

So Sean had an idea. Rather than trying to figure out how much I was owed each month, we should just all take a salary that probably reflected how much money each of us was bringing in. I say "probably" because we hadn't a clue. And again, we told ourselves the tale of a magical day in the future when accounting fairies would reconcile it all to the penny and make everything right and fair.

I could go on and on, but if you read the "Our Controller" section from the previous chapter, you know what happened next. Archer doesn't look like a fairy, but he has plenty of the pixie dust we desperately needed.

And this is when we started to do things right.

The board was wiped clean. We started over. Screw reconciliations and worrying about who's owed what; it was close enough. Archer did his mojo, and as of January 1, 2016, Sterling & Stone was officially a Texas-based LLC. We have written agreements in place as to who formally gets what when whichever items are sold, and Archer is keeping track of all our numbers, from all the dashboards, every month.

Now, here's the important part: If we'd brought Archer on in 2011 or 2012, we could have done this from the beginning. We could have formed the correct corporate structure, drafted an operating agreement, and straightened our accounting and signed royalty agreements from the start.

But I'm so glad we didn't because if we had, we'd never have progressed beyond the starting line. The task to get us up and running would have been far too daunting to even begin.

Let's be clear: In *NO WAY, SHAPE, OR FORM* are we suggesting you eschew formalities. We're not qualified to give that advice, and wouldn't. But we are saying that in our case, doing the minimum and then incrementally progressing toward the ideal was a good thing because it kept our minds where they should have stayed: not on pennies and legal agreements but on making our art instead.

When people start businesses, they usually spend a lot of time *doing it right*. For me with my first business, this meant spending days picking out the perfect business cards, envelopes, and stationery. For the infant Sterling & Stone, it could have meant sweating every single sale, making sure Dave got his 38.5 cents and Sean got his 38.5 cents rather than Dave getting 39 and Sean getting 38 — or, Heaven forbid, Dave's share rounding up to 40 cents. Or one sale getting lost over the course of a thousand sales. We could have dotted every I and crossed every T, but instead we just made sure we were legal with the tax people and didn't sweat whether the three of us were always, to the penny, getting our fair share — or maximizing the best of many possible corporate structures.

Instead of doing it right, in other words, we did *good enough*. Then we focused on getting a little better over time, never sacrificing our new company's momentum in the name of being anal.

Again: Don't listen to us on the details. Talk to your accountant, lawyer, the lady from the local IRS office. But once you assure you're legal, don't sweat the small stuff beyond that. Get your work done first. Don't sacrifice your business in the name of making your business *right* at every little turn.

I mean, my kids today are still working through the stationery I got for that first company of mine, drawing pretty pictures. It's going to take a while to deplete it. I doubt I used thirty pages throughout that entire business's life.

Our Imprints

At the start of 2014, we weren't really Sterling & Stone. Sean and I were Realm & Sands, and Sean and Dave were Collective Inkwell. We had a few other irons in the fire (a kids' line and a romance/erotica line with a different author/partner), but those two verticals were the biggies.

If you're an artist working alone, without our level of inventory, this section's title, "Our Imprints," easily could have been "Creating Harmony." Because that's the core of what happened in 2014. So please keep that in mind as you read.

The CI/R&S thing felt natural at the time. They were two different micro-companies, both unofficial, but that seemed logical. Why should they meet in the middle? They were distinct.

We built a Realm & Sands website, going so far as to register all the phonetic variants of the domain name: romansands.com, romansans.com. CI already had its site. Each had a mailing list and a series of automatic emails that went out when someone subscribed. We talked about both verticals on our podcasts but otherwise each lived in a vacuum. Why wouldn't they?

But as Sean, Dave, and I built more and more together based around the central *Self-Publishing Podcast* hub, we realized that maybe the right and left hands should know what each other were doing. We *could* keep building on two fronts, but doing so wasn't coherent. We were three people creating something under a shared ethic with a common style, albeit in different voices and genres. But in a way, Realm & Sands projects were still Dave, and CI projects were still a bit Johnny. Because we were all friends and partners.

Sean pulled the Sterling & Stone company out of mothball. He'd used it with other partners for a different purpose and was running his Guy Incognito imprint under the umbrella already, but decided it could be our catch-all. So one of 2014's biggest iterations was to stop treating CI and R&S as separate ventures and combine them — to make them two imprints under one central publishing company.

Throughout 2014 and 2015, once the precedent was established, we added four more imprints to those first two:

Our biggest collective venture was the *Self-Publishing Podcast*. But there were things that naturally clumped together, like our *Fiction Unboxed* Kickstarter and our nonfiction books like *Write. Publish. Repeat.* So those things became our *Smarter Artist* imprint.

We were also managing that romance/erotica line with an author using the pen name Lexi Maxxwell. So Lexi Maxxwell became an imprint, too. As of this book's publication, we've stepped forward again and decided to retool that line. It is now called Eros and stands for more than just Lexi. We expect big changes in this line in 2016, but as of right now it's mostly dormant.

The last of our first six lines is called LOL, and it's for humor pieces designed to make readers shoot milk through their noses. More on that in a minute.

In late 2015, we'd inched forward again and decided to add another two imprints to Sterling & Stone. This is all progressive, driven by new ways to sensibly harmonize our varied offerings and keep everything organized so we could market and cross-promote where appropriate (and no, there still isn't any Lexi/Guy crossover).

We added:

Our fantasy imprint, Legendary, which began when we brought Garrett (see the last chapter) into the fold, and

Portfolio, which is, for now, described rather inelegantly as "everything else." My solo first novel, *The Bialy Pimps*, doesn't fit anywhere else, and neither does Sean's *Four Seasons*, so they ended up under Portfolio.

The story of why the LOL imprint is an outlier is, we think, an excellent example of iteration. It didn't exist until Dave convinced us it needed to. So here's that story.

Our New Pen Name

Sean and I like to write everything. *EVERYTHING*. We haven't written historical fiction yet, and there are a few others, but just about any genre you can think of, we've written in it.

Of course, we wanted to write funny stuff. Books that were *only* funny, with no other redeeming value. If our stories were irreverent and made the right readers laugh, they were doing their job.

So we wrote them: *Greens, Everyone Gets Divorced, Space Shuttle,* a really raunchy series called *Adult Video* that makes my wife snort, and assorted shorts like "Decoy Wallet."

Writing them was smart. To "ship," as the saying goes. That's the hard part. But we did something dumb without meaning to, publishing them under our own names: Platt & Truant.

Dave told us we were idiots. "People won't take the rest of your work seriously when they see that shit beside it," he said.

We rolled our eyes. Dave hates everything.

But he was right, and inch by inch, during our Optimization year, we saw it. *We* thought *Space Shuttle* was hilarious, but it did look odd beside our serious work like *The Beam*. And honestly, it made that serious work look not so serious to people who weren't as immaturely giddy as we are.

Did seeing *Space Shuttle's* ridiculousness right beside *The Beam* on our Platt & Truant pages hurt sales of *The Beam*? Hell, did it hurt sales of *Space Shuttle*? There's no way to know for sure (data analysts, we're not), but I'm non-qualitatively convinced it didn't do any of our books any favors. Every genre is different, but I think back to a comment a romance author once made about the equally confusing, multi-genre page for author Lexi Maxxwell, which S&S manages: "There's too much here that doesn't seem to go together, so I wouldn't buy any of it."

The reason Dave was right on this one and Sean and I were wrong was this: We'd been assuming that readers would look past titles they weren't interested in and zero in on ones they were. But that's not how people's brains work. The entirety of your catalog says something in addition to what each of the books themselves say, and ignoring that fact is risky. So while *The Beam* was trying to tell our potential readers, "This is thoughtful science fiction," the presence of comedy titles beside it was shouting, "Or maybe not!"

So during during 2015, we moved our comedy titles under a brand-new pen name: Max Power, residing under a new imprint we called LOL. Anything that came *laughs first* went under Max, not Platt & Truant — even though Platt & Truant were doing all the writing. The change made both lines (Platt & Truant under the Realm & Sands imprint versus Max Power under the LOL imprint) internally consistent. We stopped putting chocolate in our peanut butter, in other words, assuming that anyone not interested would just pick the chocolate out.

The lesson here is a good one that we refused to see until it punched us in the face: *Reader expectations matter a lot, and your catalog is constantly setting expectations.* It's not just any individual title. It's also how the entirety of your library presents itself. Your catalog helps form a reader's impression of how they think of you as an author, rather than the whole of that impression coming from any one book you've written.

Reorganizing Our Websites

We needed an integrated, central website to house all our imprints.

You may or may not choose to do the same. This is a sticky issue that has to be decided on a case-by-case basis. Let's say you write nonfiction productivity books on one hand and sci-fi novels on the other. Do you create a common website for both kinds of books? Maybe (although in that specific case of very different subjects, my gut says no). In the end, it comes down to what you want your brand to be and if those two messages bear on each other — or if people manage to like *YOU* as much as they like your varied works. Because if so, people interested in one might be interested in the other — your sci-fi readers somehow becoming so entranced with you as an author that they want to know what makes you tick. But it's also possible (and perhaps more likely) that you'll just confuse people, noting the case of comedy and serious work combining in the section above.

We decided to centralize because there was too much harmony in waiting to ignore. True, our children's and adult lines weren't likely to share an audience (though who knows; romance/erotica readers often have kids), but we were also talking about all of these moving parts every week on our podcast. That quirk in our brand *made* those incoherent bits cogent, and we found more often than not that listeners either wanted to know about more than one or at least wanted the opportunity to do so.

As of right now, we still have individual websites for several of the imprints, but their purposes will change. A Realm & Sands reader shouldn't be forced into the mothership that is SterlingAndStone.net; he or she probably only cares about Realm & Sands books. But at the same time, that reader *might* care — and more importantly, attention often comes from the other direction, from the top down. Meaning we meet people and talk about Sterling & Stone because we have our fingers in all of it and need the ability to show our whole hand at once.

What we slowly moved toward — and now have mostly in place — is a thing that looks like a solar system. In the center is our sun: the Sterling & Stone website, which has all our books, all our imprints, all our podcasts, and generally all we do. The imprints orbit around it, each with their own reader-centric (but largely stripped-down) websites. They'll tell you about that specific imprint then send you upstream if you're interested in more.

For us, the move makes sense. The new model keeps separate identities for all of the imprints, but they're streamlined into portfolio sites. Most of the heavy lifting has moved to SterlingAndStone.net, where we can reap economies of scale. And as a publisher, this means we can point people who like one imprint to other imprints — without shoving discordant imprints in the faces of people who might only be interested in one.

Harmony is one of those things we've had to march progressively toward, and still don't have quite right. There's always the question of what to share and what's an irrelevant distraction to any given reader.

Good thing none of us have to get it right from the start and can always tweak to improve.

CHAPTER SIX:
Going Wide

One of the biggest issues facing Sterling & Stone — and believe me, only a corner of the larger debate makes it into our public forums — is that of wide versus narrow distribution.

Sometimes, the ideas are simple, even if there's much to discuss: Should we *go wide* with a title or grant someone exclusivity? Others are more layered and break down to whether something is on the 80 percent side of the 80/20 rule or the 20 percent side. If time, money, assistance, and mental bandwidth weren't an object (HINT: they always are), our mandate would be simple: *Put everything we have in front of as many audiences as humanly possible.* Unfortunately, there's more to it.

In this chapter, we'll break down the ways in which we've decided to go wider since publishing *Write. Publish. Repeat.* at the end of 2013.

This chapter serves a dual purpose: showing you how we iterated and optimized while updating what we said in *WPR*. Because our approach to things like multi-platform selling has definitely changed.

Let's begin.

Off-Amazon Distribution

In *WPR*, we paid lip service to the non-Amazon platforms. I feel kind of bad about that now, given how things have shaken out, but hey — that's where we were back then. That's where a lot of people were and where a lot of people still are.

Today, our firm stance is that for Sterling & Stone, single-platform exclusivity for more than a few experimental titles is a terrible idea. We always want to *go wide* if we go at all.

This is an incredibly difficult position to hold. If you're an indie author, I probably don't need to tell you this, but as of late 2015 Amazon's KDP Select holds most of the cards. There was a golden age for Select in 2012, and it's come roaring back. Today, it seems like certain authors need only to drop their books into Amazon's Select (which requires pulling them down or never distributing them on competing platforms) and throw some traffic at them. Amazon takes care of the rest.

It's annoying for those of us not in Select (who choose to also sell our titles on iBooks, NOOK, Kobo, and others) to be lapped by people with exclusivity. In no way do we fault anyone who opts to enter their books in Select, and usually suggest this strategy to new authors because it's a great way to get initial traction. But it's still obnoxious.

The glory days of Select have come and gone and come again — and in our opinions, the sky won't always refuse to fall on today's golden times. But for now, Select is a money machine for many authors. Skip putting your book anywhere other than Amazon, and you'll get all sorts of benefits to help you sell. And all things considered, you'll be way ahead.

This is a good *and* a terrible thing.

For Author X with her new book, Select can be a terrific boon in terms of exposure. She can run free promotions to claim readers, advertise in exclusive ways, offer her book as a borrowable title — getting extra money from readers who don't have to pay to read a new book since their membership to Kindle Unlimited is an all-you-can-read situation. It's a real advantage if you can get paid even when the reader didn't have to spend money on your work.

But what's great about Amazon exclusivity (and again, this is as of 2015; I can already hear this section ticking its way toward obsolescence when things change yet again) is also terrible. Not for individual authors directly, but for the indie community as a whole.

The better Amazon makes exclusivity, the more authors will try it.

The more authors try it, the more cards Amazon gets to hold.

And then they can make exclusivity even better.

At a certain point, authors won't be able to start out *without* being exclusive. The algorithms work in such a way that the rankings count a borrowed book as a sale. Books that get borrowed a lot climb the charts much faster than books that aren't exclusive and can't be borrowed. Look at the top charts. Those books are almost all Kindle Unlimited, which means that all but a few are exclusive to Amazon.

We could make an evil empire argument here, sort of like how people talk about Walmart: "If we all keep buying from Walmart, they'll run everyone out of business." But that's not what we're saying.

Amazon isn't evil. We love Amazon. Amazon changed the game. Amazon made indie publishing a real and viable thing, and for that we're forever grateful.

But Amazon isn't looking out for your interests. They're looking out for theirs.

And that means that if it suddenly suits them to cut KDP Select benefits, they'll do it even if it cripples your business. They've done it before, the last time Select became a four-letter word.

And if you're exclusive — and you almost certainly would be unless you're one of the anointed few allowed to offer your books through Kindle Unlimited even without exclusivity — you'll be fucked.

Fucked.

If 100 percent of your sales come from Amazon, the fate of your career is in their hands. That's stupid. Sorry, but it is.

Unfortunately, the non-exclusivity path is much harder. Which is why this problem keeps getting worse. In the end, we suggest a hybrid approach: each term in KDP Select is ninety days, so if you're new, you may want to do one or two terms for each book then pull out and start building audiences on other platforms. This will be hard. The way things are right now, you stand to lose a lot of marbles when you do it, and you'll wonder how the hell you can justify things when you're making two NOOK sales a month to offset all your lost revenue.

The choice has to be yours. We won't and can't decide for you. But if you choose to stay exclusive to one platform and allow that platform to dictate your success, consider yourself warned.

We've toyed with a few Select experiments, but for the vast majority of our stuff (and certainly continuations of series with existing readers), we default to going wide.

One of the best Optimizations we did in 2015 was to push everything out to all the big platforms. Now, I'll admit that we had an advantage here that you might not — but before you dismiss what we're about to say because of that advantage, hear me out because this is yet another iterative thing.

The best way to sell on non-Amazon platforms is to have a representative at those other platforms, and in the beginning of 2015, finding those reps was something we focused on a lot.

BUT — and this is where I ask you not to roll your eyes and say, "Well, of course. They had an in." — the only way to get a rep's attention is to have a catalog *worthy* of consideration. There are a lot of books out there, and an author without an audience platform won't sell to anyone.

Which means you need at least a few books. With great-looking covers, in series, so there's natural buy-through from one book to the next. And you need existing fans. If you aren't selling on Amazon, why should Barnes & Noble think you'll sell on their store?

In order to get promotional help, you need to show the reps that you can make the platform money with your titles.

By the time we started sniffing for reps, Sterling & Stone had over fifty books with dramatically upgraded covers. Many (not all) had solid sales records. We had sensible funnels and, apparently, impressed them as people who understood marketing.

Turn yourself into the kind of author who's worth representing. Put yourself in a rep's shoes. They don't work on commission, but it's the same basic idea. If you want to feed your family and keep your job, you need to find authors who will kill it.

So be that author.

Which means you need to — wait for it — iterate into that person, or that business.

This was the single best decision we made, after three-plus years of chugging forward and mostly being exclusive, unable to get anyone off-Amazon on the phone. Or *at* Amazon, for that matter; an Amazon rep is the only one we still don't have.

Now, you don't *need* a rep to make it. Free books are big on Apple, so if you have the first book in your seven-book series free, Apple will be inclined to like you. Kobo is huge in Canada. In Canada, they say, "Amazon who? I like my Kobo, eh?" If you're in Canada and have a fan base, Kobo will want to know that. We've also found Kobo to be the most open and accessible of the platforms, so by all means reach out if you have something worth seeing. Apple is the hardest. They seem to wear all black and move soundlessly and unseen in the night, like ninjas.

Show those other platforms to your audience. It's amazing how many authors only have Amazon buttons on their websites. Tweet the link to your book on iBooks and include *@ibooks* in the Tweet so they see you doing it. Nurture your NOOK audience. Search iTunes podcasts for *"Self-Publishing Podcast* Classics #160 — Multi-Platform Distribution with Draft2Digital's Dan Wood." Listen to that episode. Do what Dan says.

Maybe, if you're bold, you'll choose to offer an exclusive to someone *other* than Amazon for a while, just to treat those readers and possibly snag a rep's attention. We've done that.

It will take time (maybe a long time) to build your readership on the other platforms, but *holy shit* is it worth it. Imagine not waking up in cold sweats, wondering if KDP Select's sky will fall like it has in the past. Trust us, it will.

Imagine seeing someone reading on their iPhone, as more and more people are doing these days, and knowing your books are available in the iBooks store that now comes native on every new iOS device.

Imagine walking into a Barnes & Noble — America's only significant remaining chain bookstore — knowing you're available to those loyal audiences.

Imagine going to Canada.

(Just *going*. It's really nice there, and everyone is so polite.)

But then imagine knowing your books are in the store that Canadians use more than, as Mark from Kobo says, "the world's longest river," and all the international markets they reach that Amazon doesn't.

This won't be roses. You'll go nonexclusive and curse us after seeing your sales. But are you building a short-term business or a long-term career? And if you're building a long-term business, does it make *any sense* to put all of your eggs in a basket that's owned and controlled by someone who would tell you to your face that it doesn't have your best interests at heart?

It's taken years, but Apple is now our number two sales platform behind Amazon, and the gulf isn't wide. Sometimes,

Apple's numbers are even greater than Amazon's. NOOK and Kobo, depending on the month, often aren't far behind.

Those are readers we once left on the table. We won't make that mistake anymore.

Multi-Format Distribution

We in the indie publishing community sometimes act like ebooks are the only thing in the world. They're not. My grandmother is never going to pick up a tablet to read, and neither will my mother-in-law. Nor will my children, despite protests that kids are all digital all the time. They both read print, and Austin (age 11) listens to audiobooks, too.

We hear all the time from people who've found us on Audible or iTunes, and they'll ask when the next season of *The Beam* is coming out. We'll tell them the ebook release date, and they'll reply by asking for the audiobook release date. And then, instead of reading with their eyes, they'll wait.

We haven't had the same reaction with print, but we're looking into ways to sell the hell out of print in the coming years.

But I'm getting ahead of myself. Here's how we've upped our game in non-ebook formats, starting with the one that's borne fruit first.

Audio

The standby for indies to create and distribute audiobooks is Audiobook Creation Exchange — a quasi-DIY service that pairs writers with narrators. We started with ACX through our first iteration, hitting audiobooks hard in 2014 while trying to learn the process. This was a terrific first step for us, and we started seeing immediate sales, especially for our nonfiction.

But as with all things, we kept asking how we could get bigger and better. There were three major concerns: How do we reach a broader network of listeners with our audiobooks, how do we do it all more efficiently and effectively, and (the importance of this one wasn't apparent at first) how do we make *much better* audiobooks?

That last one didn't hit us in the face because we honestly thought we were doing well enough quality-wise — considering and remembering that you're supposed to iterate through everything, not make sure to nail it perfectly the first time. (Because "perfect is the enemy of done," as Sean always says.) So yes, there were amazing audiobooks out there. But ours were *good enough*.

Turns out quality matters a whole lot in audiobooks. Just as people have favorite actors in movies, they have favorite narrators. When the audiobook for *Invasion* hit the market, we got a ton of Tweets, emails, and Facebook messages saying, "Holy shit, RAY PORTER is narrating? He's my favorite!" And those people bought in droves, based on Ray as much as us.

Our first audiobooks, through ACX with relatively unknown narrators, were good enough at that time. And if you aren't doing audiobooks at all, we suggest you try ACX. The process is simple, and if your book sells even reasonably well, you can probably find a narrator willing to read the book for free, then you'll revenue share on the finished audiobook to split the profits. Your investment is nothing.

But in 2015, we upped our game. We already knew the guys at Podium Publishing and gave them first dibs on any audiobook work across the board. If they wanted to produce one of our books, they got it. Only afterward would we consider ACX — and this despite the fact that our royalty percentage with them is much lower than we'd get if we made the books ourselves.

I've already told you about Podium, but once we partnered with them for audiobooks, we started getting better sales. Because we had partners who understood the market, had the connections to get those books in front of people who wanted to hear them, and could take work we didn't quite understand right off our plate. We didn't have to find and screen narrators then check their work. We signed papers and trusted our partners.

This arrangement has been one of our favorite partnering success stories and is a perfect example of iterating and optimizing. We didn't go with Podium first. We learned through ACX, with no barrier to entry. We did and continue to sell books that way (Write. Publish. Repeat. and Fiction Unboxed were both via ACX and sell great), but Podium is a big step up.

In 2015, *The Beam: Season One* and *Yesterday's Gone* were both finalists for coveted Audie awards. We geeked out a bit when Neil Gaiman announced it on Facebook. And that kind of thing never would have happened if we hadn't leveled up to taking a smaller percentage of a bigger, better pie.

Regardless of how you do it, get onto audio. Seriously. Your sales may flatline until your other formats start selling, but once they do, you'll be glad you can be in this highly consumable format. *Many* people suffer commutes. You want to be on their devices or in their ears, helping them to enjoy what might otherwise be a miserable time.

Print

As I said, print has always been a 20-percent activity for us. We do it for two reasons: reader perks and pride.

Your reasons might be the same, and that could well be enough to justify print. If you use Amazon CreateSpace, there's no reason not to, so long as you're still getting your art done.

CreateSpace, as of this writing, is free. If you can do the process yourself, it's a *Why not?* sort of thing. If you choose to hire someone, which might be smart, you'll need to weigh the cost against expected benefit. Their books have steadily improved. They now do matte covers, and their paper quality and binding is damn close to anything you'd see in a bookstore.

If you do the above, it'll cost you little or nothing, and you'll have a solid paperback available for purchase on Amazon, seeing as Amazon owns the company. That's great, and it was our first step, and we've definitely managed to advance the professional look of our formatting, thanks largely to Garrett. Sometimes, people even bought those books — nonfiction more than fiction, just like audio. But even better, you'll be able to do things like order print copies to sign for your readers. These make great giveaway prizes to reward your most loyal fans, and if you speak somewhere, you can distribute or sell them. Lastly, they'll look great on your bookshelf. You can show Grandma that you're a real writer.

That's what we did at first.

Our next iteration added hardback printing. Now, if paperbacks are a 20-percent activity, hardbacks are 20 percent or less *of that 20 percent*. Almost nobody buys them. But holy shit do *those* look great on my bookshelf, and, to justify the cost, setting hardbacks up on IngramSpark or LightningSource for print-on-demand isn't free — they also make even better reader perks. The *Invasion* hardback, with a glossy cover and tidy size, is a sexy beast. I feel professional as hell holding that thing, and readers will feel the same.

So that was print for quite a while. We sold enough to recover our setup costs; we satisfied readers who loved us enough to want print; we looked like pros — an Amazon page listing ebook, paperback, hardback, and audio formats looks super-professional, all other things considered; we had nice perks to sign and raffle off to keep readers engaged; we got pride pieces to rest on our shelves. But it wasn't a profit center.

But we see that changing soon.

If you listen to "*SPP* #174," you'll see what I mean. We now *believe* in print. Not this second and maybe not even in 2016, but slowly and someday. It makes sense. You may read digitally, but look around. There are libraries, airports, local bookstores, big chains like Target and Costco. I was recently walking through Atlanta airport and saw a paperback of *The Martian* propped on a shelf in one of those little stores. Do you think some people will discover *The Martian* because they see it in a bookstore on their way to catch a plane? You bet. And do you think tons of travelers just looking to pass the time might pick it up on a whim? Again: you bet.

Print is still on the cusp of its next iteration for us. Not much has changed *yet*, but we expect it to change from *Why not?* to a major distribution avenue and profit source in the coming years.

Multi-Language Distribution

Big tip of the hat to Joanna Penn here. (If you don't know Joanna, her interview is in Part IV.) Everyone bow for Joanna. Good? Good.

Joanna is nowhere near the first indie author to start talking about translations and selling in foreign markets, but she's the one who had our ear most.

It's always smart to grab low-hanging fruit. But as you grow, you'll need to consider which fruit from the higher branches is worth climbing to get.

Remember, it's all stepwise. If your business is young, you should probably spend the maximum possible time making your art and not much time stepping outside your sweet spot. You can focus on Amazon in the short term (as much as it pains me to type that) because that's low-hanging fruit. You can focus on ebooks to the exclusion of print. And you can hit English-language distribution because in 2015 that's where most of the ebook sales are — the United States, Canada, the UK, and so on. India reads mostly in English as well. Not a small market there, even if it's still adopting digital.

But the more you build your team and the more you hit that 80-percent stuff, the more you owe it to yourself to take another small step to get better and reach further. Then another. And then another.

We ignored translations for a long time after Joanna took the dive — not because we didn't believe in those foreign markets but because it was too much work. I speak decent German, and Sean knows enough Spanish to order tacos (or at least to say hello and thank you). We recently informed Dave that there was a whole world outside his office. But regardless, none of us were competent to proofread in any language other than our own. So finding a translator? *Ugh.* Getting the work done? *Ugh.* Paying for it? *Double ugh.* Having any idea if the translation was good and figuring out distribution? *Ugh squared.*

What recently changed our mind — and I'll repeat that it's only been since we've grown reasonably proficient at our 80-percent stuff — was finding a partner. Same as with audiobooks.

You can translate your books yourself, pay for it, and try to distribute in other countries that speak those languages — it's not always as simple as just putting German books on Amazon. de. Or you can do what we did and sell your foreign rights.

As with our new print iteration, this is still in its infancy, but we've partnered with an agent who's finding buyers for our foreign rights. You don't keep your German rights, translate, and distribute yourself, to extend that example; instead, you simply sign some paperwork, and let a German press do it for you. They know the language. They know the market and how to distribute within it.

As with audio, this means we get a much smaller slice of the overall pie than we would if we did it the fully DIY way. But we like how much work this way requires. Specifically, none.

Because so much of this is still in the works, we can't discuss details here, but we've sold French rights to one book so far and have various EU rights on the table for several other titles. We get an advance, as with any traditional deal. Then if the book sells well, we get an ongoing percentage of those sales after we've earned back our advance.

Think about that. If you have a book that's a best seller in the US and your foreign rights agent can find buyers interested in French rights, you get an extra stream of income on work you've already done. But that's just France. They can sell to Germany, too. Spain. Italy. And on and on.

This is an intoxicating idea. Dean Wesley Smith calls the whole books-and-rights equation "the magic bakery." You bake a pie once, then you can keep taking slices forever. Consider all those language rights that can keep piling up new income streams. Then think of the cross-permutations if your book sells well enough: French audiobook rights, for instance, instead of just ebook rights. The mind boggles.

CHAPTER SEVEN:
The Pre-Creation Process

Sean and Dave have worked together for a long time and are quite prolific. But Sean and I, as a creative team, seem to consistently publish 1.5 million words per year or more. A full Harry Potter series, one and a half times over per year, takes *prolific* to *kind of nuts*. We did that in 2013 and ended the year feeling like we'd been towing a barge. We figured it was an oddity, never to be repeated. Then we did it another two years in a row, with no signs of slowing down.

What's funny about 2014's production was that our 1.5 million-word encore came *after we'd decided to slow down*. My demand made Sean sad. "I want to keep going fast," he said. And "I want to not die," I replied. What did Sean know? I write the rough drafts. Asshole.

My point here is that 2014's production sneaked up on me. I realized halfway through the year that we were on 2013's manic pace despite my insistence.

The reason? Because that pace *felt so much easier* in 2014 than it had in 2013.

In 2015, we began work on a first-of-its-kind writing app called StoryShop (available at SterlingAndStone.net/storyshop). The app's tagline was *Better Stories Faster.* And around that same time, as part of the promotional effort for the app, we released a free instructional audio series, also called StoryShop. And again, the entire series was about how to write better stories faster. Throughout that audio series, we kept trying to explain how we write so fast — and, if you can forgive me for not being humble here in these pages, I think we're writing *better* at the same time.

In a nutshell, the secret sauce is *planning better beforehand.* The more you know your story, world, settings, and characters, as well as their motivations *prior to* writing, the faster you can go — and the better your stories will be.

Once that became obvious, we iterated our pre-planning. That advance in *knowing our stuff before we get started* has reaped the biggest rewards out of anything we've done so far.

Here are the highlights of how that all happened.

Beats 1.0

If you've read *Write. Publish. Repeat.,* you already know about what we call story beats. I described *WPR*-style beats as "CliffsNotes written in advance by someone who wasn't paying very close attention." They're more like a summary than an outline. And the *not paying attention* part comes in because the story always diverges from what's detailed in the beats. That's why beats aren't restrictive to your creativity — because if you use them, you'll find they barely matter past a certain point as the story finds a life of its own.

We're collaborative in almost all work at Sterling & Stone. There are a few exceptions *(Penny to a Million, Fat Vampire, Four Seasons, The Bialy Pimps),* but just about everything we do these days — and everything we plan on doing in the next few years

— has two or more writers. That's because we find two heads are better than one (and that one plus one has a way of equaling ten), but that's a topic for another day. You can use everything in this chapter as a solo writer. Just substitute all mentions of me and Sean with yourself, with *you* covering all bases.

I'm sticking to the Platt and Truant process in this chapter. It's the most systems-oriented of our methods and the one that's iterated most — something we've streamlined enough to make our heavy word count feel relatively easy.

Once upon a time, Sean would write a bunch of short chapter summaries for each of our books. They were around one hundred to three hundred words, and it was my job as the first-draft writer to expand the events of those summaries into a two thousand-plus-word chapter. Late in the books, Sean's sketches mattered less and less because the story would have found its rhythm. By then I'd be on my own, but I always referred to Sean's beats to make sure I was hitting any still-relevant high points. For instance, the story might have evolved to the point where the hero no longer had to meet the villain's accomplice in person to double-cross him — but I *did* still need to remember that in the end, the hero would have to rescue his captured bride.

In this way — using the story beats process we now refer to as beats 1.0, I found my path by keeping an eye on the big events that still had to happen while tending to ignore the little events along the way. It made sense. Sean had written those smaller happenings before the story had found itself under my fingers. (Even those big events weren't written in stone. The first season of *The Beam* was supposed to end with the Ryan brothers meeting in secret on the moon elevator, plotting their shared plan. That's very much not what happened, and the WTF/OMG cliffhanger we did write was born out of the blue.)

And beats 1.0 worked great. You can read all about that process in *WPR* because it's still an excellent place to start — and, if you write by yourself, might be the *good enough* you need to get going without becoming mired in details and procrastinating forever.

But of course, we didn't stick with beats 1.0 for long.

Beats 2.0

In June of 2014, we were slated to deliver on the promise of our *Fiction Unboxed* Kickstarter campaign: writing a novel from scratch, publicly, in thirty days. It's the only time we've had a firm starting (and ending) point for a book that couldn't be moved, and it provided a scheduling obstacle.

As things stood, we were slated to start our literary mind-bender, *Axis of Aaron*, in late April or early May. Around that time, Sean gave me the story beats so I could learn the characters and get familiar with the world.

What I didn't know until I saw the *Axis* beats was that Sean had been trying something new. He didn't just write a bunch of summaries as he had in the past. This *beats 2.0 package* — much more than text — was something new.

It caused a problem for us, with June 1 looming and only a few weeks to write the project that would have to begin and end before then.

Specifically, the beats were *too good*. Too detailed. I understood the characters so well, they felt like old friends. I could picture the island, Aaron, where our story would take place. I knew the bridges. The seaside carnival that had fallen to ruin over the years. I knew every bit of Aimee's father's cottage — the one our story dictated would seem to shift in front of Ebon's eyes, at times appearing new and at times falling-down decrepit. I knew Ebon. And Aimee. And Ebon's late wife, Holly. I knew how they interplayed, and the world was so real to me I could practically smell the salt in the air.

After seeing the beats, I couldn't write *Axis*. Not yet. Rushing the story would have broken my heart. You may think I'm being dramatic, but listen to the *Self-Publishing Podcast* episodes from those days, and you'll see I'm not exaggerating. The story affected me. And okay, fine, stories affect us, and that's not strange. But this story wasn't even written. It existed only in beats.

This new way of pre-planning allowed me to see the story so clearly in advance, I already knew what writing it would feel like. There was no friction. I knew it well enough to know that it couldn't be rushed.

So we put it off. I didn't start *Axis* until July, after *Fiction Unboxed* had finished.

I don't think we could have written that novel — which is so thick with twists and mind fucks that you can't tell which end is up — without evolving our beats. It simply wouldn't have been possible. I needed to know it inside-out before typing the first word. I needed to feel it. To live in it.

Here's how Beats 2.0 — which I will hereby begin capitalizing in honor of their awesomeness — differed from the beats 1.0 you may have read about in *Write. Publish. Repeat.*

Full Character Profiles

We've been working with Beats 2.0 for a while now, and it's taken me a while to learn the best ways to digest them. If you're working alone, this process may differ for you. But with our collaboration, there are two sides to the equation: the creator's and the consumer's (I consume the beats before writing the draft).

When I get a new beats package, I always start with the character profiles and never the plot. Because it's more important for me to understand who the people are than what Sean thinks they will do throughout the narrative. If you want to know why, the answer is in that last sentence: "What Sean *thinks* they will do." He's wrong more than he's right. Sean tells the truth about the characters, and it's my job to translate that into the truth of what happens.

We developed a full (and inexpensive) course on Beats 2.0 that you can check out if you want to see this in a lot more detail, but basically Sean creates comprehensive written backgrounds for each of our key characters. This is never limited to information that we expect to appear in the story. On the contrary, the most illuminating information on characters has nothing to do with the narrative and serves only to let me know who these people are — and how they'll react. He does this using a master list of questions that he *asks* characters in order to write these profiles. The list is something we call Character DNA and contains questions like, "What is your earliest memory?" and "What's your favorite thing to do when you're alone?" Indirect questions that tell us about *them* not necessarily about things we'll tell the reader.

For instance, let's say a character is shy. You can just kind of know they're shy, and that's great. But what if the *reason* you know they're shy is because their mother was domineering and their most vivid early memory is of trying to order a Happy Meal at McDonald's but their mother shouted at them for stuttering while doing it and embarrassed the living hell out of them?

Our Beats 2.0 character profiles tend to be long. Thousands of words of background — little of which ever sees the printed page. The more central the character, the more exposition I get in their profile. The smaller the character, the more likely their profile is but a few-hundred-word almost-footnote.

Casting Characters

If you've been following Sterling & Stone and/or the *Self-Publishing Podcast* for a while, you've heard us talk about casting a lot. But if this is the first time you've encountered us, it'll likely strike you as strange. Hang in there. It's worth it.

We touched on casting a bit in *Write. Publish. Repeat.*, but *WPR* was written in the beats 1.0 days. Beats 2.0 made casting mandatory and evolved it, just like everything else.

Nowadays, we pretend that every story is a movie and we're the casting directors. Well, Sean is. I sometimes tweak, but he handles almost all of this. We ask, "Who do we want to play this role?" The answer helps to inform the character him- or herself.

For instance, *The Dream Engine,* our YA fantasy/steampunk debut, features a "dirty scientist" named Daw Blackburn who works beneath the law in the underground city of Pavilion.

(Sean handles the names, too. I'm terrible at names. I once named a character Jerome figuring he'd change it because the character is very much *not* a Jerome. He made the mistake of trusting me. Now that poor character is forever Jerome.)

Anyway, Daw is a gritty sort, prone to bursts of anger. He's highly intelligent but carries a rather large chip on his shoulder because he knows something of what the polished city of Waldron's Gate above has done to his people.

If *The Dream Engine* were a movie — and someday, maybe it will be — Sean would have cast Daniel Day-Lewis as Daw Blackburn. But not just Daniel Day-Lewis in any role. Specifically, he'd be DDL as he was playing Bill the Butcher in *Gangs of New York*. Not *Last of the Mohicans* Daniel. That's a very different character. And so when the beats arrived, the Daw Blackburn section was topped with this big photo of Daniel Day-Lewis as Bill the Butcher with his big curly black mustache and his oily hair. Sean gave me links to a few representative scenes from *Gangs* so I could get a feel for Bill the Butcher because I hadn't seen the movie. And immediately, I knew a bit more about who Daw Blackburn was.

Now, I want to be careful here. The idea is not to ape existing characters, nor to hamstring your characters so they can't grow beyond the individual another creator and actor worked together to make. The idea is to give yourself shorthand as to the character's starting point — or, if you work collaboratively, to have that shorthand in common between the two (or more) of you.

Characters always grow beyond their starting points. If you watch *Gangs of New York* and then read *The Dream Engine*, you won't see a lot in common between Bill and Daw. They look and dress similarly, and they share some mannerisms. But beyond that, they're nothing alike. But because I knew what Sean had in mind for Daw, I could hit the ground running. I didn't have to draw Daw on a blank page. I could write him and learn the rest of him as I went.

Cast with caution — and again, we talk this out in detail on the free StoryShop audio series linked earlier. You don't want to mimic. You want to start on familiar ground, taking cues that you understand right away — and can then build on as you write.

Location Scouting

Location *is* a character in your book, too. Or rather, we feel it can and probably should be. Many stories could take place anywhere. But if that's the case for your stories, we'd urge you to consider whether creating a strong location might make them that much better, or at least more compelling.

In the StoryShop audio series, Sean talks about the TV series *Breaking Bad*. At its core, *Breaking Bad* is about a good man who becomes desperate enough to start cooking and selling crystal meth then slowly spirals down to the dark side. That story, really, could be told anywhere. And at first, little thought was given to setting. It was going to be set in Los Angeles, where any number of untoward things could happen.

As things turned out, New Mexico made it attractive for the creators to shoot there instead of LA. So the story was changed in a way that, if you're not paying much attention, feels merely superficial. Walter White and his family now lived in Albuquerque. So what?

But if you've seen the show, you know what a difference that change in setting made.

Walt in the desert, burying his stash … and bodies.

The Mexican cartels, just over the border.

All those scenes in the barren outlands, beyond the gaze of intrusive eyes.

The dry, dusty feel of everything, coloring the world.

I can't imagine *Breaking Bad* in Los Angeles. It wouldn't have been the same. And given that LA was presented as a *why not LA?* sort of proposition rather than something intentional, I can't imagine it would have been as good. Because the setting would have been background instead of another interesting character in itself.

Our Beats 2.0 packages pay intense attention to location. For some stories, it matters more than others, but it's always considered.

To this end, Sean always *location scouts* our projects — another filmmaker's concept to follow casting. *Axis of Aaron* was originally supposed to take place in a small seaside town, so he found lots of images that delivered the vibe. He just so happened to stumble on images of a pier carnival and decided on a whim to include it, but that carnival (which became known as "Aaron's Party") became a key and creepy part of the narrative. Same for the house images he found: one set of a pristine cottage, the other of an old place falling to tatters. Key to the story.

Though Sean originally meant for *Axis* to take place in a seashore town, I quickly realized it had to be an island. So I modeled it after a real, existing island that meant something to my past: Pelee Island, just north of the Canadian border in Lake Erie. Aaron became an amalgam of what Sean had found and my real place, isolated in the water — ocean instead of lake, in the case of Aaron versus Pelee. And if you've read the story, you'll know why I changed it; if I'd left Aaron on the seashore, it wouldn't have worked. *Location matters.*

Location scouting is mostly photo driven. There are sometimes a few paragraphs of explanation, but I usually only get images: key buildings (interiors and exteriors), townscapes, land features, and so on. Anything that will help me get the feel of being in that place and walking its streets. Nobody other than us sees these images, but they help us form pictures in our heads.

Sean mostly finds photos by searching online for places that have the feel he has in mind, and the right photos will give me the same vibe so we're in agreement. If the world is unreal (*The Dream Engine* books are an excellent example), Sean pulls from art websites, where illustrators have drawn worlds we'd like to inhabit.

From Outline to Tagline

During the initial part of the beats creation process, Sean likes to tell himself the story first by taking his general outline and unspooling that into a story. The first version of this narrative is long and undiluted, hitting all of the primary character arcs and plot points without much of a filter. This version of the story can be anywhere from two to five thousand words.

Once he has that first version of the story, he'll trim it down to a much neater one-thousand-word-or-so version of the same story, minus all the fat.

After that, he'll reduce it even further, down to a one-paragraph elevator pitch. This can serve as the foundation for a strong product description and help to frame the writing itself.

And finally, he'll reduce that elevator pitch to a single sentence or two, which can ultimately serve as the book's tagline.

This exercise helps Sean to *truly* understand the story *before* staring the beats process, both on a micro level (*what happens in the story*) and in a macro level (*what the story is actually about*).

Going from outline to tagline was the final part of the process that made Beats 2.0 what it was, and one of the primary elements that helped us to improve the craft of our stories.

Beats 3.0

As of the time this book hits the virtual press, our story-planning app, StoryShop, isn't yet live. But by the time you read this, it *might* be out there in the wild, helping thousands of authors write better stories faster. And once it is, *that's* where we'll be doing our story planning. Not manually but inside the app, which makes everything easier, better, and faster. It's the next logical iteration, really.

It's worth noting that we created StoryShop for ourselves first, to fit our story-planning process. So of course we're going to want to use it and keep helping it evolve for the users. It's by writers, for writers. And that means we have high standards and insist they be met if we're going to use the thing every day as our most valuable tool.

The big-picture process won't change. We'll refine it, of course, but I don't see the day when we'll stop creating better character profiles, casting for common ground, scouting locations, and doing our best to create a fluid and logical outline.

But the app will make it better. It will evolve our process even further — from today's good to tomorrow's great.

It's going to show us relationships between characters and allow us to know and jump to each scene in which they appear.

It's going to allow us to draw from known templates and worlds.

It's going to guide us in the character-profile-creation process, so it's not so ad hoc. It asks the Character DNA questions, and we answer. It creates profiles we'll intuitively understand, as if our characters were real people sharing too much on social media. Then it exports to Scrivener, our writing software, so we can get started.

I'm keeping this section brief because we don't know what the future will hold, but we know it will be different. Always evolve. Always step forward. Always get better.

Once your stories grow in number and quality, it's time to position them so they'll sell better. And that's the subject of our next chapter — what we optimized next.

CHAPTER EIGHT:
Book Covers, Descriptions, and Metadata

This chapter begins the really juicy stuff. If you do things right with what follows, you'll likely see an immediate return.

More sales. More money in your bank account. Or, less tangibly, more readers looking at your books with optimistic eyes. I don't know if you've ever picked up a book with a terrible cover and sloppy description because a friend asked you to, but I have. And let me tell you, *those books never had a chance*. Fair or not, my brain went in expecting to hate those books because they were so terribly presented.

If you're an *SPP* listener, this is probably the chapter you've been waiting for. So enjoy. But do remember that all of this stuff has its place, and none of it's magic — *it won't work in isolation*.

The greatest book cover in the world won't make your book a best seller if you can't send it traffic (see upcoming chapters on advertising, social media, networking, and podcasting), the most gripping, testimonial-filled description in the world won't net you buyers if nobody reads it. And the whole shebang is nearly useless if you only have one book, have many titles but haven't connected them sensibly (see the "Series Structure" and

"Product Funnels" chapters), or don't gather any of those leads into an email list while they're paying attention. None of the optimizations in this chapter will be worth anything if your book is terrible. Yes, you'll get a sale. Once. Then you'll get bad reviews and be blacklisted by popular vote.

Read this chapter, and be excited by the possibilities. Apply what you can. But if you only have one fifty-page book of poetry and no plan behind it, please don't go out and commission a $1,000 book cover thinking it'll be salve to your woes. You'll only be wasting your money.

Always optimize intelligently and as part of a larger strategy for growth.

Book Covers

Updating our book covers was the most visible and obvious, most expensive, and most valuable change we made during 2015's year of Optimization.

People ask us what's the most important element in selling a book. Kin to that question is what they can do to increase their sales. We don't believe in simple answers even to seemingly simple questions, so we hem and haw at this pair of inquiries, giving various qualifications before answering — qualifications like the ones you just read, about making sure to optimize only when it makes sense and spend when you can reasonably expect a return.

But at that point — all things being equal and assuming you understand that your book has to be good and you should have all your other, less sexy ducks in a row — we'll tell you that getting a better book cover is the best thing you can do.

We've always been ready, fire, aim sorts of guys. You've seen it from us before, and you've seen it in this book. Hell, it's right there in the title: *Iterate*. We've beaten you over the head with it. *Ship first, and ask questions later. Perfect is the enemy of done.*

All of that is still true. And even with book covers, it might still be true under certain circumstances. But with covers, the 80/20 rule doesn't seem to apply. It's the one case where we've found that good enough … simply *isn't*.

In *Write. Publish. Repeat.*, Dave talks about how he designs (now *designed* — past tense) a lot of our covers. This made sense at the time. Dave is a talented visual artist. He understands design and is, in most cases, very good at it. *But Dave is not a cover designer.* And between that last book in our *Smarter Artist* series and the one you're reading, we came to realize just how much that matters.

We used to have covers that were good enough. But that wasn't, well, good enough. People *do judge* a book by its cover, like it or not. That first glance, almost always as a thumbnail amid many other thumbnails, determines if the chronically ADD eye of the online book customer will even click to give you a chance. If they don't, forget all the effort you put into your description to try and sell them. And, much more heartbreakingly, forget all the effort you put into *your book.* Nobody will open the preview. Nobody will use Amazon's Look Inside feature. If someone encounters your book in a physical shop, even a *good enough* cover will likely keep them from picking it up to read the back.

So I figure we'll just show you some of our own before-and-after cover reboots.

Here are the key elements a good book cover needs to have in order to best sell your book — or, more accurately, to get it past the first elimination round in a potential purchaser's mind.

Your book cover should:

Be Attractive and Eye-Catching

This one should be obvious, but good book cover design is a bit like that quote about pornography: You can't always describe it, but you know when you see it. You won't necessarily even know you'll need an upgrade until you decide to get one and then realize how much better the new cover actually is. Only then will you cringe and wonder what the hell was wrong with you.

My favorite example of this is one of the first covers we optimized — for a title that will, when it reappears, no longer bear the name Lexi Maxxwell because the line is undergoing further optimization: *The Future of Sex.*

FOS is science fiction first, spicy second. Some of the stuff in it is explicit, but it is without question a science fiction title. It takes place in the world of our political sci-fi serial *The Beam*, and Sean and I wrote almost all of it. It's smart but sexy.

We had no idea what to do with this book. *None.* We literally said, again and again, "What the hell are we going to do for *FOS?*" And there was no answer.

Dave gave the cover a shot. He did the best he could do, and it was okay. Not really right, but it was kind of slick and … sure, we guessed it could work.

Then we gave it to one of the designers we work with. The before and after are below, with Dave's version on the left:

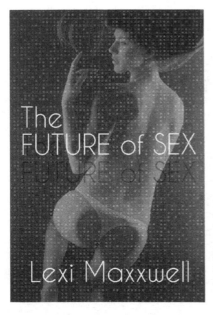 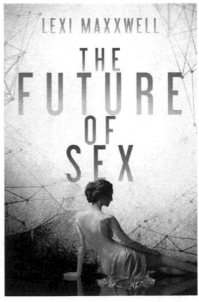

If you're on a black-and-white reader (or print), you won't be able to get the full effect, but in the color version you'll note that the orange sheet is sharp among the teals. The palate is right. The fonts — *very* tricky for almost anyone but a professional book designer to get right — are perfect. We had no idea how to catch a reader's eye with this title, but this cover does it. It draws the ideal buyer in, broadcasting the right things and encouraging them to read on.

And what's more, it perfectly delivers on the story's themes. It's understatedly seductive; it feels sci-fi with the web of nodes and choices of color. It makes you look at the title and description. Only *then* do we have a chance to sell the book, whereas all those potential buyers were clicking away almost immediately before, because the cover didn't snag them.

The next example is for *Yesterday's Gone,* the flagship series in Sean and Dave's Collective Inkwell imprint. The original cover is *good enough*. The series sold well with that cover — in 2012, when self-publishing was new. Nowadays, you can't be *good enough for an indie*. Now readers see you beside traditional books and expect you to look equally pro.

Here's the before and after of *Yesterday's Gone*. And I mean … just look at how much more dynamic the one on the right is. How much more it draws the post-apocalyptic sci-fi reader in to learn more by reading the description and maybe a sample of the book itself:

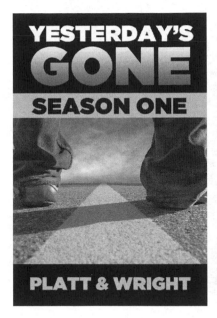
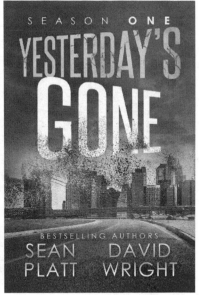

Much more interesting than the boots on the road. Much more magnetic. *Now* the book has a shot — and, of course, sells much better.

But having an attractive cover isn't enough. There's more on that checklist of what makes a book cover compelling enough to help sell your book, so let's move on and point out that covers must also …

Be Genre-Appropriate

A lot of book covers look great, but are still wrong. That's because they're the perfect covers to attract a reader you can't or won't reach (or wouldn't be right for your book if you did).

We all want to be unique. We all want to be different. Nobody wants to be just like everyone else. And believe me, Sean and I are prime examples. We wrote a western mashed with a fantasy and figured it'd be unique enough for everyone to easily see its awesomeness. We wrote a romance without a happy ending then were shocked when it didn't sell because we knew it was an excellent story. We put irreverent comedy next to our serious work and pooh-poohed Dave's protests that we'd confuse and deter our readers — *something about which he was absolutely right.*

But book covers are a place where you don't want to be too different. You don't want to stand out too far. You'll look out of place, not unique. People won't look at your cover and think, "That one isn't like any of the others! I want to check it out!" They'll think, "That one isn't like any of the others! What the hell is it doing here?" before passing it by.

Our best example is from the cover reboot for *The Beam.* Here's what it looked like before:

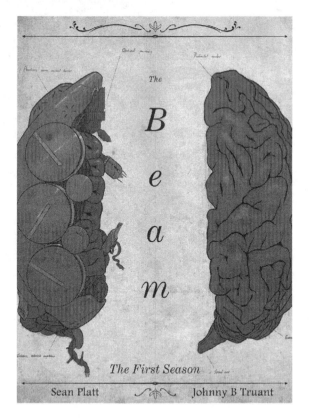

When we got that art back, Sean and I both thought it was great. As a piece of art. We'd hang it on our wall. And it perfectly fit the *aura* of *The Beam;* it's not a shoot-em-up, buttons-and-chrome sort of sci-fi, so this quieter cover made sense. The book is downright philosophical in parts. The original cover, which combined a cybernetic brain with an organic brain, felt perfect. The idea of *upgrading biology* is heavy in the series.

But there was a big problem. As much as we liked this cover *as a piece of art and as a vindication of our story,* it stuck out like a weed in sci-fi, where people expect buttons and chrome and spaceships and circuitry.

So we got a new cover:

The reason the new cover works is that it *actually looks like sci-fi*. It's still thematically correct: *The Beam* is about power and politics in a future world where a super-Internet immerses people in its omnipresent web. This cover broadcasts all of that, but now it fits in as well. Now it's not so unique that the right readers click away. Now the book has a chance to sell and thrive on its own right.

And speaking of making sure the cover fits the book, that leads us to the fact that a cover should ...

Promise What the Book Actually Delivers

Your cover can't and shouldn't be deceptive. That would be stupid. If your cover suggests it's a romance, but the actual story is about a zombie horde, expect some bad reviews. (Unless the horde is extraordinarily romantic, there's a happy ending, and none of the zombies cheats on their partners with other zombies.)

One of the fastest ways to ruin your chances as an author is to attract the wrong readers while repelling the right ones. The right reader is one who will like your (well-written, professionally edited) book. The wrong reader is one who won't like your stuff even if you do everything right.

Your cover needs to make a promise you can deliver. Look back to *The Beam* cover. Yes, we added glitz to the new cover that wasn't in the first. But it's not like the story doesn't deliver the glitz. There's plenty of bang-zoom cool in *The Beam*. It's not a thoughtful treatise on humanity and nothing else.

We have a cover example to go with this point of delivering what you promise, but before we give it, let's address a twin consideration ...

A Cover Should Promise What the Reader Expects, Too

There's what your book is.

There's what *you* feel your book is.

And then there's what your book could be seen as if you look at it from a different angle.

Take our book *Unicorn Western*. Is it a western, with unicorns and magic added? Or is it a fantasy with a bunch of western motifs? Our default, because of *Unicorn Western's* origin story (Sean and I wrote it when Dave said we couldn't write a western without doing research) was to think of it as a western. That's a mistake because western readers want *westerns*. They don't want unicorns. But on the flip side, fantasy readers are okay with authors getting chocolate in their peanut butter. Stephen King paired gunslingers and magic in *The Dark Tower,* paving the way. All things considered — seeing as *Unicorn Western* could be positioned as either — it behooves us to call the book a fantasy not a western.

That's what we mean in this section. Don't make your book look like something it isn't. Don't make promises your book doesn't deliver, but *do* show its most appropriate side to those readers who are most likely to buy and enjoy it.

My example here is *The Dream Engine* — the first in our young adult fantasy/steampunk series.

The original cover was illustrated by Erin Mehlos, the same artist who did our cover for the *Unicorn Western Full Saga* — one of few that survived our cover overhaul. I really like that cover and resisted changing it. It's a cool image, and I love the way Erin conceptualized the Blunderbuss (the big steampunk engine in the book's title) behind our heroine, Eila.

But it sold as steampunk, and that wasn't the book's best positioning.

The story *is* steampunk (an imagined world where the dominant innovations remained steam based rather than microchip based), but only half so. It's also fantasy. It's about dreams and their intersection with reality. It features dragons, trolls, and evil spirits. The long-term trajectory for the series is fantasy, too; it was conceived with Sean's one-liner "steampunk *Lord of the Rings.*"

There are people who buy steampunk, for sure. But given the target audience for this book — the sweet spot is teen girls, though the audience is definitely wider than that — we needed to put its best fantasy foot forward. Steampunk moved to the background because the key demographic tends to pick up fantasy books more readily than steampunk.

So here's the cover revamp for *The Dream Engine*, with the original steampunk version on the left and the improved fantasy look on the right:

 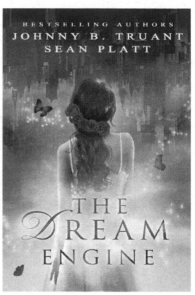

Remember, this isn't a case of good versus bad. It's a case of good versus *more optimized.* Many of our covers became better, but some — like this one — were simply adjusted so they'd have a better chance of hitting the target and delivering what the genre was asking for.

A Note on 3-D Covers

This is one of those sections that could change tomorrow but bears mentioning because it's something we changed during our year of Optimization.

When Sean and I released *The Beam*, we were using an episodes-and-seasons release model that we cover in *Write. Publish. Repeat.* That method — releasing individual episodes of a serial then bundling them into a full season later — worked great for *Yesterday's Gone*'s initial seasons but was becoming obsolete by the time we published *The Beam*. Still, we released it that way, with individual novella-length episodes for $2.99 each and bundled into seasons of six episodes for what felt like a bargain price at $9.99. You'll see our pricing arguments and Dave's objections in *WPR*, too.

Because $9.99 is a high price for indie authors, we wanted to go out of our way to make it clear that *this was a collection of books that would be twice as expensive purchased individually.* We put *Complete First Season Collection* in the title. We indicated that it was *Episodes 1-6* to connote a bundle. And we made 3-D cover images to convey the same message.

Then two things changed. First, we stopped releasing individual episodes. The system simply didn't work anymore, so we began releasing all of our serials in full seasons from the get-go. And second, it seemed like 2014 was the year of the 99-cent box set. Everyone was bundling a ton of books then selling that big box for under a buck to scurry up the charts. Box sets became shorthand for cheap. If you had a box set that wasn't 99 cents, it got a lot harder to sell.

Because we were no longer releasing singles, the need to say "bundle" with our cover images went away. And one by one, we returned to plain old 2-D cover images, showing our serial seasons to readers as the singular experience they'd become.

We still use 3-D covers for true box sets and fight the battle that comes with offering them for above 99 cents. This could all change tomorrow but is our MO for now.

But Where Do I Find a Good Cover Designer?

You have to look around. We use a few different sources — both freelancers and agencies — with a few favorites among them. You'll need to find the source that works best for you.

Our first-stop recommendation tends to be 99Designs. We use them ourselves, and they sponsor our podcast. To answer your question, yes, I suppose the sponsorship biases us a bit, and yes, we get credit (not a commission) if you use the 99Designs.com/SPP link we give out on the show. So if that bugs you, go direct to the site and skip our link (though you will miss out on the FREE PowerPack upgrade!). We love them regardless because it's a crowdsourced contest setup with a results-or-you-don't-pay guarantee.

For illustrated stuff, we really like Donovan Scherer. We've used Donovan mainly for humor and children's books, but he does plenty of other stuff. Check him out at RatatatGraphics.com.

Failing that, look around. Find covers you like. Ask your friends. It's worth the hard work to find someone whose work represents you best … and then pay them what you can afford. Not a stupid amount; you should have some realistic expectation of return on your investment. But don't be cheap. This is your book's most important sales and marketing asset.

Book Descriptions

Descriptions matter a ton. Your book cover and title hooks people in and makes them curious, but it's then your description's job to convert that potential buyer to a sale. If your description is awful or uninteresting, readers will think, *Well, that cover was nice, but this book clearly sucks, so I'll move on to other books with nice covers and non-sucky plot lines.* Congratulations: you've lost the sale.

Descriptions, like everything we've done, have gone through an iterative, optimized process.

Admittedly, our first iteration was terrible, and you shouldn't follow our lead. Because we were in publish-as-fast-as-possible mode during 2013, we sort of winged stuff out there without taking time to consider whether our descriptions were appropriately hooking the reader. Spoiler alert: They weren't. We lost a lot of sales because we half-assed so much of it. But that made sense, seeing as it was step one.

True to the Iteration year, we left the old descriptions alone for time's sake and did everything we could to make our new descriptions better. That was step two.

Step three, which we began during the Optimization year, was for me to rewrite them all. This was a horrible option. Not only was I busy and couldn't get to them, the task was thankless and thoroughly sucked.

We had a guest on the *Self-Publishing Podcast* around who taught us a lot about descriptions. Her name is Libbie Hawker, and you should absolutely pick up her book *Gotta Read It!* Search your favorite bookseller, and buy yourself a copy.

The long and short — what you'll see in *Gotta Read It!* — is that your descriptions need to be written as teasers, not synopses. You need to introduce the main conflicts then leave them dangling so readers will want to read the book to find out how they resolve.

Our current iteration of writing book descriptions is so much better than the last one. Right now, Garrett is writing them for us. He knows our books (he reads almost all of them) and was smart enough to figure out that reading the beats would let him write descriptions for books that he hadn't yet read. He's read Libbie's book and knows the right way to craft descriptions. And holy crap, I don't have to do anything. It's brilliant.

Metadata

Metadata is all the behind-the-scenes stuff you enter into publishing dashboards when filling out your book listings. Here, we're talking specifically about stuff that the bookseller sees that readers don't — or at least not in the same way.

We used to ignore most of this, but we've slowly been optimizing as we go through our catalog because it really does matter for visibility and search.

Most of what we learned about metadata we got from Nick Stephenson, author of *Supercharge Your Kindle Sales*. We highly recommend picking that book up and giving it a read. It's a great, fast little primer on making your books more visible.

We'll give you a brief bit on two key metadata components here then leave you to pick up Nick's book for a whole lot more.

Categories

Every seller has a category system for its books, and you can usually plunk your book into around five categories. The primary category should obviously be the best fit, with *fit* decreasing as you descend the list. But try to stick that book into everything you can without lying (i.e., don't put your thriller into erotica just because erotica gets a lot of eyes).

That's about as far as we used to go, and I'll be brief on categories, seeing as the real category stuff that matters is covered in the next section on keywords. But first, I'll point something out that should be obvious but isn't always: *the more categories your book exists in, the better chance someone will see your book.*

But also keep in mind that *your best bet is to put the book in front of people who will actually be interested in reading it.*

Sounds simple. But it isn't, the way most authors treat it.

Take my solo series, *Fat Vampire*. There are definitely funny scenes throughout the series, and the humor is a hook I can hang the series on if I want to. But only the first book is satire first; the rest becomes a much more action-and-blood-rich vampire tale about a war between the undead and humanity. So it would be a mistake to make the full series' primary category satire. Assuming it's positioned right (and the cover reboot for the full collection does a lot of that), it should be put in front of *horror* readers. *Occult* readers. *Dark fantasy* readers. Maybe *action* readers. And sure, if there's room down the pike, satire can get in there too, but the earlier categories are for the people most likely to pick up the book with its new cover and truly enjoy it, rate it well, and share it with their friends.

But satire readers? Humor readers just out for a laugh? Not so much.

Now, you may have one big objection: We said that most platforms let you put your book into five categories or so but not Amazon. The biggest bookseller gives you only two.

That's where categories and keywords intersect, so let's go there now.

Keywords

If you want to know what categories a book is listed in on Amazon, scroll down toward the very bottom of the product page and look at the links under Look for Similar Items by Category. Those links, as of publication, list where a book is appearing, not necessarily where it was placed by the author in their publishing dashboard.

Here's that category list for our book *Invasion*:

Look for Similar Items by Category

- Books > Mystery, Thriller & Suspense > Thrillers & Suspense > Suspense
- Books > Science Fiction & Fantasy > Science Fiction > Alien Invasion
- Books > Science Fiction & Fantasy > Science Fiction > Colonization
- Books > Science Fiction & Fantasy > Science Fiction > First Contact
- Books > Science Fiction & Fantasy > Science Fiction > Galactic Empire
- Books > Science Fiction & Fantasy > Science Fiction > Military > Space Fleet
- Kindle Store > Kindle eBooks > Literature & Fiction > Action & Adventure > Mystery, Thriller & Suspense > Suspense
- Kindle Store > Kindle eBooks > Mystery, Thriller & Suspense > Suspense
- Kindle Store > Kindle eBooks > Science Fiction & Fantasy > Science Fiction > Adventure
- Kindle Store > Kindle eBooks > Science Fiction & Fantasy > Science Fiction > Alien Invasion
- Kindle Store > Kindle eBooks > Science Fiction & Fantasy > Science Fiction > Colonization
- Kindle Store > Kindle eBooks > Science Fiction & Fantasy > Science Fiction > First Contact
- Kindle Store > Kindle eBooks > Science Fiction & Fantasy > Science Fiction > Galactic Empire
- Kindle Store > Kindle eBooks > Science Fiction & Fantasy > Science Fiction > Military > Space Fleet
- Kindle Store > Kindle eBooks > Science Fiction & Fantasy > Science Fiction > Post-Apocalyptic

Now I don't know about you, but I count fifteen categories. Or, if we stick to Kindle Store categories, nine. That's a few more than the two you're allowed.

Their help pages move around, but if you Google for *Amazon keywords categories,* you'll find a help page that lists keywords you can enter into your KDP dashboard to access certain hidden categories. There's no way to select most of the category paths you see above, for instance — and certainly not in the cascade order shown. If you want to get into the First Contact category, you have to select a category with the Science Fiction root category (ours is Science Fiction > Alien Invasion) then type *Contact* as one of your keywords. Do that, and you'll appear in the First Contact category.

There's a whole other aspect to keywords that I'll only mention and again direct you to Nick Stephenson's book for more. And that's the idea of treating booksellers like search engines rather than stores.

Meaning people search for phrases. They might search for young adult vampire books. I don't know; I haven't checked. But just like any search engine, there are phrases people search for more and some they don't use at all, even though you'd think they would. One goal, if you want eyes on your work, should be to *search engine optimize* your books (including keywords) so you appear at the top in those searches. That means finding popular search phrases without a ton of books in them or with only some poorly keyword-optimized titles.

Spend some time optimizing your keywords. Use them to come up in search and appear in additional categories, like we did. All other things being equal, more eyeballs mean more sales.

CHAPTER NINE:
Series Structure

If you want to maximize your chances of making money as an author from the start, you shouldn't do what Sean and I did at Realm & Sands by playing hopscotch with genre. You shouldn't even do what Sean and Dave did at Collective Inkwell, seeing as they still hopped between different series within their genre.

Really — and this is short-term thinking, with the need for eventual diversification always close behind — you'll want to stick to *one* series in *one* popular genre if you're looking for maximum chances of *immediate* success. It hurts a bit to say that, but it's true.

Maybe you like thrillers. Write a thriller. Then write a sequel to that thriller, then another, and another. You'll compound your gains. It's the opposite of what CI did by hopping between series and *really* the opposite of what R&S did by jumping between series in widely different genres.

Because we'd spooled out so many threads with our series, our Optimization year also called for whipping them into order.

Here are a few of the ways we did it.

Deciding What's a Series and What Isn't

Sean and I started our collaborative partnership by writing the first *Unicorn Western* book. It was twenty-five thousand words, making it more of a novella than a novel. Then we wrote *Unicorn Western 2*, so called because it was the second book in our series. Then came *Unicorn Western 3*. Seeing a pattern? We just knew that each came after the other. We'd always envisioned it as a nine-book series, with each book using the same basic arc as a classic western. And when we finished, we had books one through nine. We bundled them into the giant fantasy volume we call the *Unicorn Western Full Saga*.

The series then suffered a bit of an identity crisis. We realized that nobody thought of the *Saga* as a collection. We did, but that's only because we'd written the parts as distinct books and had separated them as such inside the master volume. Readers didn't see it that way. Intellectually, they understood. The first book was permanently free, so people would read that then decide to buy the *Saga*. Nobody bought *Unicorn Western 2* for three bucks. There wasn't any point.

So in iteration number two of *Unicorn Western* (or perhaps optimization attempt number one), we de-listed all of the individual books except for the free first volume. We only left the *Saga*. And that was fine.

But then we thought about our children. *Unicorn Western* gets a bit complex at the end, but there's no swearing, sex, or overt violence (other than gunslinger-style fisticuffs), and the intention from the beginning was to write something our kids would love. They did. But my son reads in print, not digital, and you should have seen his face when I gave him that enormous, two hundred and fifty thousand-word doorstop.

I grew up reading the Hardy Boys. Sean read *Babysitters Club* (true story) and many others. The model was the same: smaller, more consumable books. Considering the audience (and I'll admit *UW* ended up skewing older, but whatever), we knew it should be little books after all — but there was something wrong with how we were originally doing it.

Which brings us to our next point.

Making Series into True Series

We hamstrung *Unicorn Western* as a series of smaller books because we didn't treat them as parts of a proper series. We treated them as derivative. There was one custom book cover, then Erin changed the background colors and the numeral on the front. The titles *(Unicorn Western 2, Unicorn Western 3)* were also derivative. No wonder the series had an identity crisis. We were calling it one thing and grooming it as another.

The best example of the proper *series-ization* (I know that's not a word) done to optimize our titles isn't *Unicorn Western* because we're not ready to rebrand and relaunch those books just yet. But fortunately, we have another great example in *Cursed*.

We handled *Cursed* exactly like *Unicorn Western*. The idea was to have a string of adventures for our hero, Ricardo, and each time he'd face a new challenge. The original concept was *The Fugitive* with a chupacabra. We figured he'd have one adventure after another.

But, of course, the series got all Realm & Sands on us. It stopped being about an adventure of the week and gained a coherent arc. The books became true sequels, but we weren't treating them that way. Because they were so quick to produce, spending a ton on covers (and time on names and descriptions) felt like a hassle. We half-assed most of it, asking Dave to design some basic covers. Naturally, we got results commensurate with the corners cut.

Here's what the first three *Cursed* books used to look like:

And here's the reboot:

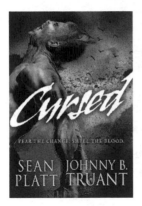
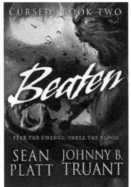
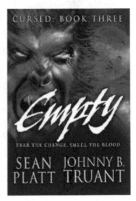

Here's what we changed and why it now makes *Cursed* a proper, consumable series from a reader's perspective:

Better Covers

Let's state the obvious: The new covers are just … better. And sure, it's possible you don't agree, but believe me, most of the horror genre does. The images are much more compelling regardless. They draw the eye. They earn the click. They pull in the right readers for these specific books. Which brings us to …

More Aligned Covers

I'm not kidding that *Cursed* started out as *The Fugitive* with a chupacabra, which is why we originally called it *Chupacabra Outlaw*. We also thought it might be kind of funny. It turned out to be dry and sparse and violent and bleak. It's the only series we have with literally no funny moments. Usually, even in our darkest stuff, characters will make amusing remarks here or there. But not in this series.

Starting out, we didn't know if the series was funny or serious, action or horror, chupacabra or whatever the opposite of a chupacabra is (a groundhog, maybe).

Once we got some distance, we realized: Of course; this is a werewolf book, except we call our werewolf a chupacabra. We'd made the mythical beast into something that was dark and demonic — cursed, if you will. But it was a shapeshifter with sharp teeth and talons, legs that bent backward like the devil. Our hero was tortured, not happy-go-lucky as an otherworldly beast. He didn't like being what he was. It was torture.

The new cover (and the non-stupid title) sells that story. It also sells werewolf instead of chupacabra, which harkens back to last chapter's discussion of positioning your book as what readers want and expect rather than point-blank what you have. It's really a werewolf book at heart. So the new cover sells that and lets the reader figure out that we're using a chupacabra once they're already immersed in the story — once they're past pre-judgment and are far less likely to care.

More Aligned Descriptions

Garrett wrote the first description for *Cursed*. We can't blame him because Sean and I okay'd it, but it hurts me to say that the first line of the original description was ...

(Wow, I *really* don't want to admit this.)

... *"Chupa-what-now?"*

Ahem. Yes. Well, anyway.

So obviously that changed. Because we didn't want to sell chupacabra (something the reader usually ends up liking but would double take before giving it a chance) and instead wanted to sell shapeshifter, which the genre already knows it likes. We removed all chupacabra mentions. He's a *shapeshifter*. And he's *cursed*. All good things that align with the genre.

Oh, and did you notice what else we added to the new covers? It was the first line in the new description, too, making a marked improvement over the what-now business.

It's ...

A Killer Tagline

I love the tagline: *Fear the Change. Smell the Blood.*

For the right reader, that tagline makes *what Cursed is* smack them right between the eyes. *Blood?* That's good. *Change?* That's shapeshifter stuff right there. Combine that with the cursed-looking guy transforming on the cover amid the many shades of red, and the book positions itself, giving it an excellent head start when presented to the right audience.

Non-Derivative Book Names

Here's something that took us too long to figure out, across several series: *If you want people to treat books as their own thing rather than pieces in a collection, maybe actually call them by different names.*

Originally, we did better with *Cursed* than we had with *Unicorn Western*. Book 2 in the *Cursed* series always had its own name *(Beaten)*, but in the 1.0 version it was still *CURSED 2: Beaten*. Now it's *Beaten*. Oh, and by the way, it's book 2 in the *Cursed* series.

Whether *Cursed* soars or falls flat in the short term has yet to be determined, but at least now it's optimized as a proper series. Meaning: whether it does well or not will no longer be hampered, at least, by our own failure to give it an optimized fighting chance.

Writing More Traditional Series

People's reading habits seems to be changing. Folks are reading more on the go; more people these days are consuming books on their phones. And maybe that means they're gravitating toward shorter, more consumable works.

It all makes sense, except that it's not jibing with our experience. At least not in terms of what sells and what doesn't.

We don't do anything only for the money; we're always searching, even with our most commercial properties, to find the intersections between *what sells best* and *what we want to write*. So when I say this next bit (and when you read the paragraph before this one, about what sells and what doesn't), please understand that we're not trying to play the market. As guys who like to write all sorts of stuff, we're asking what our readers want because they're the people who appreciate our art most of all.

Contrary to the first bit in this section, we're finding people respond to longer books in traditional series just as much as they always have.

Meaning: Yes, we can do a series like *Cursed*, with twenty- to twenty-five thousand-word installments. But people complain when we do. They tell us they want longer books. They don't want the stories to end so soon.

So we started writing a few projects as normal series. Not short series with frequent installments; not serials; not stand-alone novels; not episodic novellas. Just plain old normal-length *books*, strung together in a series.

We're gravitating more toward publishing exactly the same kinds of books that traditional thinking would have had us writing twenty years earlier: books in the range of eighty thousand to one hundred thousand words for the first installment, growing slightly longer as the series progresses.

(Side note: on membership-based audiobook sites like Audible, audiobooks shorter than this have an additional handicap because people don't want to waste their credits — which spend the same regardless of book length — on less meaty products.)

I couldn't say why given our increasingly ADHD culture, but our longer books *just sell better*, assuming they're in a popular genre and all other things are equal. This may not be your experience, but it has been ours.

And so when we decided to write *Invasion, Contact,* and *Colonization* (books 1-3 in the *Alien Invasion* series) we wrote them as three books of around eighty thousand to one hundred thousand words each. When I wrote the draft of *Dead City* — our *The-Walking-Dead*-meets-*All-the-President's-Men* zombie thriller that will debut on our *Indie Fiction Podcast*, which you'll hear about later — we were shooting for around one hundred thousand words. Same for the *Dream Engine* series and most of our forthcoming projects.

Your mileage may differ, but in our business, readers keep asking for complete, immersive experiences. So a big part of our iterating forward is in creating more expansive works, and giving our fans exactly what they want.

CHAPTER TEN:
Product Funnels

Product funnel basics have been the same since before anyone *called* them funnels and certainly haven't changed since late 2013, when we published *Write. Publish. Repeat.* You still need an entry product that's widely available and an upsell to the next logical purchase if that person liked what they got the first time around. You still want clear connections between products ("If you like this, you might like this other thing") and some sort of a call to action, obvious and visible accompanying the widely available product, that ensures people know that product A leads to product B.

Optionally, product B (then products C, D, and E to follow) can be more expensive or more advanced in some way: a bundle, an upgraded offer, a more select or funneled-down experience. Because that's another thing about funnels: They narrow as you move through them. There are many people entering a funnel at the top and relatively few making it all the way to the bottom.

In *Write. Publish. Repeat.*, we describe the default S&S funnel as starting with a free book and then upselling to a bundle — or, in some cases, the next book in our series. Nonfiction funnels are a bit different; the entry points were the *Self-Publishing Podcast* (free) and *WPR* (normally $5.99). We had deeper ways to get down the funnel, too, but as with anything, nonfiction funnels have improved with time.

In case you're missing a dominant theme throughout this book, it's that the creative entrepreneur's world is *constantly changing*. We say that "Self-publishing years are like dog years." "X event happened eighteen months ago," we'll say. And then we'll add, "But hey, that's like five self-publishing years."

Read through the next chapter, but don't take it as gospel any more than you should have taken *WPR*'s funnel advice. Take what might work for you, try it out, and note your results. Then stay nimble because we're constantly adjusting ourselves.

The biggest change in our funnels is in the way we use FREE, so let's start there.

The Changed Role of Free

I still like my Angry Birds example from *Write. Publish. Repeat.* about how that company mined so much of my family's money only because the first game was free and that made it easy for all of us to get addicted. The magnetism of "But it's free!" is hard to ignore, and we're still using that model for some of our funnels. So let's be clear: It's absolutely *not* the case that we no longer believe in the free-to-upsell model, whether that upsell is to the next book in a series or a full bundle.

But that being said, the ways in which we use free products have definitely changed. *First book free* remains a viable strategy for us but is no longer our default. As with anything you do as a card-carrying Smarter Artist, whether or not to offer your first-in-series book free is something you should analyze and question — then do only *if* it makes sense.

I'll break down some things we've learned and tried regarding free in a moment, but first I should point to an episode of

SPP where we talked this stuff out at length: "Episode #166 — Is Free Still a Viable Strategy?" It aired on July 15, 2015 and summarized our thoughts as of that date. But stuff gets obsolete fast around here, so it's entirely possible our minds will have changed by June of 2017. Use with caution, and if you want to keep abreast of the latest-breaking information out there, your best bet is to subscribe to the *Self-Publishing Podcast*.

Here's what we've discovered after using free as a key strategy for two years:

The Perception and Visibility of Free Books Has Changed

One discovery we made (and adjusted to) was the way the ideal *free books* strategy shifted between 2013 and 2015. What follows might not be true of you, in your unique situation, today, but it was definitely true for us.

When we began in 2012 and 2013, free books were unique enough to get some respect. Or if they didn't get *respect*, per se, at least they got *interest*. Amazon in particular was big on free books a few years ago and used to feature a Top 100 Free list that appeared right beside the Top 100 Paid list in every genre. You could be the most downloaded free book in the store (or the most downloaded free book in the Horror > Frightening Small Creatures > Toothy Dwarves subcategory), and you'd get this great place of honor *right friggin' beside* the top-selling paid book in the store (or subcategory). It made you look like a rock star, and it got a lot of readers to notice your book who otherwise might never have seen it.

Shortly thereafter, things changed. Amazon hid the top free books behind a tab, and only people who were specifically looking for free books began finding them.

It also used to be that if you had a free book that had got a lot of downloads, you could rank highly in the Amazon algorithms and end up appearing near the top of the popularity charts even after your book returned to paid status. But that wasn't true in the year immediately preceding *WPR*'s publication. And perhaps most damaging of all, we realized in 2015 that Amazon was no longer showing free books in the list below paid books where it says Customers Who Bought This Item Also Bought, commonly referred to as "also-boughts" or by the bastardized (but commonly used) bastardization "alsobots."

This perfect storm was a mortal blow for free titles. Because free books became all but invisible to casual browsers, it meant for the most part that only free-seekers found them. Paid-book buyers used to see the free ones, too, but no longer.

Everyone is making their books free these days. If your strategy is simply to make your book free and wait for the world to find it, you're begging for disappointment.

Which brings us to the next topic.

First Book Free Is No Longer Automatic

We've already implied this, but here's the finer point: We no longer automatically make that first book in a series free without further thought. That used to be the way we did things, but it doesn't make sense today.

Now, just because it's not automatic doesn't mean we don't do it. Far from it. For some reason, iBooks seems uniquely amenable to free books, especially if you can get some sort of featured placement on the store. It also seems to be the case that iBooks readers don't horde as much as other stores' freebie downloaders: They tend to read what they get. And perhaps because they're used to forking over extra cash for Apple products, they're also not cheap. They'll buy your next book or bundle if they like what they read.

During 2015, *Yesterday's Gone: Season One* had a featured *first book free* tile on iBooks. It was also featured in the Barnes & Noble NOOK store on "NOOK Free Friday," and we also bought a BookBub ad to go with it. That trifecta has resulted in a metric crap-ton of downloads and subsequent follow-through sales — so yes, with enough exposure, the first-book-free model definitely still works.

But what we did with *YG* isn't what we do for everything, in every circumstance.

Invasion is our most popular series. "Three books in the series" used to be the point where we'd make the first book free, but well past the fourth book's release, book 1 was still full price.

So why didn't we make it free earlier? Honestly, it's because we didn't really need to. Even without any promotion, there was seldom a day that *Invasion* didn't sell thirty copies — and there were waves that pushed that number much higher. It's also a highly commercial series. That meant it was much easier to get big advertising placement when the book was simply discounted, not free. BookBub featured *Invasion* at 99 cents twice before we even considered going free … and because it was still a *paid* book, that meant it remained visible in all those lists and also-bots, whereas free wouldn't have had that benefit.

But we did make *Invasion* free eventually, after it had been out for a year. But it won't be free forever, and that brings us to the next topic.

Temporary Free Might Be Better Than Permafree

The model we like more than permafree is *temporary free*.

When not being advertised, permafree books tend to saturate the group that they're exposed to. Once all the free seekers in your category have seen and grabbed your free book, it'll likely slide slowly into oblivion. This had happened for *Yesterday's Gone* before the big push we just told you about.

By contrast, when something is *temporarily* free, the people who see it tend to think, "I'd better get that now before it goes away." You won't lose all of your sales momentum on the paid charts (assuming you had some), and going free again later will still be something worth telling people about because it's not *always* free.

If you're temporarily (not permanently) free, you're also in alsobots (as a paid book) before and after the promotion. That means you're visible and maybe top-of-mind for some readers. When your book goes free, people might recognize and get it because they've been exposed to the cover and title before.

Lastly, we like what temporarily free says to readers: *These books are worth paying for, so this won't last forever.* That strategy positions you well in buyers' minds.

As with anything, you have to consider your own unique situation and what you want out of it. We're not crapping on permafree. What we've described for *Invasion* and *Yesterday's Gone*, in fact, is something between a quickie free promotion and true permafree. Rather than making your book free for a week just so you can run some ads (keep reading) before raising the price back up, our strategy is sort of "This can stay free as long as the download numbers remain solid and buy-through to the later books in the series is still good." When that stops being true, we end the quasi-permafree run, return the price to normal, and wait to repeat the process some time in the future — once going free with the book will again be noteworthy, or allow us to book even more ads.

The game is constantly changing, so you should be asking yourself, "Is the free strategy I'm using truly working for me?" If it is, awesome. If not, don't keep banging your head against the wall, assuming something will magically change to save you.

You Need to Advertise Your Free Book to Get It Seen

Making a book free used to be an easy button. You'd make your book free; people would see it; people would download it, and new readers would enter your funnel, soon to purchase full-price sequels and bundles, assuming your writing was good. But that's not how it was after Amazon's changes. At all. And we don't see it changing anytime soon.

You can no longer count on traffic to automagically just show up when you make a title free. You might see a small uptick when a book *first* goes free, but for permafree books there's a dungeon of diminishing returns. Because it's so much harder to simply *bump into* free titles when browsing, your book tends to be downloaded mostly by the kind of people who *never* buy.

To get your book beyond the eyes of only free-seekers, you have to advertise. Doing so will push interested traffic to your offer. The players in this space are shuffling all the time, but if you search around for free book advertising venues, you'll find plenty. But some work better than others. Ask your author friends or forums what's working now. Don't overspend. With a very few exceptions, it's seldom something that should cost more than $30 to do. Be sure to subscribe to the *Self-Publishing Podcast* for the latest info here.

Advertising gives your book the nudge it needs to get it in front of people, turning a first-in-series free book (or some other kind of free product) back into a sound strategy. The message to readers is something like, "Try this sample. It's free. Why not?"

A Bigger Focus on List Building

A few years ago, *first thing free* seemed to be the best way to chug new prospects through our creative funnels. For fiction, we made our first book permafree and let interested readers click through the CTAs in the back of that title to buy the next book or a bundle. For nonfiction, the *Self-Publishing Podcast* was our free thing. Many listeners bought *Write. Publish. Repeat.* and the *Fiction Unboxed* book. A thousand of them supported *Fiction Unboxed* when it was a Kickstarter campaign (and some continue to buy the *Fiction Unboxed* experience after the fact).

We still use first thing free across the board, but the *way* in which we use it — for fiction, at least — has changed.

Now, we'd much rather use free books as an enticement to join our list.

There are four basic ways we do this. I'll give you our examples at Realm & Sands below, but we use similar methods in our other imprints as well.

Get the Sequel Free (In-Book)

My favorite listbuilder is the one that offers *Contact* (book 2 in the *Invasion* series) in both the front and back of the *Invasion* book. We learned this strategy from Nick Stephenson, so let me drop another plug for his book *Supercharge Your Kindle Sales*, which is awesome.

We put a call to action showing *Contact*'s book cover and a link to get it free on the first page of the book. (If you use Scrivener, put this item inside main binder before the story begins, NOT in a "front matter" folder. On most devices, front matter is skipped when a reader first opens the book.) This way, our CTA is the first thing people see when they open *Invasion*: "Oh, snap! I can get the second book free right now!"

Then we repeat that exact same CTA in the back of the book, after the story ends. So they've just finished the book and read the cliffhanger. Again they say, "Oh, snap! I was going to buy the sequel, but now I don't have to pay for it!"

(Yes. They all say, "Oh, snap!")

The CTA takes them to a page on our website where they can enter their email address and join our list to get the free book. The first email they get after confirming they want to join our list gives them the link to download the free book with instructions on how to sideload it onto their device.

I love this listbuilder. It ensures that only people who like us join the list. By definition, only people who downloaded *Invasion* enter the funnel. Most of the time, that person joining our list has also read *Invasion* and liked it enough to want the sequel — seeing as it's the reason they joined the list.

This method gives you a pure, aligned list. We've also found that this is a great way to get a *grateful* and *responsive* list. Our email service sends a "just checking in" email the day after people get their free book, and it's amazing how many people respond to that email with a thank you, along with stories of how they found our books and how much they enjoy them. This is author/reader bonding at its best.

Get Two Books Free (In-Book)

We have a crap-ton of books at Realm & Sands, so we're not precious with any of them. Your situation may differ, but as we've optimized our systems, we've decided we'll always trade a sale for a list-add. *Invasion* sells well, but we'll happily give *Invasion* away if we can get that person to join our list — which might mean capturing the attention of a lifelong fan.

The previous section only works for *Invasion*. Putting an offer for "book 2 in the *Invasion* series" into anything other than book *1* in the *Invasion* series doesn't make sense, because no one wants to start at book 2, and the need to buy book 1 is therefore an obstacle to joining our list.

But we want *all* of our books funneling people into our list. Not just *Invasion*, with its offer of *Contact* for free.

So we made a separate offer for all other books. Take *The Beam*, for instance. *The Beam* doesn't have an offer saying "join our list and get *Contact* free." We needed an offer that was more logical to put in *The Beam*, so we created a "join our list and get *Invasion* AND *Contact* free."

The mechanics are the same except that obviously the link goes somewhere else and we need a different list to deliver the two books. But this way we can get readers of the other titles in our catalog to consider joining our list, seeing as they'll get two free books if they do.

Now, three questions may be arising. Let's answer those:

We give both *Invasion* AND *Contact* away because *Invasion* is sometimes "quasi-permafree" as mentioned earlier

in this chapter. "Get *Invasion* free" is a terrible list bribe if it's free anyway. Giving both books away at all times — including times when *Invasion* isn't free — is our way of future-proofing the process and keeping us from needing to shuffle CTAs each time a change is made.

No, we're not worried that people will get mad if they already bought *Invasion* and are now getting it offered for free. Yes, we're taking that chance. But you can't build a business on what-if.

And yes, it *would* be most aligned to always offer book 2 in whatever series the person happens to be reading at the time rather than this offer of *Invasion* and *Contact*. *The Beam: Season Two* is the most attractive list bribe for someone reading *The Beam: Season One*. But man, that's the opposite of optimization. That's making things more complicated and inefficient, not streamlined and effective. (We'd also never sell books because everything would always be free somewhere. There are limits on our effort and generosity.)

Get a Different Book Free (In-Book)

If you're paying close attention, you might have noticed that there are still a few books left for which neither of the above offers make sense. Namely, every other book in the *Invasion* series besides the first one (which contains the "get the sequel" offer). Because what good is it to put a list bribe for books 1 and 2 in a series into book 6 in the *same* series? That reader has already read books 1 and 2. Offering them free now will only annoy her.

But hey, it's entirely possible that someone will have bought their way through the *Invasion* books and never bothered to join the list. That's actually the norm. We want to keep tapping them on the shoulder …

Hey, you're reading book 6. Don't you like us enough by now to try more?

And sure, a lot of people will never join a list. But we still want to let them know we're there.

So we have a third offer, for *Robot Proletariat: Season One.* It's our default offer at RealmAndSands.com/joinus, so feel free to go pick up a copy. It's on us.

Because we have the offer in place anyway, we use it whenever our main offer doesn't make sense. *Invasion* and *Contact* are both fast, page-turning sci-fi reads, so they're great offers … for the kind of reader who's apt to like fast, page-turning sci-fi reads. But Realm & Sands books aren't all like that.

Consider *Axis of Aaron* or *The Devil May Care.* Both titles are longer and slower. They're more mental, and literary. Those books and others don't overlap with *Invasion* all that much. They don't overlap perfectly with *Robot Proletariat* either, but the fit is better for sure. *Robot Proletariat* is sci-fi, but it's not a page turner. It's slower, more thoughtful, more psychological and philosophical. An *Axis* reader has a better chance of liking it than *Invasion*, so this is the offer we make when *Invasion* isn't a fit.

Get Two Books Free (Facebook Ads)

This listbuilding offer is identical to the in-book version. The only difference is that instead of people coming to the page on our site to get *Invasion* and *Contact* free from the front or back of one of our books, they come via a Facebook ad. The ads are varied and never work the same way two weeks in a row, so I won't say much more about this here. In five years, we might not even advertise on Facebook and may instead advertise on Goodreads or Google.

The point is that once you have a solid, compelling offer, you can use it to advertise and build your list. It's not something you should ever do when money is tight, but you may want to consider once you have deeper funnels — when each person added to your list might prompt the next thing you offer them to buy. We pay around $1 in advertising for every person who joins our list and confirms. At Sterling & Stone, that's money well spent.

Using Our Email List As Our Main Funnel

We're only seeing it in retrospect, but all our iteration has led us here: to the point where our email lists are the linchpins for our product funnels.

Which is why we've focused so much on filling our lists with readers who love our stories — or, on the nonfiction side, with podcast listeners who want to get our *Write. Publish. Repeat.* conversations for free.

You got those for free, right? You should. Go get 'em, then you'll be in our funnel, too (insert evil laugh). SterlingAnd-Stone.net/repeaters

Once someone is on your list, you control the funnel. The funnel becomes flexible. You can take it where you want it to go, where it benefits your people most and makes them happiest.

So yes, we still use the "get one book (or podcast) into a lot of hands (or ears), then funnel those people into an upsell" type of funnel as described in *Write. Publish. Repeat.*, and you can still read about the mechanics there. But these days more emphasis is placed on building that list.

Here are some details:

Our Lists Are Built Separately

You've just read all about how we've optimized the process of building the Realm & Sands email list (a specific group of one imprint's readers). The same basic MO is in place at our other imprints to some degree ... though we're still chugging our way through this giant process a bit at a time, iterating through the same small daily improvements we keep urging you to make rather than getting overwhelmed and giving up, *even though that would be easy.*

Regardless, we keep our fences up. There are — or will be — lists for every one of Sterling & Stone's imprints, both fiction and nonfiction. In addition, there's a master list that covers everything we do in the company. So here and now, that's nine email lists.

Not *one* list.

Our iteration here has gone both forward and backward. The process is trial and error, and at one point we were building a single list to rule them all, like Frodo's ring. This was actually a step up. We'd been assembling our lists in a vacuum — building Realm & Sands in a way that pretended Collective Inkwell didn't exist. There was a ton of duplicated effort and no harmony between works that may, in some cases, have appealed to the same readers.

So we decided to consolidate. One list. CI readers and R&S readers would join the same list as the *Smarter Artist* nonfiction readers and listeners of our podcast.

Fortunately, it didn't take us long to realize that this was a terrible idea. It was convenient for *us* to shove everyone into a single pot, but it would be a hideous experience for readers. If you join a list because you liked our post-apocalyptic fiction, do you want to hear about a new romance release? A children's release? A new app we're developing to help writers plan stories?

Ultimately, we settled on the best of both worlds. As of now, yes, our funnel entrances are distinct for each imprint. You join the Realm & Sands list. Or the CI list. Or the Guy Incognito children's list. You join that list, and that list alone, with the walls between them firmly in place.

But then there's the other component to the way our lists have been optimized, which I'll get to after a brief detour.

Our Lists Get Readers Up to Speed and Cross-Sell Automatically

When all of our separate list funnels are finally finished, each will have an attached autoresponder series. Autoresponders, if you're not familiar, are a series of timed emails that are sent relative to the day a person joined the list — a day later, a week later, two months later. Those emails are automatic and go out at different times for everyone, based on join date. Most email list service providers can do them, though they tend to call them by different names.

If you join the Realm & Sands list, you get a series of R&S autoresponders. If you join the Collective Inkwell list, you get a different series. If you join both lists, you get both.

Autoresponders are great for two things: 1) getting people up to speed with who you are and what you do and 2) informing people about things automatically — stuff for sale, things that may interest them, whatever. Autoresponders let us put it all on autopilot. The CTAs in our books or podcasts send people to join our list, and after they do, they get emails that (over a period of time so they're not overwhelmed) tell those people who we are and what we're up to. Then, later down the chain, they can offer items for purchase — putting some of your selling on autopilot as well.

At Sterling & Stone, where we always have a zillion things happening, this "slowly getting people up to speed" is like boiling a frog. If we put everything about S&S into a CTA somewhere and ask people to join us, we'd surely overwhelm them — the frog dropped into boiling water and hence hopping right out in this metaphor. Autoresponders bring that same *boil* a degree at a time, letting people digest all we do like a frog slowly getting used to ever hotter water.

(I realize it's macabre to compare familiarizing our readers with what we do to boiling a frog to death, but whatever. We don't boil our readers. Whoever told you that is a dirty liar.)

If you have a diverse catalog, autoresponders are your friend. Don't deluge people from day one; let them slowly but surely get to know you over time.

Our Lists Are Prompted (But Not Forced) To Intermingle

Okay, detour over. Now that you know that each of our lists has its own sequence of separate autoresponders, I can explain the compromise with our lists from two sections ago.

We build our lists separately. And for a while, all a given reader will hear from us is about the list they joined. If they joined R&S, they'll only hear about R&S: what we write, who we are, what we have for sale. It goes on that way for many weeks.

But eventually — after they've hopefully adjusted to us and aren't likely to be overwhelmed — we tell them a bit about the other things that we do at Sterling & Stone.

We introduce the other imprints then invite them to join the Sterling & Stone master list, which is like a sampler platter — that list hears a bit about everything happening in the company but not every detail, numerous times. And from time to time in those individual series, we suggest joining a different specific list: joining R&S from the CI list, for instance.

We've found that this is best done slowly and always positioned as "if you're interested; no big deal." Many people simply stay on the list they originally joined and continue getting only that imprints' emails. Some cross to the main S&S list and hear about the other imprints as well.

We want to offer that other stuff without ever giving it to someone who hasn't expressed an interest. This way, we can have our cake and eat it, too.

We Also Sell (And Interact, and Build Loyalty) Manually

The final piece of the email puzzle, of course, is simply sending out emails when we have something to announce. These broadcast emails (which, unlike autoresponders, go out to everyone at the same time, regardless of when they joined) are what we use to let people know about new releases, time-sensitive happenings, giveaways, and so on.

It's important to play nice with your list. Put yourself in their shoes. Never hammer them with requests to buy your stuff. Sometimes, just give them updates. Sometimes, just share something that may interest them. Don't waste their time, and never treat them like walking ATMs. We like to conduct the occasional giveaway. We'll ask people to enter by clicking a link then raffle something off and give it to the winner. It keeps people engaged, opening emails and generally liking you.

So yeah, our funnel structures have changed here at S&S since *Write. Publish. Repeat.*, but it's more of a series of iterative steps than an overthrow of all we did before. Ultimately, the goal is still to have something magnetic that attracts people to you en masse then capture their attention in some way and see if they'd like to go farther down the rabbit hole. Or down the product funnel.

We still do the permafree-then-buy-the-bundle sort of funnel, but our recent focus has been on building our email lists and using *those* as flexible funnels. Because we're more adaptable that way. We can build one-on-one relationships.

Give it a shot. We'll bet there's something here you could tweak to better results, too.

CHAPTER ELEVEN:
Podcasts

If you don't have a podcast and don't ever anticipate having one, this is one of those chapters we mentioned in the introduction that you may choose to skip. But these days more and more creators have podcasts and we're constantly asked about ours, so we're leaving it in. Skim through it, read it all — whatever works for you.

We optimized many things in the past two years, but we optimized the *hell* out of our podcasting. We're far from perfect, and there's still plenty to improve (we all need professional mics; we sometimes have Internet connection issues; someday, it'd be awesome to live in the same place and have a studio), but podcasting is a much better and more pivotal outreach vehicle for us today than it ever was before.

If you don't have a podcast, it's absolutely *not* a foregone conclusion that you should have one. And actually, this is one of those chapters that may be more for nonfiction authors than it is for you novelists out there. It's hard for a fiction author to make a podcast worthwhile — worth stealing time from your writing, in other words. There are ways to do it for sure, but know what you're likely to get out of the time you spend. In those cases, only start a podcast if it's something you think you'd enjoy, and on a topic where you have plenty to say.

At the time of *Write. Publish. Repeat.*, we had two podcasts, with one of them being more for fun than anything we'd expect a return from.

As I write this, we have nine podcasts, with another two actively in the works and many more (from us and trusted partners) in various stages of planning.

For Sterling & Stone, podcasting has become a central marketing avenue and key community builder. We're all verbal people, so podcasting comes naturally to us as a way to broadcast information — in, really, the way that blogging used to. But now that we all spend so much time writing during our working lives, the last thing we want is to *type more.* So we decided to turn our mothership SterlingAndStone.net blog into a podcast network. Because why write when we can get together and chat instead?

A podcast may or may not be right for you. We love it because it feels like hanging out — and, with a podcast producer on the team, really doesn't require much more of us than showing up and opening our mouths. Podcasting is also an intimate medium; we meet people all the time who say they feel like they know us and hence feel bonded. That's a hell of a thing in terms of building community around you.

But it's also another thing to do — another way that resistance keeps you from making your art. Podcasting makes sense for us. It helps us reach fans and prospective customers in ways that are comfortable because it aligns with who we are. It's also easy for us, whereas you'll likely have to figure out the process and do the tech work yourself — at least at first. This might be a good place to suggest going to iTunes and searching for "*Self-Publishing Podcast* #170 — Podcasting for Writers without Wasting Your Time."

We'll tell you how we upped our podcasting game, then you can decide if you want to up (or create) yours.

We Improved Our Quality

Most of the improvement you hear in the *Self-Publishing Podcast* over the early episodes comes down to simply putting in time. By the time you record two hundred episodes of anything, you're either going to improve or you're a stubborn idiot who refuses to back down. (Don't say it.)

If you want a fun experience — and here I should put "fun" in quotes — go back and listen to *"Self-Publishing Podcast #1"* in the *SPP Classics* feed. Sean, Dave, and I had a decent rapport even in that first show, but it's light years from what it is today. I've always played host because I have the mixer and the recorder, and in that first episode you'll hear me fumbling with the reins. I cringe a little listening now.

Sean and I knew each other, but only passingly. Dave and I had barely spoken — and it's a running (but true) joke on *SPP* that he was still suspicious of me back then, sure I was a marketing scam artist whose intention was to ride his and Sean's coattails long enough to release a $97 How to Self-Publish info product. Our transitions are awkward. We talk over each other a lot. I sound timid, and our information is probably way too 101.

But hell, we had to start somewhere.

And you'll hear other differences between those early shows and today. Our mix isn't the same, and I've since turned down the treble a bit to make our voices more tolerable and less pitchy. The show's sound took a noticeable leap forward when we hired our producer, Audra — something it took 170 episodes and three years of podcasting before we were able to justify. Audra performs audio ninjitsu to the show in addition to cutting out places where we ramble too much, adding intros and outros so professional, you'd think *we* were professional and not just her.

But mostly, we simply improved with time, and so will you if you put in the hours.

We Hired a Producer

Our producer, Audra, has twenty years of radio experience. She *gets* audio in a way that we heathens don't. It's not just about the auditory experience. It's about creating theater for the mind. In addition to simply dealing with what we throw at her, Audra is always making suggestions on ways we can improve. *Close some of these conversation threads you guys leave hanging. Give real takeaways whenever possible. Self-contained mini-stories are audio gold.* Stuff like that.

Hiring Audra this year flat-out made our current podcasting trajectory possible. Not only were our podcasts far less professional before her, they were also more work. Especially for me. I had to add all the music, record and process all the files, edit whatever needed editing, write the show notes/blog posts to go with them, add all the metadata so people's players would label us correctly, and so on. But now, it's simple. We talk; I record; I drag the recording into Dropbox. Audra does most of the rest; Amy schedules the episodes in our master calendar; Maya posts them and makes sure they show up when they're supposed to. It's like magic.

The point here isn't that Audra saved us (or me) time and work. The point is that we'd never have been able to add more shows to our network lineup if that time and work wasn't saved, because we were tapped out. Adding her to our team let us put more effort into what we did well (putting on the actual shows) rather than all the backend that a pro could do better.

In addition to leveraging our team's skills to make Sterling & Stone's shows happen, having a producer makes everything we do sound so much better and more effective as marketing vehicles. Audra created all of the imaging for the podcasts, which is the audible branding you hear when you listen: music, mood, intro, and outro. She adds CTAs to our episodes depending on what's most in need of promotion. When edits are required, she makes them happen. The combined effect is to turn what used to be a hassle into a smooth-running content marketing engine for our company.

We Tightened Our Format

Most of our shows are new and hence needed creation from the ground up, but the BIG podcast we already had was doing mostly fine. It had an engaged audience; it was quite popular; it had most of what it needed in more or less the right places. So it simply needed a facelift.

We officially rebooted the *Self-Publishing Podcast* with the release of "Episode #170," but up until that reboot we'd been telling subscribers what to expect from what we casually referred to as *SPP 2.0*. Nothing caused more concern than the idea that we were going to *clean up the format.*

Which meant, in essence, that our most loyal listeners were saying, "NO! Don't make the show GOOD!"

There's actually a lesson there, before I get to my point. Trying to be overly professional — especially as a creative entrepreneur — is almost always a mistake. You're a creative person; what makes you *you* is one of your most valuable assets. And yet a lot of people think they need to iron out all that difference and sound (and act, and write) like an anchor on the evening news.

Nope. Just be yourself. You need to be quirky. Improve your quality by iterating and optimizing your articulation, not your so-called professionalism. By speaking better and making better points, not by flattening your personality out into a boring cardboard cutout. Our listeners didn't like the idea that we'd clean up because they thought we'd be stiff. They thought we'd stop tripping over ourselves, stop starting stories that spiraled into nowhere, always stay on topic, and stop telling questionable dick jokes. They thought we might stop discussing suicide and ayahuasca in our ad reads.

I understand their fear. I've heard many podcasts that are so bland, they make oatmeal engrossing. I hate shows like that, and we'd never want to kill what made our show special — to the right audience, not to everyone — in the same way.

When we said we wanted to clean our format for the 2.0 release, what we really meant was that we'd tighten the show. For one, we wanted to trim our opening rambles, which had grown like The Blob to swallow half of our show, down to fifteen minutes. We wanted to get the guests in on time. We wanted to stay on topic a bit more so we weren't as annoying (and yes, we absolutely were sometimes). We wanted to be sure to stop the show by fifty-seven minutes, so it would still be 59:59 or less when Audra was done. Our previous shows had a way of rambling on to an hour and twenty minutes or more. Not only is that harder for a listener to digest (the one-hour mark is a psychological barrier between listenable and "Holy crap, when will I find the time?"); it was often hot air. It's not like we were adding only good stuff in those extra minutes.

We tightened up. But we still tell stupid stories, give horrible, awkward ad reads, and act like fools who can't stay on topic.

We Commissioned New Art

We got new art for all of our shows, using book cover logic: We needed a step above *good enough* to capture a listener's time. So unlike last time, we didn't try to make the art ourselves.

We commissioned new art and went through several versions for most of the shows before settling on art that we liked. Only two of our shows were officially rebooted: the *Self-Publishing Podcast*, as already mentioned, and our irreverent travesty, *Better Off Undead. BOU* — which started life as a horror podcast to support our fiction but derailed within five shows to become the "Dave's foibles" show — was renamed *Worst. Show. Ever.* Both it and *SPP* were snazzed up by Audra and relaunched on new feeds. Both got pro art to match, although I love the podcast art for *Better Off Undead* and was sad to see it move to the archive feed.

We Launched a Network

We've already mentioned this one in an oblique way, but here's the formal explanation.

If you go to iTunes and find any of our podcasts, click on Sterling & Stone beneath the podcast name (or our actual names in the case of *SPP*) and you'll be sent to a page that's essentially "other content by this artist." That's our network page, and it's different than a single show's podcast page. If you're curious but don't feel like hunting, the direct link to our network page is SterlingAndStone.net/fm, so linked because the network's official name is Sterling & Stone FM, like a radio network.

Having a network is a game changer for us. First of all, the existence of the network page itself means we're cross-pollinating our shows without having to do anything. You might have seen The *Smarter Artist* when it was on the iTunes front page as New and Noteworthy then grown curious and clicked the name to see what else we had. Then BOOM!, here's this professional-looking page with our logo and several more shows. And that's not counting the cross-pollination we do ourselves (by mentioning other shows in the middle of any one show) or Audra does for us (by mentioning other shows or the network page in the closing CTAs.)

Each of these shows is a new way to reach a slightly different (or entirely different) audience in a unique way. Linking them via the S&S FM podcast network compounds our efforts so that one plus one can equal three.

Future iterations of the network will have us taking on shows where we're not the hosts, starting with our inner circle of SuperFriends. This is leverage where everyone wins — people can use our promotion to find an audience, and their quality content sends new people our way.

We Got Ears on the Podcasts We Have

Podcasts aren't *If you build it, they will come*. You can't just release a show and expect it to benefit you — or even find an audience.

We often say that the *Self-Publishing Podcast* succeeded in spite of itself. We began with no real promotion beyond telling our lists and social media — two groups who, honestly, weren't even writers or creative entrepreneurs as a whole. We were mediocre at the whole podcasting thing and didn't know what to request from the listeners we had. We didn't ask for reviews and ratings. We didn't have sensible CTAs of any kind. We didn't hit iTunes coveted New and Noteworthy list or even come close.

You might get lucky and pull off what we did, but it's a crapshoot. It's much better to have a promotional plan, and with our team's help, a solid community, and a bit of thought, we cobbled one together for our fledgling network. We didn't want to create several great shows and have no one to hear them.

We won't detail how to launch a podcast here because it's a huge subject, and there are lots of books and websites out there that will tell you what to do. But I will say we *had* a plan, and that was a big part of our iterating forward in 2015. And I'll add that having a preexisting successful podcast makes a *huge* difference. Given that *SPP* already had a fantastic community, telling our listeners about the new shows meant we could skip well ahead of where we would have been without that following. If you already have an audience for your topic (a blog, a speaking gig, a TV show, whatever), be sure to include *Tell those people about your new podcast* in the promo plan.

Anyway, it worked. The only podcast in our network that hasn't hit the New and Noteworthy list is *Backstory*, and that's because we specifically avoid promotion — read the description of that show further on to find out why. Even the *Self-Publishing Podcast* and *Worst. Show. Ever.* (formerly *Better Off Undead*) hit New and Noteworthy following their reboots. They weren't *new*, but our optimization efforts and the power of our existing audience *made* them *noteworthy*.

Introducing the Sterling & Stone FM Lineup

Because this part of the book is all about Sterling & Stone's 2014 and 2015 Iteration and Optimization, we thought about listing our shows for you and telling you a bit about each of them. Amy told us we'd just bore you if we did that. Her comments were numerous and caustic enough that we eventually relented.

To see the entire Sterling & Stone FM lineup, go to SterlingAndStone.net/fm. Most of them are nonfiction, how-to, inspiration-heavy kinds of shows, meaning they'll be right up your alley. If you're *Smarter Artist* — and we think you are — then you'll probably get a lot out of listening to them while you drive, take walks — or wherever you could use some auditory accompaniment.

We've got a lot going on, and any podcasting you choose to start will, at first, probably feel complicated and overwhelming.

But remember: as much as we have going on at Sterling & Stone FM today, we started with just one show.

We did it all by ourselves, without staff or help.

And we had no audience.

Iterate and Optimize, baby.

CHAPTER TWELVE:
Advertising

The definition of wishful thinking: *assuming someone will find your work out of the blue, without knowing who you are in advance — just sort of stumbling across it.*

Too many creative, otherwise intelligent people do this. They write their books, make their music, craft their art — then wait for something to happen. Authors have some grease, and I suppose indie musicians on major platforms do as well; there are algorithms in place to provide buyer suggestions. But even that's chicken-and-egg. Because how will anyone find you in alsobots without someone buying your stuff in the first place?

Nope. Ain't gonna happen. Not in ways that make you a self-sustaining artist, making your living sans day job — or in ways that create a nice sideline income or get your name out there. The world is noisy. There are too many people already competing for your ideal audience. We live in a distracted world filled with people who are too busy for their own good. The odds of significant numbers of buyers poking around endlessly until they just so happen to discover your gem are so thin they're practically see-through.

You have to get in front of people who don't already know you — right in front of them so they practically trip over you. In their email inboxes, in their earbuds if you have a podcast, in their social media, in the damned alsobots and bookseller recommendation emails.

You can do some of that yourself. A *lot* of it, if you're like us. We iterated our way to so many podcasts because we wanted to reach a wider audience. That's why we spent the chapter before last talking about using free books to gain exposure then using product funnels (including a well-crafted email autoresponder series) to hang onto those new people once we've captured their attention. That's the reason we pour so much stuff into the world without charging for it: because we want to be top-of-mind, in our readers' and listeners' heads, hacking through the noise.

You might form partnerships. A common mini-partnership we used to do a lot but have mostly backed away from (because it gives us a poor work-in-versus-results-out ratio, though your mileage may differ) is guest-posting on other people's blogs. But you can do things like that, too — ways of reaching out that require your time in exchange for access to another person's audience.

But you can't do it all alone. You only have so much time, and your network only has so much reach.

And that's why over the past two years we've spent so much time, effort, and money figuring out ways to crack the advertising nut. Advertising is a way of reaching audiences who might love you — but you have no way of touching. But *someone* has a way to get in front of those people, and if you're willing to pay, they'll put you in front of them, too.

You can win big with advertising or lose your shirt and get nothing in return.

In this chapter, we'll walk you through what we've found works for us and why, as well as what doesn't and how you can hopefully avoid some of our mistakes.

Facebook Ads - Iteration #1

We didn't exactly start using Facebook advertising before it was cool, but we did start before we had any idea what we were doing. This is the way we do most things. Don't laugh. Yes, we fall down a lot, but there's that Gretzky quote about how you miss 100 percent of the shots you don't take and … and … okay, fine, maybe we should have been smarter and done a bit more research.

Our first shot at using Facebook advertising came before we did our *Fiction Unboxed* project. As the Kickstarter campaign for that project was funding, we decided to throw away several hundred dollars just because. We did it by hiring someone to help us with Facebook advertising to writers who might be interested in paying for what we were doing. The ads did nothing. *At all.* In fact, I'm pretty sure Mark Zuckerberg showed up at Sean's house and punched him in the face then laughed.

The thing about Facebook advertising (and we did actually know this and made a conscious choice to take a shot, all jokes aside) is that you can't just nail your ad campaign the first time unless you're extremely lucky. You generally try something, tweak, then try something else. The people we know who successfully use Facebook generally have dozens of ads going at once, and that's narrowed down from hundreds of trial balloons. They monitor those ads, adapt, then kill the ads that aren't performing and throw more money at those that do.

We had one ad. *ONE AD.* It was sort of like making a retirement plan that consists of "Head to Vegas and put it all on 13 at the roulette wheel."

Lesson number one learned: Advertising doesn't work immediately. If you aren't willing to spend some time and money to keep experimenting, you're probably best not even taking a shot.

So before returning to the type of mass-audience advertising you do on Facebook and other places — which we were certain could work given the right context; both of us knew people who were making a mint selling stuff there, albeit not $5 ebooks — we took a honeymoon by trying much safer venues.

List-Based Book Advertisers

We initially stuck our toes into Facebook ads because we were, for the first time, advertising something that wasn't a book. It should have been easy to get a return on our investment considering that the live *Fiction Unboxed* project had a base price of $49, but it wasn't. And conversely, it should have been hard to get an ROI on ebook sales — something that cost one tenth as much. But we already knew that was possible, if you did things correctly.

And by do things correctly, we mean buy an ad on Book-Bub.

We've titled this section "List-Based Book Advertisers" instead of just BookBub as some sort of a vain wish that one day, a challenger to BookBub will appear and give authors more than a single decent option. So let's all pretend that BookBub isn't holding all the cards.

Ahem.

In case this is the first you're hearing of advertising through book-specific venues, the idea is that various websites have spent a ton of time and money collecting email addresses from a dedicated group of readers. These are people who have joined a list or frequent a blog because they're looking for new books to read. *Discounted* books, to be specific. So if you can get those websites to tell their lists and readers about your book, you stand to sell a bunch of copies, seeing as that's exactly what those people signed up for.

This is and probably should be the first stop for authors looking to advertise — always in conjunction with some sort of a sale, typically reducing your price to either 99 cents or free for a short period of time. You know you're hitting a receptive audience if you advertise on one of these platforms. It's up to your book's cover, title, and description to convert browsers to buyers of a 99-cent purchase or a free download. But as far as audiences go, you won't get much more receptive or surefire.

Now, as we casually stated above, you do need to discount your book to use these advertisers because a deep discount is what makes this type of buyer respond. So consider your endgame. If your book normally sells ten copies a day at $4.99, your commissions at 70 percent are around $35 before various fees. At 99 cents, with a 35-percent commission, you need to sell one hundred books to make that same $35. So if all the ad gets you is ninety extra sales and you have no back end on your book, you're treading water and wasting the ad fee.

There are three basic benefits to these kinds of ads. Consider them all as you think about spending your money:

Your book's ranking and visibility will rise if you sell more copies. The example above is a bit of a cheat. Technically, you will see a benefit even at $35 versus $35: you'll get a ranking boost as a result of those ninety extra sales, and you should show up in a few more alsobots (though not necessarily; your sales need to sync with purchases of another book for that to happen). But the ranking spike won't necessarily mean more sales, and neither will the alsobots. But it is something.

You might get more sell-through to the sequels. This is the main reason we like list-based book advertising and the one thing we always consider when placing ads. We rarely advertise stand-alone titles with no sequels and almost never try to advertise anything other than the first book in a series. You should see some uptick in the book you're advertising unless the advertiser is a total dud, but the real benefit is that if your book is good, some readers will then buy the sequel(s) at full price. That kind of thing can make a mediocre ad run successful. So we're willing to take a loss on the first book if we have to. Advertising that book for free might feel like a waste — until some of the people who downloaded it start to buy books 2-6 for $5.99 each. Now, be warned: Buy-through is far from a given. Maybe 10 percent of the people who get your first book will buy the sequel — possibly more but possibly less.

You might add more people to your mailing list. Before running a big ad, we always spiff up the list-add CTAs in our books, making sure to place one *before* the story in addition to after. If the ad flops but we get a bunch of new people on our list (because those downloaders see they can get something else by signing up with you), it's usually a win. Sometimes, those subscribers are cheap or free-seekers, but that's the case less often than you might think. We hear from a ton of our most loyal readers (and full-price buyers) that they joined our list after a BookBub ad.

Oh, yes. Well, speaking of that, let's break it down. We talked about this kind of advertising in *Write. Publish. Repeat.*, but as with anything, we've optimized our way of looking at and using it. So from a two-years-later perspective, here's how we view the players in this space:

BookBub

I remember the first time I saw the prices for BookBub ads. None are cheap, and some are well over $1,000, depending on genre and your advertised price. I thought, "Well, that sounds great. But where am I going to get that kind of money for an ad?"

Then we ran one.

You'll almost for sure get your money back on a BookBub ad and then some. If you have sequels, the effect is greater. If you've optimized your book prior to the ad and have an offer to join your list and get something cool by doing so, all the better. We'd schedule a BookBub ad every day if they'd let us. Unfortunately, they won't. Which brings us to some things you need to know about advertising with these guys:

1) BookBub is very selective. I'll be frank: You'll probably get rejected if you try to place an ad. Maybe you'll *always* get rejected. You might bang your head against them for years and never get anywhere. It's just how they are. We swore a blue streak about this for a long time and struck out endlessly before finally scoring a hit, but we also understand *why* they are the way they are. The choosier BookBub is about the titles it advertises, the better it works for everyone. BookBub knows their readers, knows what they like and respond to, and knows that overwhelming those readers with too many choices at once will lead to analysis paralysis. If BookBub let people advertise books that didn't fit their audience and/or sent too many choices every day, people wouldn't buy as much and the machine would stop working. It's incredibly frustrating to get rejected. Our optimization here was to *keep trying*.

2) BookBub is a black box. We love BookBub, but still ... what a bunch of assholes. They'll reject you, and you won't even know why or what you can do differently next time. We understand why they do things the way they do, and we probably wouldn't do anything different, but talk about *frustrating*. They'll usually tell you that your book "isn't a good fit," if they tell you anything at all. Break a stated rule (like submitting a book under 150 pages long), and they'll tell you that, but other than that you'll get zero guidance. We have books we think their audiences should love that are always rejected — and when we get emails and see some of the strange stuff that *was* accepted, we barf in our mouths. You can reply to your rejection and ask, but we've never received anything more than a vague response.

3) BookBub is an excellent way to get traction in off-Amazon stores. Some of the other advertisers have started asking submitters to include links to their titles on iBooks, NOOK, Kobo, and others, so this may change, but until then BookBub is unique in its ability to reach readers everywhere. If you manage to get an ad, don't be an idiot. Submit links to your book in every place it's sold. You may find yourself gaining slow and steady traction on that store afterward now that those readers know who you are.

Everyone Else

We don't mean to be dismissive. We truly don't. With all our hearts, we hope that one of the other players in the book advertising space (we won't list them; they change all the time and you can Google to find them) rises up to become another force like BookBub. But if you asked the other guys right now if they think they're anywhere near as effective as BookBub, I doubt any could approach a *yes* without flinching.

Facts are facts. We love the other advertisers and use them, but there's only one BookBub.

There's a guy we know, named Brian Meeks. Brian is a data guy. He'll tell you he acquired this skill working at Geico, where fifteen minutes could save you 15 percent or more on your car insurance. And yes, he'll say it exactly that way, before launching into an hour-long story about his buddy Flippy, who died on a golf course in "the most awesome death ever." Every time Brian runs a sale of any kind, he closes himself in a room and giddily fills a spreadsheet with numbers, surely with a delighted cackle. And if you're anywhere near him and *you* run a sale, Brian will watch your numbers, too. In this way he's data-leeched his way through a group of our inner circle, trying to reckon what works and what doesn't when it comes to advertising.

According to Brian's extensive analysis, nothing provides a reliable return on investment other than BookBub. Not even ads that only cost $10. He says, on average, you don't make your money back.

We find this hard to believe, but if we doubt him, Brian will show us more spreadsheets and possibly pull us into more endless hilarious stories.

Regardless, our own anecdotal and non-data-driven experience shows that he's probably right. But there are a few reasons we still feel paying for non-BookBub ads can be an excellent idea.

1) If you schedule a few non-BookBub ads after a Book-Bub ad, those extra sales will help prop up your rankings boost. iBooks, NOOK, and Kobo seem to have *stickier* rankings than Amazon, where the algorithms are such that a one-day sales spike will result in a big rankings boost … followed by an immediate crash. Sustained spikes, on the other hand, tend to be rewarded. You'll sustain your rankings longer if you can spread sales out over a few days, and you might even get Amazon to send some recommendation emails to potential buyers on your behalf. Other ads can toss you a few hundred extra sales and provide this rankings support.

2) There's still sell-through and list-adds to consider. Maybe you can't ROI on most ads for standalone titles with anyone but BookBub. But *Invasion* has a great buy-through percentage, and even if a campaign only gets us one hundred extra sales of that book at 99 cents, it's hard to imagine we won't sell fifty more books at full price when you combine sales of the three others in the series. And if that doesn't ROI, consider when the *Invasion* series is done, at seven books. A good enough buy-through rate on six full-price books would, you'd think, justify the expense. And of course there are the people joining your list, assuming you plan right. We also feel this point is extra-valid if, again, the supplementary ads are scheduled around an initial BookBub ad to magnify the effect.

3) But we use these other players differently now. We used to take ads wherever and whenever we could get them. But we've discovered that if you put the same book on most sites or lists a second and third time, you'll get diluted results because buyers have already seen it. BookBub isn't *quite* the same; you'll get a good spike the second time you use them because they're constantly adding new subscribers, and their list is ginormous, but you will still see a diminished return. We'd try a given book twice a year on BookBub but might only try that same title once a year on all other venues. Otherwise, the questionable return on investment becomes an in-the-toilet ROI.

Facebook Ads – Iteration #2

After finally solving a lot of the list-based-advertising puzzle and getting a few big 99-cent book advertising wins *(The Beam, Yesterday's Gone, Invasion, Contact,* my *Fat Vampire* bundles, and more), we returned our attention to figuring out Facebook ads.

It's worth noting that this wasn't a this-then-that process. We didn't decide to try Facebook advertising again because it was, chronologically speaking, time to do so. It wasn't like we'd solved the other advertising issues and this was next on our list — possibly because we'd failed before and felt the need to get back on the horse.

No. We were smarter in round two. We didn't delve into Facebook ads (a medium that it's spectacularly easy to lose large amounts of money in, not unlike a Vegas craps table) willy-nilly and uninformed. We came in with a line of products that was already mostly optimized (new covers, new descriptions, etc.), arranged in sensible funnels (so that even if we didn't ROI on the first product, there was a chance subsequent purchases by the same person would mean we'd get a return overall), and had a clear outcome in mind.

Our Facebook ads spark was reignited when we had Mark Dawson on the podcast, who reported using Facebook ads to sell books and get people onto his mailing list with tremendous success. That got the ball rolling. We couldn't quite get our ads to work in the same way as his returned profits, but we started digging.

Then we met Julie Huss, a romance author who writes under the name J.A. Huss. Julie's a hoot. She's a total badass about everything she does and kept very casually mentioning things on *"SPP* #161" like the fact that she was using Facebook ads to see a return on investment selling $3 books, which seemed impossible. Julie plunked down an insane amount of money on ads for her *New York Times* best seller *Three, Two, One* (which is excellent but filthy). We probably shouldn't say how much it was, but many writers would be pleased to make as much income as she spent on that one book over the course of a year.

For us, this was like hearing about the four-minute mile. We knew Facebook ads could be cracked even though we hadn't yet done it ourselves. So we delved deeper. We hired a consultant. We added "make Facebook ads work for S&S" to Garrett's plate, seeing as he'd already managed to get a return for his series *Nightblade* and has since been killing it on all of the books in Legendary, our fantasy imprint.

The following sections detail what we've learned — but keep in mind that we absolutely are not experts and that we continue to inch forward on Facebook ads as with everything else. Small improvements, iteration and optimization over time, and all of that.

You Can Use Facebook Ads to Build Your Email List

Most people want to use Facebook ads to sell books. It can be done (see subsequent sections), but it is often difficult, and inherently a gamble.

But many people forget that these ads can also be used to build your list. And then, if you have a smart autoresponder series and/or you're good at using that list as a sales tool, this is a roundabout way to make money on Facebook ads via the back end.

We mentioned in the "Product Funnels" chapter that Facebook ads are one way we send new people to our fiction mailing lists. We advertise the free books; people click over and join our list to get those books; we then have their attention unless or until they unsubscribe. That happens, of course. We get unsubscribe notifications sometimes that say, essentially, "Just wanted the free books ... see ya, suckers!" But we also regularly hear from people who say they found us via an ad and are now hooked on our way of telling a story. In those cases, we've earned a customer for around $1 on average — or maybe, to be generous, $2 if you factor out all the people who unsubscribe or will never buy. But still, two bucks is cheap. The first time that new fan buys a book at a $2.99 or more, we've earned our money back. From then on, it's profit.

Facebook Ads Require Constant Monitoring and Tweaking

Do you remember the Ronco Rotisserie? Ron Popeil said the thing was painless to use: you "set it and forget it." Well, that's not how Facebook ads work. Try to set it and forget it, and the Facebook rotisserie will short-circuit and burn your house to ashes.

Let's begin with the monitoring part of this subsection that concerns your costs because that's where the most pain tends to surface.

When you run Facebook ads, you set a daily budget. You may say you only want to spend $10 per day. And that's great, unless you realize it's not working for you and forget to turn the ads off and suddenly owe Facebook $300 at the end of the month for nothing. Pay attention. Don't forget that every day that passes, money is leaving your wallet.

Second, you need to monitor the ads' performance. Facebook will tell you how many people are clicking on your ads so you'll be able to see if they're even getting any interest from the people seeing them. But that's only half the equation — or, honestly, far less than half if we're talking results. What you really need to know isn't how many people are *clicking* on your ads versus what you're spending; you want to know how many people are *buying* (or joining your list) from those ads. You can use Amazon affiliate links to see how many sales are coming through your ads and watch your lists to see how many new subscribers you're getting. Take your total daily spend on a campaign and divide it by the results (dollars in sales or number of subscribers). Then watch that number like a hawk. Make sure that you're okay with it — *daily* — and that the campaign is still worth the spend.

Great ads won't perform forever. Don't make the mistake of thinking they will. Even successful ads atrophy, with a lifetime of a few weeks at most. Then you'll need to tweak them. You'll either change the ad itself to see if you can increase the number of clicks (better ad copy, a better image, adding a testimonial, etc.), or you'll notice that people are clicking but not buying or signing up. Then your job will be to work on your sales page or list signup page to get people acting more reliably on what they thought was interesting when they clicked the ad.

Facebook Ads Require a Ton of Experimentation

Fair warning: In order to find a campaign that works, you may end up creating a hundred images to use in your ads. Don't expect to get it right the first time — remember the title of the book your'e reading. You may end up writing dozens of variants on the ad copy and the headline. A lot of this will feel blind at first. Julie told us that when she uses a book cover as the ad image, the ad performs more poorly than if she uses another image and a quote. But that's the kind of thing you only discover through trial and error, so you need to take your small wins and build on them, always just trying to get a little better.

But it's not just the ads that need tweaking and constant, incremental improvement. There's also the targeting inside the Facebook ad console. You might target men in the US who like Neil Gaiman's page who read on Kindle and find it fails, then target men in the US who like Neil Gaiman's page who use Android OS and find it's a stunning success. You can target desktop users of Facebook or mobile users. We've heard stories of people for whom one works and the other fails miserably, and stories of people for whom the situation is exactly the opposite.

If we didn't have Garrett manning this process for us, I honestly doubt we'd even do it. We just don't have the time to keep tweaking and experimenting to discover what works.

If this and the section before it haven't convinced you that Facebook ads are far from an easy button, I'll say it outright again: FACEBOOK ADS ARE FAR FROM AN EASY BUTTON. Most authors are probably wise to avoid them. Others, with their lines optimized and their intended outcomes clear, maybe should — if managing the ads doesn't consume all their writing time. And the situation may be different for musicians; we don't know. Maybe there's a thriving Facebook community that would buy custom-painted kilns through ads. You'd have to try and see, if you're willing to lose some time and money finding out and can schedule vigilance into your day.

Too often, we see desperate creatives looking for ways to flip a switch and hit a home run, but it's always far better to take baby steps and be *very, very patient* as you make slow, steady improvements on what you do over a period of time that's probably long enough to make you want to pull your hair out. So if anyone tells you that Facebook ads (or any ads, really) are this switch, run away from those people and get back to making more great art instead.

Ads' Effectiveness Varies Wildly by Genre

This should be obvious, but advertising is only effective to the degree it can reach the correct audience in the place you're advertising.

Look at BookBub. The people who want to buy good, temporarily discounted 99-cent horror-genre titles are easy to find with a BookBub ad on the horror list because those people joined the list because they were looking for exactly that.

The offer-to-ad-recipient match is nearly perfect. You have what they want. All that remains is for your book to look interesting enough for them to commit.

I'm going to take a stab in the dark, but I doubt Facebook ads for a book that tries to convince senior citizens they should be on Facebook would work very well. Why? Because THEY'RE NOT ON FACEBOOK!

Now, edging back from these two extremes and finding the more sensible middle, do you know who's on Facebook? In *huge, teeming droves?*

Romance readers.

Facebook just happens to be one of the places where that demographic hangs out. They join groups; they like author pages; they post about their latest reads. It's also a famously ravenous and dedicated audience: When they find an author they like, they read everything by that author then bang their forks and knives on the table demanding more. They post photos, share favorite quotes, discuss characters as if they were real people. Facebook is where romance authors market. Julie Huss recently told us about something called page takeovers that happen when romance books launch on Facebook. They're huge deals and don't exist in other genres.

The romance authors we know have a much, *much* easier time seeing ROI on Facebook ads. Same for the fantasy ads we run — not necessarily because Facebook is their home base but because the targeting of like audiences (ex: ads targeting Robert Jordan fans) is so much clearer. But Sean, Dave, and I, as primarily sci-fi authors? Not so much. Those readers hang out somewhere else, and they're a lot harder to target. Fantasy has far less internal variability than sci-fi, meaning that it's far harder to find sci-fi books that are *a whole lot like ours* than it is for Garrett to find books that are a lot like his. Better targeting of ads means better results. Sci-fi is just too broad, with too many sub-niches, to work as as well as fantasy and romance.

So just because your friend is doing well with Facebook ads doesn't mean you will, or vice-versa. Refer back to the previous section: *experimentation is key.*

Nonfiction Is Usually Easier

We've played with nonfiction ads too. And we have plans, once our *Smarter Artist* autoresponder series is fully built out, to invest heavily in advertising. Because nonfiction is so much easier to advertise. If you're offering some kind of nonfiction information — books, courses, free online seminars — you're going to have an easier time with just about any kind of advertising, and not just Facebook.

Here's why:

The solution you're selling is clearer and more pressing than with fiction. You're selling solutions. *Learn to play Neil Young songs on the guitar* isn't a nebulous concept like entertainment or escape. You don't need to convince anyone whether or not they want a solution. You only need to convince them that your solution is good enough to be worthy of a potential buyer's time or attention.

Ad targeting is much more straightforward. Fiction is so subjective. We can say that people who liked *Ender's Game* might like *Invasion* and target those people with our ads, but it's by no means a certainty because so much depends on nuance and mood — and on impossible-to-determine factors as to why that person liked *Ender's Game* in the first place. They might like it because they once saw Orson Scott Card at a party; you never know. Nonfiction doesn't have this problem. If you like playing guitar and are constantly looking for hints on how to do it better, there's not a lot of subjectivity there. You're either the ideal audience for an ad or you're not.

The prices in nonfiction tend to be higher, making ROI easier to achieve. I'm not even talking about books. Let's go back to guitar lessons. I know nothing about playing guitar, but let's say an instructor with a solid reputation sells lessons via Skype. I'm guessing she'd charge more than the $5 we're asking for an ebook, with at most $3.50 of that price being profit to us. Let's say the instructor charges a paltry $35 per hour for that lesson. She can spend ten times more than us on the ad for that sale because her profit is ten times higher per conversion. And unless she's terrible at ads, reputation, targeting, or something else, it shouldn't take ten times the ad impressions to earn that conversion.

Back end profits are bigger in nonfiction. Let's say we sell *Invasion* on a Facebook ad and break even: The price of the ad offsets our profit. There are three more books in that series, so in a perfect world our new reader might grab all three, netting us maybe $10 after fees. And hey, let's be generous. Let's say that reader loves us, joins our list, and buys another $20 in books over the course of a year. We've just made $30 on one person from a Facebook ad via back end sales. Hooray!

But now think of the nonfiction ad buyer. Maybe that first ad was for a book about increasing your company's organizational efficiency. And forget about breaking even; let's pretend that on average, our hypothetical person is *spending* $10 to nab that conversion. A net loss of $10 on the ad.

But then the person reads the book and signs up for a course on business management for $499. Or attends a seminar for $1,500. Or hires the author to speak at a corporate event for $5,000. That's not bad shakes on a $10 net loss.

Other Types of Ads

We're on the ground floor and iterating forward, so this is a section we're including just to be thorough even though there isn't yet much to say here at Sterling & Stone.

In 2015, Amazon began offering advertising opportunities exclusively for KDP Select members. In general (and sort of on principle), we don't like the idea of being in Select, but our catalog is broad enough that we can afford to experiment. And that's something S&S has never been afraid of: *experimentation*. Our approach to strategies is a bit like my personal approach to food: we'll try just about anything once, assuming it's not obviously ridiculous or overtly disgusting.

At the urging of Garrett Robinson and previously mentioned data fiend/raconteur Brian Meeks, we decided to remove a few titles that don't sell well anywhere from non-Amazon platforms and enter them into Select. The feeling here was like, "We don't love the idea of going exclusive, but what can it possibly hurt, given the sales?" And then Garrett began running Amazon Select ads for those titles.

There isn't much of a conclusion yet, because it's far too early in the game to say either way. Both Garrett and Brian report success with advertising this way, so we'll see what happens. And if you want to hear more, just keep listening to the *Self-Publishing Podcast*, where we'll report our findings if and when we have any.

Being Our Own Advertiser

This is where we step outside the box because that's another thing S&S is known to do.

We cheated in the chapter's opening, talking about how using your existing platform could, if you really wanted to look at it this way, be considered a form of advertising. But really that's not advertising. You're not creating an ad; you're simply talking to your audience.

And advertising, then, is something distinct: you're putting your offer in front of someone else's audience, usually for a fee.

But we've created a middle ground — a situation where we're both the ad's buyer and seller — because now we have all these podcasts.

The *Self-Publishing Podcast* has one advertiser at the time of this writing: 99Designs. They pay us money, and in exchange we do a live (and always awkward) ad read in the middle of our show, plus a shorter read in the beginning.

It's a good idea to let a podcast get its legs before selling ads, and many podcasts are never attractive to advertisers at all. On *SPP*, we waited nearly two years before selling ad space, and before 99Designs decided to work with us, they wanted to see our stats and test the waters. If advertising with us wouldn't net them new sales, they didn't want to do it.

We figured that after a while we'd add sponsors to a few of our other podcasts as well, as they gained popularity and became attractive to advertisers. Not full reads like we do on *SPP* but shorter mentions at the beginning and/or end. It would be a nice little income stream to offset the cost of creating the shows.

But then we thought, *Why don't* we buy *some of that ad space? Be* our own *sponsor?*

This, like the previous section, is only in its infancy, but right now the debut of the *Indie Fiction Podcast* is our best predicted example. If that show blows up big — and we think it will; we have a lot of bombs set to blow on that one — it's exactly the sort of advertising venue we'd seek out as a publisher.

Rather than creating the *Indie Fiction Podcast* on one hand then seeking out targeted podcasts on which to advertise on the other, we figured we'd just close the loop. Be both buyer and seller.

We'll see how that goes, but why not? It's the ideal audience. People who regularly listen to the *Indie Fiction Podcast* (which contains only S&S content) are, by definition, the kind of people who'd be interested in the books that we write. Perfect alignment. And so at least in part, the *Indie Fiction Podcast* will be "brought to you by" our latest projects, books, and initiatives.

Be creative with your advertising efforts. There are no rules, really. You need to get your stuff in front of the right people, spending what you can justify for a return but only when you can keep an eye on and feel that it's worth it.

CHAPTER THIRTEEN:
Networking and Meeting In-Person

There's no substitute for meeting people face to face.

Sean and I talk on the phone for a few hours every week, and all three of us end up pow-wowing for another few hours weekly on the podcasts and afterward. You'd think we'd know each other really well by now. And yeah, we do. But I only met Dave in person for the first time a year ago, and before that *I just didn't know Dave*. I can't quantify that statement or make anyone understand it who doesn't. But it's true. Until you sit across from someone in real space, they're only a concept to your brain. You aren't getting *all* of them. And because of that, fewer great things are able to happen.

Every week, Sean and I hash out details of our business — both for Realm & Sands and *The Smarter Artist*, but also in Sterling & Stone as a whole. We make this note, conduct this experiment, shuttle this information to Amy, email this partner. A lot of stuff gets done. It's magic.

But somehow, it wasn't until Sean and I were together (ostensibly for Austin's South by Southwest conference, which I attend most years) that we had the sudden inspiration for *Fic-*

tion Unboxed. We'd been kicking around ideas for a while, but it took an in-person adventure for something to happen.

When I went to Texas again in September of 2014, Sean greeted me with a list of company projects — things like our baffling autoresponder problem, tricky issues with a bunch of our series that we couldn't work out, the positioning of one of our lines and ways to advertise it, the question of forming a mastermind group, and creating a live conference of our own. It was all stuff we could have talked out on the phone or in one of our video hangouts. So why was it so simple to plow through a month's worth of work in two days while walking through the woods?

Sean and I had spent a few hours talking to James Tonn, from Podium. We all knew how each other thought. Yet it wasn't until we all sat in the lobby of the Renaissance Hotel together (and had dinner at a Brazilian steakhouse, where the waiters bring meat on swords) that some of our biggest ideas gelled.

And I already knew Jon Nastor, who works with Copyblogger.com, when Sean and I went to Denver in May of 2015. But somehow the idea of rebooting the *Self-Publishing Podcast* (and running it up the New and Noteworthy flagpole despite it being three years old) and launching a full network wasn't born until we had coffee with Jon in a Starbucks.

We knew our various platform reps from email and from conference calls, but we didn't hit big wins until we shared meals.

We now have a few amazing authors in our mastermind whom we knew from social media — but I doubt they'd be in our group today if we hadn't all met when Sean and I keynoted an event in Cleveland.

And on. And on. And on.

The only thing that's making me cut this list short is respect for your time. But trust me, these stories are drawn from a bottomless well.

Your success isn't isolated inside your own arena of experience and talents. In this business, it really is who you know. Or, to put it another way: *Your network is your net worth.* You need to meet people. You need to share and make connections. And you really, honestly, need to do it in person whenever you can.

Every time we travel, our business improves. Every time we meet smart people we hadn't known before, our business improves. So when we started asking ourselves what we could Iterate (in 2014) and Optimize (in 2015), networking and in-person meetings made that list. We wanted to improve and do more of the right kind. But we also wanted to be smarter because travel is expensive — not only in dollars but time.

Who are the people we should take advice from? Who are the people we most want to surround ourselves with? Who are our peers? Who's accomplished things we aspire to? Which trips are fully aligned with our goals, and which are expensive vacations disguised as work?

That's what we wanted to determine. In this chapter, we'll tell you how we did it.

You Really Are the Company You Keep

First, let's talk about *why* we did it.

We've already given you a bunch of examples of times that people — and especially in-person meetings with those people — made a big difference for us. If you do cool stuff, other people who do cool stuff tend to want to work with you. And then you can combine forces, opening doors for each other.

But it's more than that. It's about the company you keep.

Many artists and creative entrepreneurs suffer from a poverty mind-set. They believe the myth of the starving artist, and even forward-looking ventures are met with a sense of doubt and hesitation. Sometimes, those ventures are approached with fear, guilt, or a feeling of needing to hide. Because what would people think if you hooked your hopes and dreams on some foolish fantasy and failed?

But it's not just a poverty mind-set — a sense that no matter how much you try and believe making a living with art is possible, your head never really has faith. It's a *default* poverty mind-set. Or perhaps a *circumstantial* poverty mind-set. It's not something that's in their heads in any inexorable way; it was simply the inevitable consequence of *being surrounded by people who don't believe*.

My parents are both artists. Mom went a more commercial route and created a business, but she's more right-brained than left. Dad is even more right-brained. Once he left Corporate America, he decided to paint and nothing else. They both believed in me, creatively speaking. Nobody told me I was stupid to write. Nobody told me I was wasting my time or shouldn't bother. And my wife, Robin, has always believed — with gritted teeth and white knuckles through many lean times, but always with faith. She never told me to get a real job. She never told me to knock it the hell off, that what I was trying to do couldn't be done.

I was lucky. Most people aren't.

If your friends are all millworkers who think your creative pursuits are soft and mockable, you've got problems. Your network, frankly, sucks. And equally, if your peers are all poor vagabond artists who think making money is evil and that a true creator must suffer, your network sucks even harder. You have to raise your station so that you can rise with it.

Upgrade your network. Find examples of possibility. Informally, we'll be part of that support system for you. People tell us all the time that listening to *SPP* and reading *WPR* helped them to see that what they wanted to do was possible, even if they never talked to us personally.

But you live in the Internet age. It's easy to find like-minded people. So find them. And find those who aspire not just to be creative but to be creative *entrepreneurs* — even if that last word just means they're the captain of their one-person operation, striving toward improved efficiency and profit. Always iterate your network.

That's what was on our mind: How, as we elevated Sterling & Stone, could we find more exciting people doing more of what we were doing and more of what we still wanted to do? How could we surround ourselves with minds we admired and could learn from — because truly, we're all the average of the people we're around most?

We needed to travel to where great, smart people gathered.

And then we needed to find ways of bringing them to us.

Optimizing Travel

In 2014, we traveled everywhere. Sean and I still had one foot in the blogging and online marketing worlds, so we attended all sorts of events that weren't strictly aligned with where we were going and were more like artifacts of where we used to be.

In 2015, we were more focused. We asked what we hoped to get out of each trip before going. Some were broader, and some were hyper-focused (once, we flew across the country to have a single lunch then returned the next day), but there was a reason for each trip: someone we wanted to sit down with. Something we wanted to learn.

But the next iteration has to be even better. Our resources (more time than money) are finite. Every time we take our eye off creating new words and advancing our businesses at our respective home offices, we lose momentum. I have to stop the draft I'm in the middle of and lose all the steam I've built up. Sean has to stop writing beats for new stories. We miss team meetings because our schedules get wonky. Loose ends are dropped.

So our trips, going forward, need to be even more intentional.

For example, an excellent conference for us to attend would have been Novelists, Inc. (NINC). But NINC butted right up to our own in-person mastermind gathering, so it was a no-go. Next year, we'll schedule around it because we know from the start that NINC is a must. There are too many people there we want to meet and spend time with: other prolific and highly intelligent creators, reps, smart entrepreneurs, connections we want to make.

Similarly, we're in the middle of planning an April event of our own. We knew in advance we wanted to go to the London Book Fair, so we moved our event back a few weeks so we could do both.

And on the flip side, we'll drop a few *candy* sorts of events next year. This year, I skipped SXSW Interactive because although the conference as a whole is creative, it's more of my old blogging and marketing world not my new one. Next year, there are a few more we'll skip. They're fun to attend, and we have friends at each. But travel is precious, and as we optimize, we can't afford to waste it.

You may not be like us. You might only travel once a year, if at all. But you *should* travel. And if you do, make sure you get the biggest possible impact.

Of course, there was a big way to optimize our travel that Sterling & Stone was staring in the face. It's a bit outside the box, but considering that we hold two events each year in Austin ...

Moving to Austin

This is so simple. At least twice each year, I take time out to travel to Austin, where Sean lives and where our semiannual in-person mastermind events are held. I can eliminate those trips if I move from Ohio to Texas. Problem solved.

I won't go into much detail on this one because you don't give a shit about me moving. But seeing as it's something we're optimizing for the company's sake (and mine; I hate cold, dark winters), it needs mentioning. I'll be there in the Spring of 2016. *Travel: optimized.*

What's additionally interesting is that Amy and Garrett now both look like they'll be moving to Austin as well. Archer has talked about it, too. And most importantly, we want Dave here with us. His environment is toxic. He needs to ditch his old habits and move his family toward company HQ, at which point we're all convinced he'll get healthier as if by magic. This isn't sarcastic. We got a preview of Austin Dave in September of 2014 and it's a different, happier, healthier guy.

Creating Our Own Conference

So we're traveling more intentionally and with greater purpose. The team is centralizing. But the ultimate coup in terms of optimizing our networks and in-person relationships with smart people would be *bringing them to us.*

So screw it. We decided to start a conference of our own.

I wish we could report on it, but this book publishes before the first *Smarter Artist* Summit in March of 2016. But planning is well underway, and a lot of tickets have already been sold, and I'll be honest: half of the reason we're doing it is because it's a ninja way to get a bunch of smart people on our home turf.

And oh, the glory of having all those amazing, smart-artist minds right there with us — where we can all benefit, grow, and glean power from the expanded network!

The *Smarter Artist* Summit is a massive undertaking, but the leap forward it promises for the company — and, we think, the indie community as a whole — is *so* worth it.

I guess we'll need to report back on this iteration in later books and on the podcast, but if you'd like to know all about the SA Summit (we'll hold it every year; it's not once-and-done), you can check it out here: SmarterArtistSummit.com.

Creating Our Mastermind

We should step back a bit. Because the idea of doing our own live event predates the *Smarter Artist* Summit and grew out of the *Fiction Unboxed* project. Given that this book is supposed to be about taking reasonable steps forward and learning as we go rather than making larger unsustainable leaps, we owe you that story.

As we've already mentioned, June 2014 was the month we delivered on our *Fiction Unboxed* Kickstarter project. Or at least, it's when we delivered the heart of it. When you do a crowdfunding campaign (and there will be more about this in the "Crowdfunding" chapters), you typically want to promise a range of rewards. We wanted to think big and cover the gamut of what Kickstarter allows: all the way from the $1 minimum contribution level up to the max of $10,000.

It was tricky to come up with those big-ticket levels: specifically, those at $2,000 and $5,000. We wouldn't just *ask* for that much money. We needed to figure out what would be *worth* that much money to anyone who was willing to pay it. We decided that spending in-person time was the only sensible option, so it broke down that the $5,000 level would get you into an intimate group with all three of us for a weekend. We'd work out story world stuff for the Kickstarter novel — which those people would then write their own books in — as well as all sorts of strategy and marketing talk. The $2,000 level was the same, but it would happen six months later and be a larger group.

We held the first group session in September of 2014. And it was amazing. It was this tiny group (us plus five others), and it was like someone had poured concentrated brain power into a conference room. We built that whole story world, and it was fantastic. Everyone came away so much smarter and better connected.

Case in point: *two of those new people now work for Sterling & Stone.*

But by the time the second, larger session rolled around, none of the attendees wanted to talk about the *Fiction Unboxed* story world. It was too far in the past to make sense, and the world had already been well developed. So we turned our attention elsewhere, holding sessions on promotion, marketing, exclusivity, and the general business of creative entrepreneurship.

That session — which, again, was legacy from *Fiction Unboxed* and boiled down to us delivering what we owed these people — was a neither/nor event. It wasn't a mastermind because it was pay-and-you-can-come; we didn't take applications or do any screening. At around two dozen attendees, it was also larger than we'd have wanted for a mastermind at the time. We conducted sessions like presenters, but it wasn't a conference. We were definitely at the front of the room as if teaching instead of brainstorming, but it wasn't strictly instructional.

That's what got us thinking: We shouldn't do events like that one (though it was amazing) because they weren't fully one thing or another. Instead, it made us want to do both of the alternatives.

We'd do a real, official conference, with speakers and everything, in a large room with a stage. That's the *Smarter Artist* Summit you just read about.

But the small group intimacy also made us hunger for a true mastermind. Sean has been in — and paid handsomely for — mastermind attendance, so he was intimately familiar with their value. He wanted to lead one and collect some great minds into our little corner of the business world. I'm an enabler, so of course I was on board. Dave groaned and bitched about having to travel. He's not into the whole leaving his house thing but, interestingly, thrives in those situations after we drag him kicking and screaming.

So, iterating our way forward inch by inch, we opened to applications for our mastermind, called the Stone Table, shortly after our neither/nor (but awesome) gathering. And in September of 2015 we held our first official Stone Table meeting.

That meeting (with two per year to follow) was the ultimate. Our room is amazing. Every one of us walked away much smarter and infinitely more driven to expand our creative businesses. We're all bonded. We're working together with synergy, so that one plus one can always equal three.

You may not want to (or be able to) join a formal mastermind for a while, but remember: This book is about small, progressive steps. We had a podcast and an audience first. Then we had friends and people in our network. Then we had better friends and tighter networks.

It's taken years to launch that in-person group — which, of course, will hone and become even smarter in the years to come.

Meeting with Our Team

A wonderful side effect of those in-person meet-ups for events like the SA Summit and Stone Table is that the S&S team comes to them, too.

We meet, virtually, all the time. Amy is in Virginia. Garrett is in Los Angeles. I'm in Ohio, and Dave is in ▮▮▮▮▮▮. As we mentioned, most, if not all, of that group and more are gravitating toward Austin, but for now we're apart — and could easily stay that way. We could keep holding meetings via Skype and Google Hangouts. We could keep talking on the phone.

But there's nothing like sitting around a table at Z'Tejas over guacamole and cornbread, with Dave refusing to sit beside Garrett. There's nothing like discussing company issues in shared space.

If you have a partner you work closely with but have never actually met, we think seeing them in person is probably an excellent first step out of everything in this chapter. You might work well together at a distance, but just wait until you're sharing a table.

You'll be blown away by the magic that happens. We always are.

But What If I Can't Travel?

Oh, come on. You can almost certainly travel. We'd bet that 95 percent of you who are complaining about your inability to travel technically could but have found bogus reasons not to and convinced yourself they're real. So, look: We won't insist (in that impotent way bossy books sometimes try to insist things) that you go out there and travel right now, but at least begin the mental process of iterating slowly toward it. Start by analyzing your reasons for not going, and see if you can knock some of that crap out of your head so the way is clear to travel later.

You might be like Dave. Dave hates traveling. Driving infuriates him, and he's terrified of planes. He just plain hates being out of his rut. But Dave can do it, and when he does, he's glad he did. If you're meeting someone important to you and your work, it's usually worth forcing your way through the discomfort.

You might think you can't afford it. I know I used to worry about cost. But back then, I still sucked it up and paid, keeping things as lean as possible. Specifically, I just stayed with Sean's family and let Sean drive me around in his car instead of getting a rental. Total cost was the plane ticket plus maybe a slight increase in meal expenses. Like $300, tops. And yes, I get that you might not have that lying around. But what's your business worth to you? For us, $300 was the cost of a good book cover, and we knew how vital those were if we were serious about making a business out of our art instead of playing at this thing like a hobby.

Save. Scrape. Do without something. A few of you literally might not be able to pull $300 together, but that's not the majority. Most people are spending that on crap that isn't improving their lives or business: Starbucks lattes, cable TV, overage on your cell phone data. C'mon. You can find that money somewhere if you believe it's as vital to your future as it truly is.

Or you might think there's no time. This is the worst excuse of all because we're willing to bet your days are just as long as ours: twenty-four hours pretty much every single time. It's not that your time is truly, immutably booked. It's that you're prioritizing different things. What could you move? Whom could you get to fill in for you as far as important tasks are concerned? How much notice do you need to give your boss that you want a few days off — or, failing that, don't skip work and go over a weekend. The kids probably have a sitter somewhere, right? Or if not, have you considered scraping for a little extra money and taking them with you?

And hey, remember the iterative process. Start small. Go to a local networking event where you won't have to stay overnight. Just go for the day, and shake some hands, and get some business cards for an hour or three. Then, next time, go somewhere you can reach in a few hours by car, and maybe stay overnight with a friend. You'll be boarding that jet to the London Book Fair in no time.

(Note: The Americentric progression above will be less meaningful for those of you who live in London. You folks should strive for New York or something as an end goal.)

And okay, we'll admit it: Some of you *legitimately* can't travel. We get it. And for those of you, we'd suggest doing as we've already indicated: form your connections online; use Skype for faux face to face; seek out groups who are like you and like you want to one day be.

But to the rest of you and your excuses, we'll ask you: How important is your art? How important is your business? And if you could truly make a business from your art by traveling to meet people who might someday help or connect you, how much more freedom would you have in the future?

We'll close with a true story.

Sean never used to travel, for a lot of the BS reasons above. Then one day he had a chance to go to the Blogworld conference (now New Media Expo) and his wife, Cindy, forced him to suck it up and go. She bought him new clothes that they couldn't afford and pushed him out the door.

Two years later, he went to the same event, this time in New York, where he met me, Johnny, in person for the first time. Sean and I knew who each other were before that, but being together in person cemented us.

If Sean hadn't gone to Blogworld, I wouldn't have pushed him and Dave to co-create the *Self-Publishing Podcast.*

And then nothing in this book would have happened.

Or more accurately: none of our books would even exist.

CHAPTER FOURTEEN:
Social Media

This is going to be a short chapter.

If you've read *Write. Publish. Repeat.*, you know that the social media chapter in that book was almost apologetic. We mentioned the big networks because we felt we had to and because so many gurus said they were important. The way people sometimes act, it's like social media is an easy button — and *everyone* is looking for ways to push it. So if nothing else, we had to list them in *WPR* so you wouldn't think we'd forgotten, and default to spending all your time there instead of writing, unreasonably certain that was the one thing that would make your business explode.

But then after mentioning key social networks, we pretty much told you we had nothing to say. We also sort of poo-pooed them, as if we frankly didn't give a shit. Because we didn't.

Then, halfway through our period of Iteration and Optimization, we began to think we'd missed the boat. Maybe social media *could* matter to us and we were leaving leads on the table. I distinctly remember thinking, *Wow, we really need to make an updated version of WPR. And Iterate and Optimize will need a stunning social media section to cover all we've learned and what we're going to put into place that we'd ignored before.*

But then we started ignoring it again. And here we are once more, about to give lip service to the whole endeavor because we just don't care about it.

I should clarify two things:

First, we wouldn't waste your time with a chapter that didn't have value, so don't let our cavalier attitude in this intro make you think what follows is worthless. We will tell you what we know and what we're hearing from others. And more importantly, we'll tell you our story and why we feel as we do, which is ultimately more convincing than our default way of handling social media in the last book.

And second, despite our generally *blah* take on social media, please don't interpret this as us saying it's objectively stupid or a waste of time. It's not. But for us, where we are, it has a limited role. It might work for you. And in this chapter, we'll talk about one group — and one person in particular — who's using Facebook to annihilate the world. This despite our ignoring it almost completely.

Cool? Then okay. Let's begin our whirlwind tour.

Phase I: Wherein We Ignore Social Media

No surprises here. This was where we were after *Write. Publish. Repeat.* It's not (again) that we feel social media isn't worth your time or even that it isn't worthy of ours. It's that you need to know its place — and for us, that place barely existed.

Here's why:

It Felt Like a Distraction

I go on Twitter if I'm procrastinating. Fortunately, it's Twitter, and there's not that much happening. You get a few @ messages here and there, and you only get 140 characters to respond. So if I'm good at using Twitter to postpone unpleasant tasks, I might manage to waste all of five minutes. *Maybe*.

For most people, Facebook is the same. But, hell, it's *Facebook*. And Facebook isn't like Twitter. People write long missives, and then everyone responds. It's easy to get sucked into the drama. It's easy to lose hours watching inline cat videos and clicking links.

That's the number one reason we didn't do much with social media back then: Without a plan to use the networks, they'd be a rabbit hole. And that's a big danger for anyone who uses social media as part of their outreach plan: it's easy to convince yourself that you're "doing work by interacting with your fans" when, in fact, you're burning hours while you should be working.

It Felt 20 Percent

We aren't idiots; we know there's a way to leverage social media. But every time we thought about it, two questions arose:

How much advantage could we expect to get?

And *how much time* would it take to get it?

We've discussed the 80/20 rule before — the Pareto Principle, which states that 80 percent of your results tend to come from only 20 percent of your activities. We have full plates as it is. Whenever we consider adding something new, we've trained ourselves to ask whether it feels like one of those activities that's likely to give us an 80 percent return or a mere 20 percent for our efforts.

Could we make social media work? Sure, with effort, and in time. But for a long while it felt firmly in the 20-percent camp, requiring too much squeeze for not enough juice.

We Didn't Like it Personally

This might be the biggest reason of all that we didn't do much social media.

Most people who kill it on social media genuinely love it. They'd be on Facebook (or whatever) constantly anyway. They're not adding an action; they're harnessing activity they'd be spending regardless and refining their tactics. It's a bit like building a windmill: the wind is going to blow, so might as well erect a turbine so you can get something out of it.

Conversely, sending someone into social media who doesn't genuinely enjoy it requires a different metaphor. That's like shoving a curmudgeon into a room full of cheerful partygoers and demanding that he have fun. Think anyone won't see right through his artificial smiles and contrived chitchat?

Of the three of us, only Dave enjoys Facebook. I check (but don't indulge in) Twitter. Sean does nothing.

We'll get to this in Phase Three, but our first serious attempt to iterate forward into social media had me groaning. Everyone kept promising me it *wouldn't be that bad*. What kind of a way is that to enter what's supposed to be a social space?

So that's where we were after *Write. Publish. Repeat.* We didn't use social media much at all and had no plans to. But then we met someone who played the networks like a fine pianist plays a grand piano, and temporarily changed our minds.

Phase 2: Wherein We Meet Tara the Social Media Maestra

We like Tara Jacobsen a lot. She's a social butterfly, never shy, and always has something to say. We hung out a lot in person at the beginning of 2015 (see the previous chapter) and found her to be a beacon of light and energy. You couldn't sleep around

Tara. Her no-bullshit, let's-get-this-done manner wouldn't allow it.

Tara had been part of the *Self-Publishing Podcast* community for ages, and we knew she did social media. More importantly, she did it *well*. It was the opposite of what we did. She not only hit all sorts of networks all over the place; she saw real results for her business from doing so and did it in a way that seemed effortless. Almost magical. So Sean reached out to Tara and struck a deal. She no longer handled social media *for* people and companies as a social media manager but liked us enough to break her rule. She agreed to set up our systems, to take the wheel for a few months, then hand the controls over to us or our team.

It was a sensible plan. A good plan. A logical plan that would definitely work with proper implementation.

The problem was that Sean, Dave, and I were part of it.

Phase 3: Wherein We Implement Sean's Plan While Johnny Protests

So we're sitting in a meeting with Tara. And I've become The Dave.

Usually, in our meetings, Sean and I are lively while Dave seems totally annoyed. There's always so much great stuff going on that Sean and I are like puppies. Dave is the gruff old dog barking from the corner.

But not in this meeting. Now *I'm* Dave.

I remember the feeling. Tara had this amazing plan. And it really was amazing. She'd outdone herself. She had all these tools lined up that would allow us to hit all sorts of different networks in one fell swoop. We'd post here this many times a day and here this many times. Some were broadcast only; we'd find tidbits of news or snippets from our work and we'd share them.

Others were based on interaction. Answer comments here. Hit like there.

But as I'm hearing all of this, I feel like someone is stepping on my face. It's probably the same feeling office workers get when the boss tells them to put TPS reports in chronological order from a vast pile on the floor. I'm so uninterested, it hurts.

And Tara keeps saying, "I promise, Johnny. It won't be that bad."

Sean wasn't helping. You should have seen his ambitions — ambitions that Tara, who's the one into social media, kept telling him to tone down. This was the maestro talking to the student and saying, "Stop practicing Mozart so damn much." But that's how Sean is. He wants to do it all. I swear, the guy doesn't know the word *or* exists. It's *and* 100 percent of the time.

I'm tempted to link to an audio Sean made for the website wherein he detailed what he wanted S&S to do for social media. I won't, though, because I remember the gist of the plan, and it was this:

Post EVERYWHERE, ALL THE TIME.

And Tara, in this meeting, keeps interpreting Sean's ambitions for me, translating puppy dog speak into reality: "Seriously, Johnny. It'll be okay. It's not too bad."

It's hilarious in retrospect that we thought this plan had a chance of succeeding. Since, you know, we'd have had to execute for it to work.

Phase 4: Wherein Everything Falls Apart Just Like Johnny Predicted

I'm not going to say I told you so — but *holy crap, Sean, I told you so.*

I dearly love my partner's ambitions. Really and truly I do. The fact that Sean believes the impossible is a lot of the reason anything we do today even exists. He's bolder than I am, and I think I'm pretty bold. I set high goals, but Sean sets his on the moon.

But there's a downside. One of the things I constantly ask Sean is, "Yeah, but can we sustain that?" Because there's a difference between a sprint and a marathon. What we were attempting to put together for S&S wasn't *iteration* at all. It was jumping off the deep end. We did no social media and had practically dismissed it in *WPR*. Then all at once, we're launching Facebook and Google+ and Pinterest and Twitter and all sorts of other profiles for not just the three of us but every imprint as well. And we've got to maintain those, or why bother having them? Facebook's algorithms are ruthless. If there's no interaction on your page for a few days, just about anyone who would usually see your post suddenly no longer will.

And that's what bothered me about the plan. The need to sustain what Tara had built — at least after she was done handling it for us. Now that I think about it, having a dedicated, permanent social media manager might have made the big plan work, but we always knew Tara's tenure — meant to ease us through a transition, after she built systems and before we found someone to take the controls — was a ticking clock. We knew she wouldn't be handling those accounts forever, and that's all I could think of as I watched posts go up:

Sure, we're active now. We're growing all these presences. But what happens when it's time to maintain them ourselves?

It made me nervous. It made me *Dave*. We'd really spooled things out into the world. And that was great if we kept it up, but it would make us look ridiculous when we quit.

Ultimately, Tara had to move on and hand it over, just as she'd said all along. We could have trained someone to take it over, but we didn't. Mainly, this was because we weren't seeing enough results or ROI. We were engaging much better with the people who already knew and liked us and that was great, but we didn't seem to be moving any more product. So was it worth it? Not for us, not at that time, not with the effort we were willing (and, at the time, happy) to expend. It was dragging a boulder uphill, with too many loose ends dancing behind us. And when we finally got that boulder to the top of the hill, we weren't able to roll it down and smash something.

That's us *seeing an ROI* if you're not getting the metaphor.

As this phase falls apart, it's worth noting that I'm being tongue-in-cheek about Sean's grand plan. It *was* worth a shot. I'm glad we tried all of this, but there just wasn't any real reason to continue, from an 80/20 standpoint. The system, even handed over, required too much work for what we saw coming. It wasn't a bad idea. But we had so many other ideas that felt better and delivered on their promises. And there's only so much time.

I'm glad we tried the full Monty of social media, and I'm sure we'll experiment again. But at the end of that bit of misaligned iteration, we ended up back where we started.

Well, almost.

Phase 5: Wherein We Realize the Truth about Social Media, Like That of Santa

Okay, that's not true. We're not back where we started. From a to-do-list and organization standpoint, we're much better off than we were before Tara stepped in to help us. She got our loose ends cleaned up and organized: pages with dead links and blank pages, profiles that were halfway filled out and generally looked like crap. She created a system that we can start to follow again, bit by bit, if we decide to try again in a more iterative, less blitzkrieg sort of way. She made great header images for of the accounts. So, my old Twitter and Facebook account had this antiquated, Johnny-1.0-from-forever-ago look, and now they're snazzy.

And on top of all of that, Tara's tenure with S&S cleared out a lot of black-box confusion surrounding social media. It used to be the case that we "didn't know what we didn't know" — and hence that mysterious social media pitfalls might have been lurking where we didn't expect them. Thanks to Tara, we now know we aren't somehow walking around with our asses unknowingly exposed. It's as if she's a doctor who looked us over then gave us the all-clear.

It's not really true that we ignored social media, flirted with it for a few months, and are now ignoring it again. At least that's not the *whole* truth.

We've learned a few new things and crystalized others. Like:

We Actually Do Social Media Pretty Well

Hey, do you know what's social media?

Podcasts.

Do you know what else?

YouTube.

We do both of those very well. True, our YouTube presence just piggybacks off our podcasts with video-included versions of the same thing, but we have scads of videos, and each earns a few hundred to a few thousand views right away. Most people don't do that. Dave interacts with the commenters, while Sean and I focus on the show.

And with podcasting? We're killing that. We've iterated and optimized the hell out of it. It's media; it's social; it's us putting ourselves out into the world and hearing back from listeners, who send us email and talk to us on Twitter. So when we say we suck at social media, we're selling ourselves short.

In addition, I still do Twitter, and so does Dave. I don't watch more than my mentions (the main stream is information overload), but I interact with everyone who talks to me. Dave broadcasts the times and dates of our podcasts on Twitter and interacts with people during the show. Same with You-

Tube comments, as mentioned. No individual among us has the whole package, but we do okay as a team. And Sean promises to do better.

We Actually Are Continuing to Explore New Ways to Use Social Media

I've been posting on the Realm & Sands and *Self-Publishing Podcast* Facebook pages. (There's also a *Smarter Artist* page, but *SPP* has more likes and I don't know what to do with the other one.) It's a small step, and I don't do it often, but it's something.

The trick is that I'm not forcing myself to do anything. Dave already enjoys interaction on Facebook — both as his public persona and under his ▮▮▮▮ real account, shrouded in secrecy and NDAs — but I'm trying to dip a toe in ways that amuse rather than annoy me. Like posting about upcoming books and projects. I get excited and share things with the rest of the company, so why not Facebook?

Hey, it's a start.

Beyond that, we're still trying to figure out Facebook advertising. We have something brewing that's as ▮▮▮▮ as Dave's true Facebook identity, and that project will rely a lot on Facebook ads. There, we expect to succeed where we've thus far failed. But that's the point: *we don't know and are experimenting so that we do.*

We're still trying to figure it all out because iteration is a never-ending process.

What We Ignore Is Invaluable to Others

Remember how I mentioned *NYT* best-selling author JA Huss? Julie is a shining example about how our often-dismissive attitude about social media is more about us than any objective truth. For us, Facebook feels like a productivity sinkhole at worst and a 20-percent activity at best for the reasons already given. But it's a linchpin for Julie.

As I write this, Julie's pages have twenty thousand and thirty-three thousand likes, respectively. Her private Facebook group has almost six thousand members. And they're *good* members. Any group has more lurkers than active posters, but Julie has hundreds of active users constantly filling the feed, chatting among themselves, discussing their favorite JA Huss books. On our podcast she talked about her hardest-core fans: the street team who helps her launch, also gathered via Facebook. She's built a real community around her, and you'd better bet it's invaluable — not *helpful*, but *invaluable* — when launching a new book.

In addition to the love Julie's fostered, there are many things that she and other romance author friends have told us about that don't seem to exist outside the romance genre and yet are instrumental within it — things like Facebook page takeovers and page-based giveaways, both of which are near-essential tools in that genre's box. And don't make me repeat the fortune she's spent on Facebook ads … and reaped back many times over.

For us, Facebook is a footnote. For Julie, it's her major platform — more important than her blog, than her mailing list, than just about anything but the books themselves. And she's not alone. This is true of many authors, both in and outside romance.

Don't take this chapter as advice. It's *our experience*, which hangs essentially on *our unique circumstances*. Social media might be the smartest thing you could delve into, given *your* unique situation. Know your why — what you hope to accomplish through your effort. Then try stuff out to see if it works.

You Should Only Do What You Enjoy, Do Well, and Can Sustain

Social media needs to fit you and your business. For Sterling & Stone, it's a footnote if you don't count podcasting. For other authors, it's their number-one baby.

As you peruse the world of social media — and people offering to teach you "social media secrets" for low monthly payments — our advice boils down to asking yourself three questions whenever you're considering any venture:

DO I ENJOY IT?

Because if you don't, you shouldn't be doing it. Seriously. Not only is life too short for that crap, you're going to do it poorly. People can smell insincerity a mile away, and if you come into social media with a grudge like I knew I would be, you'll get a negative response if you get one at all.

AM I GOOD AT IT (OR WILLING TO WORK HARD TO *GET* GOOD AT IT)?

I think we're good at podcasting and engaging as hosts, but I also think the systems we've developed over the years make the final product excellent as well. Our shows are professionally produced and imaged. We have professional art. We've mastered the art of getting ears on new shows, and hitting iTunes's New & Noteworthy list.

Because of those things, podcasting is a worthwhile activity. But even if we enjoyed Pinterest and could somehow get an ROI, it wouldn't be worth it because we'd be terrible. We could learn and improve, but don't want to. And because we're not good or willing, we won't get results. *So why do it?*

CAN I SUSTAIN IT?

Starting anything recurring is like acquiring a new cell phone with a monthly service bill. Projects, on the other hand, are one-and-done. Writing a book or a song is one thing; you can soldier through the process then declare it finished. But social media and the like are different. You have to keep doing them indefinitely.

For me, alarm bells go off every time Sean proposes something ongoing. I say, "But can we sustain that?" as often as Dave says, "I hate you all." And Sean has a lot of ideas: *Let's start another podcast; Let's dive into LinkedIn; Let's commit to publishing something within the company every week.* I *always* push back. If I could pay my cell phone bill all at once and never pay it again, I would. I dislike taking on anything I'll have to continue forever.

Choose your commitments carefully. Casually using Facebook is one thing; starting a plan to build interaction and engage fans that has you posting thrice daily is another. You can do it, and *should* if you can sustain it. But don't start something you can't finish, especially considering that we're talking about things that aren't ever really done.

We're not down on social media. We just think everyone needs to keep it in its proper place ... and, as with everything, know what you expect to get.

CHAPTER FIFTEEN:
Crowdfunding

As with the "Podcasts" chapter, it's entirely possible that the following may not apply to you at all. If it doesn't (and if you don't care about how we iterated and optimized between our first crowdfunding campaign and the second to achieve bigger results, regardless of whether you plan to run your own), just skip to the next chapter. We're including this section in response to the many people who have asked about our crowdfunding experience — and it's definitely something we iterated from one generation to the next, and therefore merits discussion in this book.

In case you've never heard of the concept, *crowdfunding* is where you want to create something, can't justify or muster the money required to create it on your own, and so instead make an open pitch to the world, asking if they'd like to help fund its creation. If you're able to get your campaign in front of the right audience and your idea resonates, people will pledge varying degrees of support (usually anywhere between $1 and $10,000) toward your needed total. In exchange, contributors receive some sort of reward if the campaign fully funds and you're able to build your project. Rewards usually include a finished copy of the product or service itself, but creative bonuses are usually added, which ideally relate to your project's core idea in some way.

Not everyone will need to crowdfund something. And honestly, a lot of the crowdfunding campaigns you see hit the big platforms (Kickstarter, Indiegogo, GoFundMe) really have no place being there. Crowdfunding should be about rallying people behind an interesting idea — not using the populace as an ATM machine. There's a difference between saying to the world, "Hey, I have this big idea — do you think it's cool enough to help make it a reality?" and, "Hey, I want something but don't really want to open my wallet. Would you pay for it so I won't have to?"

It's a bit strange that we're devoting a chapter in this book to crowdfunding. Not just strange for you; strange for *us*, too. Because we *did* crowdfund something once: the *Fiction Unboxed* project mentioned earlier. But we never expected to do it again, and hence should have had nothing to report about iterating and optimizing a second campaign.

Although the results and end experience of *Fiction Unboxed* were great, the process of crowdfunding, in itself, was painful. The campaign lasted for thirty days and was the longest month of our professional lives. I won't go into every detail (you can read our book about the process, *Fiction Unboxed,* for that), but suffice to say it was an insane amount of work.

We had to drum up interest from our existing audience — a process that required educating them on *what exactly we had in mind* beforehand and a lot of explaining along the way. We had to write content for our blogs and guest posts for others. We had to send a ton of emails and Kickstarter updates. We had to engage in comments, create new *stretch goals* (second-tier goals with new incentives) after our initial milestones were hit, build custom graphics, create deliverables for backers, dedicate podcast episodes and field Q&As, and on and on and on. That frenzy continued for a *full month*, nonstop. And that was just the Kickstarter campaign, not even including the thirty-day-write-a-book-live month that followed two weeks later.

It was exhausting. We were incredibly grateful to all of our participants and enjoyed the hell out of the project once the crowdfunding was finished (and, to be fair, even during the campaign when our fans became enthusiastic), but we still said we'd never do it again. We told ourselves that when the next big idea came, we'd find a way to pay for it ourselves or sell direct to our audience without pomp and circumstance — no thirty-day-long sprints required.

But then we got an idea to build a first-of-its-kind sto-ry-planning app for writers: *StoryShop*. And guess which *never again* we immediately violated?

Much to our initial chagrin, crowdfunding was the only sensible way to build our app. Not only was the all-at-once de-velopment price tag ($80,000) a bit steep for our little start-up; the idea of a write-better-stories-faster planning app was an unproven concept. If we plunked down that money and had StoryShop built, how could we be sure that anyone would even want it?

That last part was what really convinced us to crowdfund again.

Crowdfunding wouldn't just get us the money to build the app. It would test the market as well. Crowdfunding — at least on Kickstarter, and we'd argue in any *pure* funding situation — is an all-or-nothing proposition. You either hit your goal and get the money, or fall short and leave with nothing. If we didn't hit at least $80k with our campaign, we wouldn't receive any funds to make the app and would have to abandon the project.

But here's the important point: If we didn't get $80K from our campaign, we *shouldn't* make the app because *the campaign's failure would have proved that nobody wanted it — and that no-body would pay for it once it was finished.*

Crowdfunding, in other words, would protect us from making a massive mistake. It would keep us from wasting money on a business venture that would ultimately fail.

So back to Kickstarter we went — with plans to compromise between the results we wanted and the thing we swore we'd never do again by *making the process easier, better, and more efficient this time.*

Or in other words, by iterating and optimizing.

Modifications Required

Sean and I were sitting in a small Austin restaurant called Z'Tejas, waiting for Seth Atwood — the guy who'd take development lead on our yet-unnamed app. Sean had promised that Seth "is super-cool and *smokes a pipe like a Hobbit.*" This last part was important enough to merit vocal italics. The words were accompanied by a drawing-out motion, presumably to indicate the impressive length of said Hobbit pipe.

We'd arrived at the restaurant early on purpose. The two of us needed to discuss pre-Seth strategy. And so over a Tejas Trio (queso, salsa, and guacamole), Sean says, "Just so you know, he's going to want to crowdfund the project. So we need to be clear on why we won't do it that way."

I got chills. *Crowdfunding.* The feeling was like low-grade PTSD. It's hard to feel bad for us when you see how well *Fiction Unboxed* did, but the process of conducting the campaign was incredibly stressful. Also, we realized in retrospect that we could have achieved 90 percent of that result with maybe 20 percent of the effort — another argument for keeping the process in-house next time. We'd put the project on Kickstarter to reach a wide audience, figuring blogs and news types might pick it up — or, at least, those having to do with writing and publishing. But that never happened. The majority of contributions came from our existing audience. These were men and women we already knew, who would have contributed if all we'd done was to put up a checkout on our own website and sent a single email.

Sean and I firmed up our arguments. We made notes to remember our objections and convictions. Then Seth arrived, unfortunately *sans* pipe, which he'd given up.

"I think we should crowdfund this app," Seth said.

Sean and I replied with various versions of, "Yeah, but ... "

And Seth said, "Okay" to every one of our objections. He's soft-spoken, one of the nicest guys you'd ever meet.

Somehow, Sean and I ended up tripping over ourselves and Seth's amiable compliance until we were all nodding, saying, "Okay. So we all agree: we'll put it on Kickstarter."

I don't know how this happened. Seriously — looking back, I can't recall. Seth didn't strong-arm us. Sean and I just sort of caved, without effort, on our own. Probably because it was the right decision and had been all along, and we just didn't want to admit it.

I probably put my head on the table and said, "Okay. But only with some modifications."

What Worked with Fiction Unboxed

We set *Fiction Unboxed's* campaign goal at $19,000. We figured that was the minimum amount of money that would justify tossing our production calendar out the window for two months: the month we'd spend working on the campaign and the month we'd spend diverting to an unplanned book and setting up all the tech and notifications that would allow people to watch us meet, brainstorm, and write live. Dave mostly kept chugging on his CI work during the project, but Sean and I were fully occupied. The funds had to keep two families eating and pay the project's overhead, or we couldn't swing it when measured against other, more company-sustaining work already backed up in our queue.

We wanted to hit our goal, do the project, have fun, and inspire a lot of writers who either couldn't get past their own internal censor or who thought that good ideas were special and rare (and that you couldn't do improv writing on any old idea like we planned to).

In that first crowdfunding campiagn, here's what went well:

Funding Exceeded Expectations

We actually hit our $19,000 funding goal within the first eleven hours of day one. Beyond that, everything was more or less gravy, and we ended up funding at $67,535 with almost a thousand backers. So as far as money and rallying the troops, the project was a success. But how much of that was due to crowdfunding? How much did we achieve because we were on Kickstarter that we wouldn't have achieved otherwise?

As we've said, we think 90 percent of what we ended up with came from our existing audience. So this, as far as reasons to crowdfund go, felt like a mixed bag. Yes, we surely grossed more. But how much more is uncertain, and we did owe Kickstarter a commission that we wouldn't have had to pay if we'd gone direct.

The Campaign's Results Proved There Was Interest in the Idea

True. The campaign's market testing provided proof of concept. But *Fiction Unboxed* was a low-overhead project, unlike the StoryShop app. With StoryShop, we needed money to pay developers. With *Fiction Unboxed*, we were paying ourselves and handling our own overhead. If we'd sold *Fiction Unboxed* direct and fallen short of our funding goal (say, hitting $15,000 instead of

$19,000), it wouldn't have been the end of the world. Because our costs were our personal expenses, a short result would have meant tightening our belts and living lean for a while. And given our audience's responsiveness when we began talking *Unboxed*, there seemed to be little chance that we'd come up flat. Raising $19,000 in a month, even on our own, felt like a reasonable bet.

So yes, the results proved there was interest in the project, whereas before it was an unknown. But we're not sure that was sufficient reason to justify a crowdfunding campaign for *Fiction Unboxed*.

It Brought the Community Together

Advantage: crowdfunding on this one. There's zero chance we could have rallied people ourselves nearly as well as what happened in the excitement of a live Kickstarter campaign. If we'd been merely selling something from our site, people would have bought it and then *maybe* told their friends. But they wouldn't have been cheering as if it were *their* own venture. They wouldn't have been as active on social media, in our email inboxes, or in our podcast audiences.

Fiction Unboxed — because it was a shared goal for our entire *Self-Publishing Podcast* community — definitely tightened our bonds in a way it couldn't have without crowdfunding.

It Was Exciting

Much like the previous point, there's no way *Fiction Unboxed* would have been anywhere near as thrilling without the campaign. Kickstarter gave us a clock for the initiative that we wouldn't have had otherwise. It gave us an opening shot and a countdown as it closed. The energy around it — especially at the beginning and end — was exhilarating. It felt like a concert, and all of our *SPP* peeps were right there with us, raising the roof.

If you've read our book *Fiction Unboxed* (the nonfiction book about the process of funding and then writing live), you'll know what I mean. Kickstarter gives you a by-the-second countdown in the final minute. You feel like you're watching a championship sporting event, waiting for the final shot before the clock runs out.

We wouldn't have had any of that on our own. And I'll be honest: as much of a pain in the ass as the campaign was, the fun and frenzy of those first and final hours almost made it worth our while all by themselves.

Almost.

What We Could Have Done Better with Fiction Unboxed, and What We Aimed to Do with StoryShop

Let's come right out and state the obvious: Our problems with crowdfunding the first time around didn't have so much to do with *crowdfunding itself* as with *crowdfunding in that exact way.* There are few things in life that are truly binary — truly *this* or *that.* There's always a third option, if you're willing to look.

The last section was all about what worked with *Fiction Unboxed,* so this section could easily be "What Didn't Work with *Fiction Unboxed.*" But what good is detailing faults for the sake of a list? That's not being thorough; that's bitching. Once we knew that crowdfunding was the only sensible way to handle StoryShop, we needed solutions, not a litany of problems. We had to identify weaknesses from our prior experience so we could mitigate them this time around.

What follows is a list of problems we had with *Fiction Unboxed*'s campaign — and what we did to mitigate them when we crowdfunded StoryShop in late 2015.

It Was Too Damn Long

I don't know who among you has ever done a product launch, but Sean and I have done many. (And Dave has watched many, while scowling with a skeptic's eye.) Product launches are a bit different from book launches. The scope is wider. The outreach and prep are bigger. There are so many details to keep track of that you feel like your brain will explode. Stuff gets forgotten. Things go wrong, and you have to scramble to fix them. The minutiae is excruciating.

Product launches are exhausting, but few last longer than a week. Usually, an Internet product launch only lasts a few days. You get your ducks in a row, you send a lot of emails, you open your shopping cart and prepare for the glitches. But a few days or a week later, you get to sigh, shut down the promotion machine, close your shopping cart, and sleep for days.

Fiction Unboxed was a monthlong product launch.

We felt like we couldn't stop. Traditionally, when you hit your crowdfunding goal, you're supposed to articulate stretch goals — new levels to your product and backer rewards that you'll turn on if a higher, secondary goal is reached. This never ends. You're always stretching, telling people about new goals, changing your sales page and adding stretch goal graphics that show your progress, marketing, placing new ads, trying to up-sell. Stretch goals, among other things, are supposed to incentivize backers to raise their pledges to reach a higher reward level with newer and better prizes.

Doing this at a weeklong sprint isn't bad. You work insanely hard for a short period of time, and then you rest. But doing it for a *month?* Holy shit!

Originally, we decided to solve this problem during Story-Shop by doing a seven-day (instead of thirty-day) campaign. In the end, we slid right down the slippery slope and ended up deciding a thirty-day campaign was still a good idea, but because we knew how exhausting it had been the first time, we set a bunch of ground rules to make sure that thirty days didn't feel like *three hundred* days as it had during *Fiction Unboxed*.

So we insisted, right from the start: We'd streamline the process. We'd eliminate stretch goals and keep things simple.

And we'd do all the other stuff that follows in subsequent sections.

We Alienated Our Audience

We had a large and extremely engaged group of supporters for *Fiction Unboxed*, but they came at a price. We also estimate that the *Self-Publishing Podcast* lost 10 percent of its listeners during our campaign because we didn't get the hint that we should shut the fuck up about it.

We made a mistake in letting our own enthusiasm for (and simple preoccupation with) the campaign infect the podcast's core content. This was dumb thinking with no excuse; we honestly didn't mean to be nonstop promo machines but have a hard time dampening our enthusiasm when we're excited about something that's in the works.

For more than a month, we beat people to death with *Fiction Unboxed*. While we were planning it, we detailed our strategies. While it was running, we reported our progress. When it was over, we discussed results and lessons learned. We dedicated a show to talking about the Kickstarter reward levels once we'd decided on them. And it wasn't just the podcast; we emailed our list over and over ("Get excited!" "Get ready!" "Buy, buy, buy!"), and our blog became nothing but *Fiction Unboxed* promotion.

Not only was this downright inhumane to our listeners and readers; it was exhausting for us. Even the month's feeling of victory gave way to an unpleasant aftertaste. We'd marketed ethically and honestly, but we'd done way, WAY too much, and felt like we needed showers.

For StoryShop, we resolved from the start to limit our audience's exposure in three ways:

1. We refused to turn the *Self-Publishing Podcast* into the *StoryShop Show*. We had Seth on the show way back when the app was a twinkle in our eyes, no selling involved. Then we had him on once during the campaign, to give a tour of the app's proposed wireframes and operation, including screenshots. It was intended to be more interesting (also giving a glimpse into our pre-planning methodology) than *salesy*. Beyond that, the campaign's only mentions on *SPP* were in closing calls to action.

2. We launched a sideways podcast series focused on content rather than selling. We launched a podcast called *StoryShop*, separate from *SPP*, to do our promotion — and didn't even do a ton of promotion on it. The *StoryShop* podcast was a nine-part series explaining how to plan your stories and hence *Better Stories Faster* — content rich, not nonstop sales pitches. Calls to action at the end of those episodes sent listeners to the StoryShop Kickstarter campaign, but promotion ended there. And then on *SPP*, instead of talking forever about StoryShop the app, we suggested people check out the *StoryShop* podcast, which people told us they'd have wanted to hear regardless.

3. We limited and segmented our email blasts. Our primary nonfiction list got a *lot* of email during *Fiction Unboxed*. For *StoryShop*, they only got a few emails, and the first of those were content rich. We didn't say, "Help fund our campaign." We said, "Here's a podcast about how to write better stories faster," and "Here's a demo and Q&A session we're doing if you'd like to join us." Only certain segments of our list saw those emails. For instance, you only got a few extra emails about StoryShop's campaign if you'd indicated that you were interested in StoryShop.

These improvements over what we did with *Unboxed* meant we were putting fewer opportunities to fund our campaign in front of our audience, but they also meant a lot less overexposure (we got angry emails and bad *SPP* reviews during our first campaign) and a lot less work for — we think — the same overall positive result.

We Burned Social Capital

We made a big mistake with *Fiction Unboxed*. We thought the *idea* of the project (writing a novel live, without preparation, and letting people watch) was intriguing enough that people with audiences would want to tell those audiences about it — not just for us but because their peeps would be interested.

But we were wrong. The folks we approached didn't hear, "We have a cool idea your readers and listeners might be excited about!" Instead, they heard, "We want money!"

Crowdfunding has a stigma. It looks to a lot of people like begging, and hence they're embarrassed to even meet your eye. We were bullheadedly blind about this with *Unboxed*. I remember emailing one authority about the campaign, hearing nothing, and checking back twice. Finally, he responded and said, "Oh, I got your email all right." *Ouch*. We worked it out, and eventually he told his people, but it didn't make a blip in our funding, and afterward I distinctly felt like we'd just degraded ourselves to merit a reluctant mention.

We saw this all in the rearview. During our frenzied asking of friends and big voices, we remained blissfully unaware of the pitying virtual looks we were surely getting. I tried to convince one prominent reporter that we weren't begging and/or scammy when he finally replied to my emails with his concerns — he'd wanted to cover it and liked us a lot but didn't care for the taste of crowdfunding. This one *didn't* eventually cave and promote *Unboxed* like the first, although I'm sure we succeeded in sabotaging any chance of ever having him cover us about anything in the future.

A social media mass-broadcast service we used to *blast the word out all at once* was our biggest disappointment. It ended up being just another way to drop our pants and look like assholes — without the satisfaction of a positive result. It did nothing. *Nothing*. And yet we'd begged and pleaded with friends to sign up for it, surely with many eye rolls. More people who might never look at us the same way again.

So when we looked at doing the StoryShop campaign, we resolved to not burn so much of our social capital by asking for favors and begging for mentions. As we've said, we're sure 90 percent of the campaign's results came from people we were *already* reaching, meaning that meant we'd begged (during *Fiction Unboxed*) for no reason. It's one thing to debase yourself for a result, but we didn't even get that much.

For StoryShop, we only reached out to people who were obviously already interested. We didn't beg or plead or even really pitch much at all. We only pinged news outlets as an FYI, never desperate for coverage. And you know what? The exposure we got without burning all that social capital was plenty.

We Spent Too Much Promotional Money

To promote *Fiction Unboxed*, we bought a high-end press release package Sean has used before with terrific results. But for our Kickstarter, the results were terrible. That was more than $500 down the drain, and the social media blast from two sections ago had cost another $250. That doesn't even include the time cost of writing the release, which wasn't quick.

We also hired a Facebook consultant to help us run Facebook ads for *Fiction Unboxed*. Cost: $700. Results: *zero*. We even had direct stats on that one. We got just a few clicks, and no funding.

If you ever crowdfund anything, you'll also find a metric ton of scammers contacting you to offer promotion. Ignore every one of them. We did, but that didn't stop us from burning through plenty of money on stuff we thought of as "smart shots." But there was no such thing.

For StoryShop, we did none of this. No ads. No consultants. No press releases. Just organic outreach. We spent nothing at all on promotion, and figured it would have to be enough. If we had to spend big to get the word out, the idea was doomed anyway.

We Spent Too Much in Other Ways

We knew some crowdfunding experts who advised us, "Don't have any lower-price reward levels that require shipping. Seriously. Don't do it. Everyone loses their asses on shipping." And so on *Fiction Unboxed*, we heeded their advice. No rewards with physical goods required shipping until the $194 level.

And still we spent a *ton* on shipping.

Seriously. It was crippling. Domestic shipping was surprisingly hefty, and international was hideous. Shipping a single T-shirt to Australia cost us $30 each. Same for bundles of books. We spent thousands on shipping, *not even including the actual merchandise.*

And speaking of those T-shirts? Some internal gaffes resulted in them being printed twice, and at an unnecessarily pricey printer. We know how to get them cheaper with equivalent quality. We just didn't.

You can limit your shipping (domestic only, for instance) and price to account for goods you'll need to have made, but the way we chose to control unpredictable costs with StoryShop was to have nothing requiring shipping at all.

If you think that makes us cheap, we disagree. There was no reason for us to ship anything for *Fiction Unboxed*, given that its heart was a virtual experience that would be consumed wholly online. We only added T-shirts and signed books because we wanted to fill out those Kickstarter reward levels and needed to come up with stuff to put in them.

For StoryShop (also a wholly virtual experience, seeing as it's an app), we decided not to clutter things along with the *iterated forward* theme of keeping the campaign simple. So we didn't add baubles that would require shipping and unnecessary manufacturing. We kept it pure, and kept the funds we raised for what needed them most: the cost of building the app itself.

Whereas our first campaign had eleven distinct Kickstarter reward levels, StoryShop had only five (plus one exclusively for corporate sponsorships). And whereas *Unboxed* had rewards that were only barely related to the project itself (like T-shirts), StoryShop's rewards *all* had to do with the app, save a Digital Summit we held for the highest non-corporate tier.

You may be seeing a theme. In *Fiction Unboxed's* campaign, we did everything we possibly could. In StoryShop, we obeyed the 80/20 rule and kept things simple — *as we should have all along.*

We used 20 percent of the effort of the old campaign and easily got 80 percent of the result. Optimization achieved.

It Was Our First Campaign

There was no avoiding this one. *Fiction Unboxed* took our crowd-funding virginity, and that opened us up to rookie mistakes. It's not like it could have been our second unless we'd been able to go back in time. But still, having one campaign under our belt when we did StoryShop made a big difference. The retrospect view let us look back and optimize what had and hadn't worked, but we were also able to leverage what we already had.

Maybe six months before we launched the StoryShop campaign, Sean got an email from someone at Kickstarter. They were looking for storytellers for a media thing they were doing, and they'd found us by searching for their top-performing fiction campaigns. *Fiction Unboxed* was the second highest-funded fiction Kickstarter project on earth at the time, and that meant something important: we'd proved ourselves once, and hence were worth paying attention to the next time.

I won't take you through the details, but having the attention of someone at Kickstarter made a big difference for Story-Shop. And that's the kind of thing that can't happen until you try a time or two or five, possibly failing along the way.

Iterate, improve each time, and leverage your wins where you can.

There Were Too Many Moving Pieces

Too many emails. Too many rewards to track and deliver. Too many stretch goals, and too many campaign changes to keep telling everyone about. Too much outreach and too many blog posts to write. We had to create the text on the main Kickstarter page for both campaigns, but did we really need to keep changing it as we had for *Fiction Unboxed*? Did we really need to keep writing all those FAQs on our blog and write-ups off of Kickstarter itself? And did we need to maintain it all for as long as we did the first time around?

By comparison, we pared StoryShop to the bone.

As a compromise between not crowdfunding and Seth's aim of crowdfunding, we decided to crowdfund — but to treat the campaign as if we were merely selling the app on our site instead of on Kickstarter.

We'd promote it, but not play the crowdfunding game. No stretch goals. We told people that our stretch goals were baked in: The more money we got to develop the app, the more awesome we could make version 1.0. We promised to keep our promotion light and manageable. We had Garrett on our team to make the Kickstarter video rather than outsmarting ourselves by trying to have someone else do it (with poor results before Garrett took over) like with *Fiction Unboxed*. And we had help this time around. We had Amy to wrangle all the cats; we had Seth to make the mock-ups and help us explain the app.

The results of our pared-down campaign were stellar. Despite our lack of overpromotion and overmanagement (or perhaps because of them), StoryShop overfunded at $83,957. All of the results, an optimized level of hassle.

Essentially, things unfolded so that we got to have our cake and eat it too. It was a lot less work and stress, for ultimately greater results. We might have squeezed more out of StoryShop if we'd pushed, but why? We wanted to know if the market wanted our app, and that meant not shoving hard enough to fudge the data. If it was a viable concept, people would show up without us knocking ourselves out. That meant that we didn't *need* a maximized funding amount; we just needed enough to build our 1.0 then iterate forward to 2.0 and 3.0 and beyond.

Now that we've finished our second campaign, our bottom-line opinion is that crowdfunding can be great — *if* you approach it your way, with the capacity you honestly have, and if you are crowdfunding the right thing. We wouldn't crowdfund a new book because doing so requires no time, cost, or effort beyond what we would expend anyway. But if we wanted to do something bigger, like a commissioned graphic novel or a movie?

The answer is that yes, we'd go to the crowdfunding well again — so long as we knew what we were getting into and what we expected to earn for our time, effort, and expense.

CHAPTER SIXTEEN:
Building Community

Talking to readers, listeners, and fans while building community is a *this-and-that* sort of thing. It's hard to slot any of it into an obvious box on a checklist. There are some things you can do that are dedicated, specific actions, and we'll discuss some of them in this chapter. But mostly it's a feeling in the air, small things you do and don't think much about. You'll either feel like you have good connections to your people, or you won't.

I guess it's worth asking if you should care about any of this. If you're an artist, maybe it's okay to create from inside your Batcave, never leaving to mingle. Maybe you don't need to feel like your fans are SuperFans (or could become SuperFans). Maybe it's not important to feel like there's a group of people out there watching your back.

Fair questions. And arguably, as an artist, there are two ways to answer them that run counter to what we'll discuss in this chapter.

The first amounts to apathy. You simply might not care. Maybe community building or fan interaction is a distraction. Maybe it's best to stay focused and make your art.

The second possible response might be that artists should actively ignore interaction and community. It seems harsh to me, but there's a definite argument there. While writing a book from scratch while everyone watched for *Fiction Unboxed*, I practically sequestered myself, refusing to interact until the rough draft was done. I couldn't keep the opinions, thoughts, and feedback from our well-intentioned community from negatively affecting my creative process. In that instance, interaction was a *detriment* to art.

But in our opinion, holding either of the above attitudes for more than brief, in-the-workshop periods is 1) arrogant and 2) extremely destructive to your career as a creative entrepreneur. If you're a starving artist type, then fine: Go be a hermit. But if you want to make a living (and, we'd argue, an impact) with your work, you need to also spend time as the entrepreneur half of *creative entrepreneur*. You don't just have adoring fans. They're your *customers*, too. And a business ignores its customers at great peril.

The Internet has democratized much of the art world. Indies can publish on their own, without middlemen. We hear the cries of "There are no more gatekeepers!" plenty. But this isn't true. The *middlemen* are gone, but there are more *gatekeepers* than ever: readers, viewers, listeners, and potential buyers. Get things in this chapter right, and those gatekeepers — people with the power to decide whether your art sells, how well it's rated, and what the public at large thinks of you and your creations — move firmly onto your side. They stop being readers and turn into fans. They stop being viewers and become your ultimate allies.

They become your community. Treat them right, and they become your promotional team. A private Army of You.

We've done a decent job of fostering community at Sterling & Stone but did it better at the beginning than we did in the middle. We're back on track now, but there's still room for improvement. As with any relationship, it's easy to take those around you for granted and stop doing the things that bonded you in the first place. Community building is deliberate. Something you have to remind yourself to do, lest apathy and atrophy become the defaults.

Something, in other words, that you have to constantly nudge forward (iterate) and constantly seek to improve for the best results (optimize). It's something we focused on intensely during both phases, and continue to inch torward today.

In this chapter, we'll show you how we've made an ongoing effort to build our communities and foster those fan relationships at Sterling & Stone — and where we still need to improve.

Opening Rant: Be a Damned Human Being

This happens to me every few weeks. Not a ton but often enough to notice.

Someone will send me an email or mention me on Twitter, so I see that they've talked directly to me. I'll reply briefly. And then they'll say back, "Oh, wow, I can't believe you responded!"

Me.

Let's back up and look at the situation.

We're talking about *me* here.

Not Stephen King. Not the president of the United States. Just Johnny B. Truant, who has some podcasts and writes some books, whatever, who cares. It reminds me of a Mitch Hedberg joke: "People ask me for my autograph after the show. I'm not famous. I think they're fucking with me. They're trying to make me late for something."

And people are shocked that I respond. To a 140-character Tweet where they've said something nice or asked me a question.

Whenever this happens, I think, "Man, if the bar for impressing fans is this low, most people who have them must really be assholes."

We talked about this in *Write. Publish. Repeat.* so we won't delve too deep here, but the idea is this: Your resources are finite, and you can't spend all day talking to people who want to talk to you. But you can be a human being. You can reply to Tweets. You can either reply briefly to emails or develop systems to thin your workload without letting people go ignored.

You'll impress people a whole lot by simply speaking up here and there. By not turning your head and pretending that no one is talking to you, because screw them: You're an artist. By being polite, like someone should have taught you growing up.

The Scalability Problem

That said, you probably won't be able to respond personally to everyone forever, no matter how much you're determined to be human and not ignore the people who want to discuss your work, or perhaps even praise you. And that leads to what we'd call the Scalability Problem.

Scaling our ability to interact as we've grown has been one of our biggest challenges. We've needed to find new, system-based solutions so we can be cool to people without losing our entire day to email. Because there simply aren't enough hours, no matter how good your intentions.

When you have a small fan base, it's easy to be personable with them. You want to do it; you might *live* to do it. *Oh, wow, someone sent me an email because they loved my book? That's my new best friend!* So you reply, and maybe even carry on with a bit of chitchat to keep things fun. It's easy because at first you only have a few fans, and even fewer who'd raise their hands to reach out and say nice things. It's easy because at the start, you probably don't have a lot on your plate — at least in your business. And it's easy because most artists enjoy validation, to greater or lesser degrees. It feels good when someone likes your art. You want to indulge that feeling, so maybe you do. And one by one, your small community grows.

But if you're successful and always making those small, iterative changes to move forward, the number of tasks on your plate will increase. You get more fans, then more and more. And one day, you realize you have the very definition of a quality problem: *too many fans to keep up with*. So you do less because how can a person keep up with all those emails and social media contacts? If you answered everything, you wouldn't have time to write or whatever it is you do.

At this point, many people just stop responding. Others offer terse responses. Objectively, no one can blame these super-successful creators for not spending a half hour each day batting emails back and forth with every fan who gets in touch. But if you were one of the first in that artist's circle — or if you felt connected to them through their art and imagined a relationship that was never there — the wrong kind of unresponsiveness can hurt.

It's a catch-22. You need loyal fans to get bigger, but once you're bigger it's hard to find time to interact with all those fans. In no way are we judging anyone or speaking sarcastically. There really isn't a good solution. You can't stay highly responsive in a one-on-one manner if you want to have any time left in your day — especially considering that you need to save some of that time and energy for yourself, and/or for your family if you have one.

As your tribe grows, you must find new ways to build that community so you can scale with the size of the tribe itself. You need to stop thinking one on one in many cases so that you can start thinking bigger.

One-To-Many Community-Building Solutions

We'd bet that the most personable and fun people you know out there in the public eye (anyone from A-List celebrities to your favorite bloggers or YouTubers) don't seem personable or fun based on your individual interactions with them.

Results may vary, of course. Maybe you constantly email your favorite people, and they email you back. But on average, most people feel bonded to and have positive feelings about people they don't know based on public interactions, not private ones. It's not that they emailed with you. It's that they did a Reddit Ask Me Anything session and answered questions — probably not even yours. It's that they appeared on a fun podcast that feels delightfully out of character — or, more to the point, maybe exactly *in* character. Their appearance on a podcast you enjoy might bring them a step closer to you, even though you never interact.

President Barack Obama's advisers were terrific at this kind of stuff. Whether you love or hate him, Obama swayed many minds into seeing him as a real person when he did both of the things we've just mentioned. Obama did a Reddit AMA and was a guest on Marc Maron's *WTF Podcast*, and as a result, a lot of folks decided that Obama was *a normal guy, just like them*. Not bad community building for one of the world's most famous and busiest people.

Now, maybe choosing a politician for our example is a mistake because politics are divisive, but hopefully you get the point. Filmmaker Robert Rodriguez was on Tim Ferriss's podcast, and Sean and I both decided he was our type of guy even though we'd never traded a word. Same principle. It's proof that mass bonding doesn't need to be done one on one.

We're not suggesting you go on a press junket. In fact, don't. You'll look like a pompous ass. Reach out to the community you already have and set up one-to-many sessions that capture the same spirit as Barack and Robert. They'll be smaller in scale, of course, and you won't be a guest on someone else's platform. You just want to put yourself out there in ways that let you reach as many of those people as you can.

Here are some of the ways we've moved into mass community building — making ourselves open and accessible without needing to take specific time for each individual person:

Our Podcasts

I know this is a bit of a cheat, but we'd be remiss if we didn't mention it.

Podcasting is an intimate medium. More so than blogging. Blogs are read without *you* in the picture as readers add their own voices and inflections to your words. Podcasts are different. We have one daily podcast now and many weekly shows. Their repeating nature makes them a habit for loyal listeners, which means *you become part of their routine*. Listeners typically listen through headphones, with your voice right inside their heads. For — in Sterling & Stone's case — a few hours each week if someone listens to every show.

Podcasts are community builders by nature. We're not stiff or overly professional; we're real people with flaws. We joke, we laugh, we take listener questions. People we've never seen run into us at live events and tell us they feel like they know us. That's the power of podcasting.

We don't need to add any extra community-building efforts here. It's automatic. But it's also not enough to foster the strong community we've been blessed with, so let's move along to the next one.

Ask Us Anything Hangouts

There was a super-busy period in the *Self-Publishing Podcast's* history where we kind of held on for dear life and tried to get the essentials done while so much else blew away in the breeze of our frenetic changes. During this period, we stopped doing the occasional evening meet-ups where listeners could join us live and ask us anything, but we've started doing them again as Amy wrangled the schedule and started cracking whips.

This was a good thing. We try to foster a few communities at S&S, but the *Self-Publishing Podcast* nonfiction community (the one that is probably reading this book) was the first, the biggest, and the most loyal. We were close with our audience early on, answering a lot of questions one on one by email, replying to tons of blog comments, and generally being out there. When some of those things became hard to scale as we grew, things like *Ask Us Anything* hangouts became much more important. We'd been letting them slide along with the rest. But we're back on track now.

The way this works is simple. Once a month, we hold video hangouts on YouTube. We typically schedule them at 8 p.m. Eastern time to give more listeners a chance to get home from work, then stay on for ninety minutes or so, answering questions. Most of the queries come from live viewers (they type them in the YouTube comments), but we also answer backlog questions that have accumulated since the previous hangout. Amy keeps a running list, and we try to squeeze a few in between live questions.

I loathe doing anything work related at night, but I actually enjoy these sessions. They feel casual and fun. We go out of our way to keep the mood light and in line with who we are as people. Dave, who comes alive when the sun goes down, is uncharacteristically un-grumbly. Somehow, Sean and I got in the habit of drinking during the hangouts, so now that's tradition. Not to excess; just one each. Sean's standard cocktail is a margarita. I have a white Russian.

Our *Ask Us Anythings* are broadcast only; we don't open them up and have everyone literally join us. But the nature of the in-comments interaction makes them feel a bit like a slightly nerdy party. There's a lot of joking and a lot of screwing around

among the viewers, which we join in on by reading and participating as we conduct the show.

Only a subset of our audience joins the hangouts live, but
they work as effective community builders for more than just
the attendees. Amy always sends a notice to our entire self-publishing list, so even if people don't attend, they know they were
invited. And since we launched the S&S FM Network, the audio of those *AUA* sessions pulls double duty, magnifying their
effectiveness. As soon as we're done on air, I pass the audio recording to Audra, who preps it for the *Ask Us Anything* podcast
feed.

Audio Author's Notes and Other DVD Extras

We produce all of our current podcasts and *Ask Us Anythings* for
our nonfiction, *Smarter Artist* audience. And it'll stay that way;
we hope our *Indie Fiction Podcast* will be huge, but it won't be us
reading the audiobooks or a forum where we're accessible to our
community like we are on the nonfiction shows. You could definitely hold *AUA* sessions for a fiction audience, but it's a harder
sell for all but the biggest authors. People would line up if Neil
Gaiman offered his fans a chance to ask him anything, but you'll
find it a less compelling offer if you're not a household name.

Because we want one-to-many ways to bond with and feel
accessible to our fiction audiences, we've tried several varieties
of bonus material for our books. We think of these as like the
DVD extras that often accompany feature films. We create this
bonus material and link to it in our books. People can then
check it out and hopefully feel the effort we're making to be the
sort of authors who want our readers to join a community.

We've kept development diaries while writing our books.
Every day after finishing work on my current draft, I'd get down
another two hundred to four hundred words about what I discovered that day and what surfaced in the pages that might have
surprised me. The development diary for *Axis of Aaron* was par-

ticularly interesting because the book was a real mind-bender and we didn't know what was going to happen next, even while writing.

We've recorded bonus video sessions and teasers to put on YouTube, discussing our books and the plans we have for them.

But the most fluid and successful of these bonus features have been our audio author's notes, which we call Backstories, so-called because we have a podcast, called *Backstory* that we told you about in the "Podcasts" chapter of this book. *Backstory* isn't meant to be subscribed to; it's composed of individual spoiler-rich episodes designed to be consumed after reading. We stick the episodes in the podcast feed so they have a place, then we link to each individual episode from the back of the book itself.

Recording *Backstory* episodes is quick, easy, and fun. A chance to debrief about the book and discuss it once the hard work is behind us. Each episode is about thirty minutes long and requires no preparation. We simply record and send the file to Audra. If you want to copy this idea, you'll need a few extra steps. But it still shouldn't be hard. Your file doesn't need much production. If you talk for a bit about your book then stick it somewhere on your website for readers to play (you don't need a podcast), that's enough to boost engagement.

Answering Questions One-To-Many

The last thing we do in this area is to answer questions publicly. It's a compromise over privately answering questions, which is the way we used to do things. We never want to be so busy that we can't help people, but we do want to leverage our time so we can help the greatest number. We do that in three ways.

We answer them in a public venue rather than responding in individual emails. That way of doing things worked when we had a small audience, but holy crap, did it eat time once we got bigger. If all we did was answer one-on-one questions, we wouldn't have time to write new books like the one you're reading now — a venue that helps a lot more people than a single email to an individual. And that right there is another reason we went to public responses where possible: We tended to get the same questions over and over. If we answered them publicly, we could respond to anyone with that same query in one fell swoop.

Obviously, we're careful to never breach privacy when answering these questions. We omit all personal details and inform the asker in advance that we're moving it to our public queue. If they don't want us to answer it that way, they simply need to tell us.

We leverage our time by answering verbally. Not everyone is the same, but all three of us are faster and better at answering questions out loud than by typing the responses. Besides, we're all writers. We want to save our typing time for books. So we answer with our voices, recording the answers in audio files.

We broadcast our answers. This is sort of a repeat of the first way above, but I'll be specific: Any question sent to us goes into a master queue, which Amy curates from email — again, letting the askers know that we'll answer publicly, making sure they don't get or feel ignored. We then pull from that queue for any number of public uses: on our *Ask Us Anything* hangouts, on the *Self-Publishing Podcast*, as topics for our daily *Smarter Artist Podcast*.

In this way, we're not only being efficient and answering many people's questions at once, we're also generating content for our various shows. It's the best, fastest, and most facile way to help a majority without eating all of our time.

It's worth noting, as we end the one-to-many section, that sometimes people truly need individual responses to questions and/or don't want us to read them publicly. When this happens, we always answer one to one.

Solving the Email Issue

For the record, we weren't the ones who became *diva* enough to put *our people* between readers/listeners and ourselves. It's not like we said (and I request that you read this next bit with a haughty English accent), "Oh, gracious, we're far too busy to chat with the hoi polloi. Let us hire someone to handle all that unfortunate mess for us."

Amy introduced herself to Sterling & Stone by yelling at us about this. By telling us to stop answering all our own damned email so that we'd have some time left to focus on creating the content those people liked us for in the first place.

We used to put our email addresses in the backs of our books and ask people to email us directly. Amy thought this was a travesty. We used to have no customer service for anything we did. This, Amy thought, was downright moronic. (Amy loves us, but that doesn't stop her from constant judgment.)

"I get that you want to be cool to your fans," she said, "but if you spend all your time dealing with customer support and answering email, you'll never write any books, which is what they want from you most."

This was a hard lesson, but she was right. In Neil Gaiman's "Make Good Art" talk he said, "There was a day when I looked up and realized that I had become someone who professionally replied to email and who wrote as a hobby." That's sad. Sure, Neil's fans want to talk to him, but I'll bet the sensible ones among them want his next book more. There are only so many hours in the day, and the more time an artist spends on even the best-intentioned social interactions, the less art he or she produces. And that helps no one.

The email address we give out these days — and the one that inquiries through our website go directly to — is the main customer service email at S&S, handled by Amy. It's not her personal address, so if we want to move her out of that loop and have someone else take over, we can.

Amy answers these emails as herself. This, we feel, is vital. We don't want Amy to feel like some sort of secretary to people who email us. We want them to understand that she's a member of the team and that her response not only speaks for us but is valid in itself. Have you ever had an email exchange with an assistant *on behalf of* the person you're trying to reach? It's obnoxious. You're trying to get through to the Grand Poobah, and here's this gatekeeper, relaying information from She Who Must Not Be Bothered.

The way we handle things is, I hope, decidedly different. You don't talk to us through Amy when you email S&S; you talk *to Amy*. She knows much more about many things than we do anyway. Amy's *smart*. We don't want anyone to think she's a puppet, because she's very much not.

In this way, Amy filters the bulk of S&S incoming email. She consults us about anything that requires our input, answers most things by herself, and copies us on pretty much everything. There's a tremendous benefit to the last one on that list. People will get in touch to say nice things about what we do. It would be kind of douchey for us to be *too good* to see those emails, so when Amy replies, we're copied. We see every single one. Often, we chime in, adding our thanks. But Amy has said most of what needs saying, which is great.

This also lets Amy be the bad guy — something she's not averse to. She can pester people that need pestering, deal with unreasonable people in diplomatic ways, and generally keep our heads out of issues that would distract and annoy us but that don't really require our attention.

(Side note: On reading this, Amy gave us a heads-up that this book makes her sound like a bully, then repeated that she was cool with it. For the record, she's not. And no, she didn't force me to write this. Really. I swear. Not at all. [Insert smiley-face emoticon here.])

We all get our own mail, of course, and that includes plenty of folks who've found our email addresses the other places we've left them lying around. Some of this is the kind of stuff that would be best handled by Amy, so we'll forward it to her. Most we just answer, being sure to respect our own time without disrespecting the sender. Dave tends to write essays in response to people, but Sean and I are more clipped. We're friendly, pleasant, and try to be helpful. But we also keep things moving.

More and more, we're trying to move email through Amy. It's a great system and not at all impersonal. Amy doesn't answer emails dryly; she's a real, friendly, helpful person. She's also skilled at customer service. When there are tech problems, she either handles them or finds the solutions. When there are purchase problems, she makes them right. She keeps us informed while clearing our plates. And it's not a blind, impersonal system, which is what we'd initially feared. We still see our fan mail. We still interact plenty when interaction is truly warranted. But in this way, everyone gets a cordial response, and nobody is ever ignored.

Best of all, *we still have time to create.*

Keeping Individual Interactions in Play … But Keeping Them Manageable

It's worth repeating: The goal isn't to be inaccessible or to remove all that pesky social interaction from your desk. The title of this chapter is "Building Community," and its point is to articulate the steps we've taken to — wait for it — *build community.* But you've got to do so sensibly, in a way that solves the Scalability Problem.

Which means that your community-building methods in year five might be different from what they were in year one.

Which means you'll want to inch forward with your community as you inch forward in your business.

Which ultimately means you need to find ways to build and maintain that sense of community around you and your work that don't require never-ending amounts of time. You want to rally your fans. You want to take care of the people who got you to where you are.

I mean, hell: the *Self-Publishing Podcast* community? They're the best. They rally behind us, cheer us on, say nice things about us, spread the word, and buy our stuff. They defend us when we're attacked. They're a huge part of the reason we've been able to do so many of the things that we have. But we can't talk to each person, one on one, every day. It's not possible — and if it was, we'd produce nothing new. They understand that. They're cool.

A lot of the solution for S&S has been to build one-to-many outlets and email-filtering plans like we explained. But I'd like to make one big point to go with everything said so far: *Despite it all, we are not inaccessible, and I doubt we ever will be.* Maybe the day will come when we're too busy to respond to Tweets, but I can't imagine it.

The best balance, for us, echoes the 80/20 rule. There's really only 20 percent or so of all possible interaction that nets us and everyone involved 80 percent of the benefit. So for most, being able to submit questions that are answered publicly and attending our hangouts are interaction enough. For most emails, Amy's response is enough. It's not that we turn away from any of this. We want to optimize it, so we're only spending time where it matters rather than on fluff that can be sufficiently handled other ways.

So of course, there are still plenty of one-on-one interactions. All three of us are responsive on Twitter because even casual interactions take seconds to respond to. And if you send us an individual email that *truly is* individual, we'll answer it. And for people we already know, the balance skews even further. Of course we'll happily answer an email from Blaine Moore or Kathy Austin because we've been emailing and Facebooking them from the start. And of course we'll make time for Kevin Tumlinson's podcast because Kevin is an *SPP* Original Gangsta.

As you grow and time shrinks, your goal is not to interact one on one less and less. Your goal is to interact with more *intention and purpose*. You don't want to scale it back. You want to purify it so that you're doing the most important things and making the greatest possible impact.

We have a ways to go in terms of building community around our work and refining the ways we do it. So for instance, we used to interact a lot in blog comments, where people discussed our podcast episodes. That's now harder to keep up with, and because we don't keep up with it, those used-to-be-vibrant comment streams have dwindled to almost nothing. To some degree, our community interacts with itself, and that's great. We don't want everything dependent on us. But there are still places we should probably find better, more efficient, more effective ways to be there too.

As with everything in *Iterate and Optimize*, our journey here isn't finished. It never will be. The thing about iterating is that you never truly reach an end. You refine. And refine. And refine.

But we're getting better, up from our interaction low in 2014, when we got too busy and lost a lot of loose ends. And that, at least, is something.

CHAPTER SEVENTEEN:
Dealing with Criticism

Criticism sucks. Even when it's helpful, it sucks. But we realized while outlining this book that our way of dealing with it has iterated forward, sometimes automatically as the other parts of our business changed (sometimes deliberately). As your business grows, so will the number and nature of your critics. So we figured it merited a chapter to show ways we've evolved to handle it.

Before we end this section, we'd like to touch on what we've learned about criticism and how our own mental processes have changed regarding it. Next we'll head to the final chapter in this section then on to the part where we take the vast deluge we've given you so far and turn it into something more streamlined. Big promises, I know.

The first thing to know is that just as not all criticism is equal, not all *sources* and *kinds* of criticism are equal, either.

Let's start with an important distinction.

Critics versus Haters

Critics are those who look at your work, judge it, and offer an opinion. We artists who consider ourselves delicate, creative flowers flinch at the idea of criticism because we assume it will be negative — casting aspersions on us as people, perhaps. But criticism can be positive, too, as we'll get to in a bit.

Short version: we owe certain critics a debt of thanks.

Critic, unlike *hater*, is seldom a static identity. A given person might be unflinchingly positive about one of your ventures and highly critical of another. The criticism has to do with the work, in other words, and not that they are your critic for life.

Haters, on the other hand, are uniformly negative. They simply don't like you or what you represent for some reason — a reason that almost always has more to do with them than with you. There is no reasoning with haters, so there's no point in trying. If you can rise above what haters say, you'll see the situation for the oddity it is: *They're not actually criticizing you in a remotely valid way because they* always *hate, no matter what.* Whether you distribute a masterpiece or a napkin with a smudge, it will elicit the same review from a hater. Isn't that strangely freeing? In a way, it removes all negativity about your work that a hater might have offered. It means you can completely dismiss their opinion as irrelevant.

If you are at all successful, you will attract both haters *and* critics. This is a good thing, believe it or not, because the only way to have no critics or haters is to be totally irrelevant. It's a fairy tale to expect every person to have only good things to say. You aren't that naive, are you? Of course not.

Let's take haters as an example because they're so loud. A solid hater might come up once every thousand readers, in our highly unscientific estimation. If that were an immutable statistic (one in a thousand), wouldn't it make you want as many haters as possible? We would. We'd be like, "Holy shit; I'm up to one hundred haters! That means I have *A HUNDRED THOU-SAND READERS!*"

We're being a bit ridiculous here, but you get the idea. Look around your favorite booksellers. Every title with even decent readership has some one-star reviews, and those reviews came from either haters or critics. Now look for books *without any criticism or hate at all.* They exist; they're just not selling. Whenever I see a book that's been out for a while with ten or fifteen five-star reviews and nothing else, I know something definite about that book: It was launched to a very narrow audience of people who knew the author — probably family and personal friends. And those are pretty much the only people who ever read it.

We'll take criticism over obscurity and irrelevance every day ending in Y.

Now. On to understanding each.

What Haters Do

They hate.

That's it.

Don't try to read more into it. Don't try to please them. Don't feel bad about them. Almost always, their cranky mood has nothing to do with you but is more about a wound they're burdened to carry inside. Let's say you write a book about luck. Unlucky people might compose your hater group — but it's probably because they feel chronically unlucky and resent you for feeling the other way around, for daring to feel you have what they lack. It has nothing to do with your book. Nothing at all.

As Kat Williams said, "Haters gonna hate."

Move on.

What Critics Do

Critics may or may not be literally trying to help you, but we suggest that's how you take what they say: as something that's intended to be helpful, whether or not it actually is. Thinking that way helps to frame the critic. If you give them the benefit of the doubt and see them as well intentioned (even if they *aren't*, strictly speaking, in every instance), it will help with how you proceed.

Critics identify the aspects of your stuff that aren't working for them. They're not telling you what's wrong — unless it is factually wrong, but that's closer to fact checking than criticism. They're telling you what they, personally, did not like.

You decide if a critic's take is something you agree with if looked at objectively and/or something you think might be representative (i.e., if your single critic might be a coal miner's canary) or indicative of a larger problem you should consider addressing.

If you can honestly stare criticism in the eye, without emotion, and decide that you don't agree, that few others are likely to agree, and/or after considering the evidence, you'd rather keep things in your work exactly as they are, then you can choose to ignore a critic's comments.

Critics raise possible warning flags. It's your decision whether to heed them or not.

How We Used to View Haters and Criticism

We're human. Negativity sucks. It'll always suck a little, but it used to suck more.

When *Write. Publish. Repeat.* launched, we got a small handful of good reviews to start from die-hard fans. Then a bunch of haters showed up and crapped on us. We'd given advance review copies to some people in our audience ahead of time, but these reviews weren't from those folks. In addition, most of the early, non-ARC reviews weren't verified purchases, which means those people were reviewing a book they hadn't bought. That told us something: Specifically, that those reviewers were probably haters, because they'd reviewed it very quickly and hadn't bought it. *They were just waiting for the book to launch so that they could pounce.*

We'll admit, years later, that it bothered us. Sean and I took turns with our fury. Sometimes, I'd have to tell him to calm down, and sometimes he'd tell me. The numbers were always in our favor: Even during the worst part of the early deluge, we always had way more good vibes than bad ones, but the bad mojo still bugged us.

More: It all made us very dismissive. "That person's an idiot," we'd say, even if some of what they said was valid (like that *WPR* was verbose and took a while to get to the point, which is true). During those final weeks of 2013, we were unoptimized. We saw everything as hate, even though some was actually *criticism* that could help us improve if we could get past our knee-jerk reactions.

It was that way in our fiction, too. And because our catalog is mostly fiction, it was a bigger issue in those titles. In those cases, people wouldn't like a book, and we'd say they didn't get it. Or that they were out to hate on us. And yes, sometimes it *was* stupid, pointed hate: We've read reviews of our fiction that have nothing to do with the book itself and instead talk about how we're scammers (or something similar) in our *non*fiction work. But some was either criticism that could help us improve in the future or criticism that pointed to a bad fit — a version of "this book just wasn't for me." We've been told that our prose is too rambling in our earlier work and have since worked to tighten our copy.

That was then. The next bits are about how we've changed our mind-set to see various forms of negativity today.

Our Optimized View of Haters

We'll talk, about our optimized view of criticism in a minute, but let's get haters out of the way first.

So, class what have we learned about haters?

They hate.

Once you really get that idea through your head, the phenomenon of being hated on is much easier to handle. It used to bug us. But now with a few extra years under our belts, we can put hate in its proper place.

We suggest you work on evolving your mind-set about haters as you remain a creator. Force them to bother you less today than yesterday, and less tomorrow than today. If you don't, hate will put you in a box. But if you iterate this like anything else, you'll be free to create what will resonate best with your fans, and grow your readership accordingly.

There's simply no point in getting agitated over haters. Here's why:

Haters Are An Indication of Success

Haters go hand in hand with fans. You can't have many fans (positivity) without attracting a few haters (negativity). It's just not possible. If you've never had a hater, then you'd better pay attention to everything in this book because you've got a lot of iterating forward to do. If you've literally never been hated on, you're not where you want to be. You're not yet relevant enough.

Make *get my first hater* your next goal if you find yourself in that position. When you finally get one, rejoice! That means you're on your way.

Haters Are Loud. Fans Are Often Quiet

Holy shit, are haters loud. They'll ring your bell because that's what they're trying to do. Because here's a secret about haters: They don't like hating in obscurity. They want everyone to know how big and impressive their hate is. What good is hating something if you have to do it silently? That's no fun.

So haters will make a lot of noise. They'll leave long bad reviews, or particularly venomous ones. They may send you nasty emails. We've had a few of those. You'll know them when you see them. They're the ones that make you wonder what went wrong with the world.

Amid all that gloriously cacophonous hate, you'll have a hard time hearing those who love you. It's easy to dismiss hundreds of great reviews and notice only that one horrid one.

But what's easy to forget — but what we now always remember — is that even your wealth of positive feedback is a drop in the bucket compared to the true positivity about you and your art, assuming your work has decent reach. Only a tiny percentage of people leave any review at all — but sadly, someone who *loved* your book is far, *FAR* less likely on average to leave a review than a hater.

Haters are absurdly proud of their hate. They won't skip a chance to share it with the world. Those who love something tend to quietly enjoy it but seldom bother to tell you or anyone outside their immediate circles. It's just not as pressing for them as it is for haters.

We've learned to keep this in mind and suggest you do, too.

Even if fully 20 percent of your reviews are negative, that means that 80 percent are positive.

And in reality, maybe 90 percent or more of people who read your book liked it, even if they fail to speak up.

Haters Are Unavoidable and Can't Be Reasoned with

Phoebe: You and Emily are in the past, and you can't be mad about the past. So are you still mad about the Louisiana Purchase?

Rachel: Pheebs, I don't think anyone's mad about that.

Phoebe: Exactly! Because it's in the past!

Ever tried to convince a die-hard conservative that liberalism is right? Ever tried to do the inverse? Or what about religion? Ever tried to change someone's religious beliefs?

It can't be done in almost all cases, and that's how it is with haters. They won't decide to like you no matter what you do. So why try? Why give it any thought? Haters thrive on attention. Why feed the troll?

You can't be mad about haters. They're like the past. They're *over* as far as their decision-making process about you and your work. Don't give them any more thought than those lingering doubts you might still have about the Louisiana Purchase.

Haters Are Kind of Sad

Think about haters for a second …

What are their lives like? What motivates them? Why have they glommed onto whatever they hate, determined to throw jabs whenever they can? Really think about it. Is this someone you're going to turn around and hate right back? Or do you, once you consider the situation, actually feel bad for them?

Most of the booksellers allow users to vote on existing reviews for a title, indicating whether they feel those reviews are helpful or not. And every once in a while, we'll notice that all of our positive reviews on a book have been downvoted by a single vote. There won't even be any new negative reviews. Someone has simply pulled up all of the good reviews and indicated that they're not helpful.

Really? Who does that? Why? What does it accomplish?

Another surefire way to get a bit of sniping hate for us is to mention that we're working on something that will eventually be sold. Most of our YouTube videos have all thumbs-up votes, but the shows where we talk about an upcoming product (like the time we talked on *SPP* about our StoryShop app) always have one thumbs-down. Who's doing that? Is it the same person? What motivates them?

Remember, for true haters, *It's about them, not you.* It helps to remember that when they attack. They're not really angry at you — not really. Something inside them is aching, and that's why they lash out.

Our Optimized View of Criticism

Critics, on the other hand, are different. Critics are sometimes as biting and caustic in their feedback as haters, but we've learned to tell the difference. For one, critics can be won over. Not always, but they're usually willing to listen because their criticism isn't based on internal wounds and instead is based on something real.

Unlike haters, critics can help you. Or they can help position you and your work more accurately. You don't have to engage with critics and *certainly* don't have to try and adapt until you've changed their minds, but it's important to remember that although a critic may be *influenced* in her criticism (a highbrow literary author might criticize genre fiction for being pulpy), they don't *identify* with it. That will help you understand how to receive criticism, and what — if anything — to do in response.

It's not always easy to hear negative things about your work, but it's one thing we've made an effort to do critic by critic. If you want your work to grow and become better, iterate your mentality around criticism until you can see it as its own kind of blessing.

Here are our current takeaways:

Some Criticism Helps Us Improve

Contact, the second book in the *Invasion* series, has a handful of critical reviews that say it's sort of slow. A few also said that they were getting tired of waiting for the damned aliens to show up, given that you don't see them at all in *Invasion* and barely as more than silhouettes in the final scene of *Contact.*

Once we saw those negative trends in our reviews, it influenced the way we wrote book 3, *Colonization.* We knew the story we wanted to tell but also wanted to please the readers who seemed to like the books but were getting bogged down. We looked at that criticism and said, "You know what? They're right. We *should* be delivering more aliens in an alien invasion series. And book 2 was a bit too methodical." So we wrote *Colonization* with a red-hot pace and ramped up the alien action. As a result, it became most readers' favorite book of the first three.

On the nonfiction side, we went a bit overboard promoting our first Kickstarter campaign, for *Fiction Unboxed.* As described in the "Crowdfunding" chapter, we were kind of promo whores. *SPP* reviews became negative. We got a long streak of iTunes reviews saying, "This show used to be good, but now all they do is talk about their shit."

At first, we were angry. We wanted to know where those people were when the show *used to be good.* They didn't leave reviews through the hundred-plus shows that they liked, but they were coming out to yell at us now?

But they were right, and with some distance we saw it as obvious. So we launched the StoryShop Kickstarter differently the following year. This earned us better results and improved conversion. It allowed us to preserve the interest of those who didn't care much about the app. Win-win, thanks to helpful critics.

Some Criticism Should Be Ignored

Your critics will disagree diametrically with each other. Some will say they want more action while others want less. It's obviously impossible to please both groups.

But even aside from the impossibility of pleasing everyone, you shouldn't try. Nor should you try to please any specific group if it goes counter to your internal compass. There have been plenty of times that people argued one of our stories should have been handled differently, and we simply refuse. We don't agree they should have been handled differently. So we listened, we assessed, and we declined the suggestion. You're allowed to do that. You're the artist.

There's a fine line here. If you ignore all criticism, you're kind of a pompous asshole. If your response to fan comments is, "I'm the artist, and I know best, so screw you," then good luck out there. You won't sell much, and worse, you won't engage with anyone or foster community. Being a misunderstood genius is awesome except for the part where you live alone in a dark apartment and keep getting angrier at the world.

But on the other hand, if you flop about in the wind and treat criticism as gospel, you shouldn't be an artist. Be a contractor instead. Get someone to give you instructions, then follow them exactly. Francis Ford Coppola said, "If you don't take a risk, then how are you going to make something really beautiful that hasn't been seen before?" The same concept applies. By taking a stand in the face of some of your critics, you're planting a flag in *your art*.

At S&S, we've settled somewhere in the middle. We hear criticism and sometimes adapt — usually going forward, though in a few cases we've made changes to stuff that was already published. The trick is to find a balance.

Just don't get emotional about it. Use your judgment.

Answering Critics Might Change Their Mind

Dave engages with critics, either angrily or sometimes apologetically. Usually rationally. But he's not shy about explaining himself fully, in most instances that irk him. He's better now; he pretty much never used to turn the other cheek.

My default is to ignore people. They don't like it? Screw them. It's a petulant response, and I'm not proud of it half the time. Often, ignoring critics entirely, if they seem set in the opinion, is the right response. But plenty of the time, I could address their concerns and am just being pouty.

Sean is perfectly in the middle, between me and Dave. He ignores things when he should and has a knack for engaging at what seems like the perfect times.

I'd say, "To each his own," and applaud Sean's interest in answering critics that I'd rather avoid as a gesture, but I can't merely pat him on the head for choosing his own path. Because, like, ten times now, Sean has responded to someone I figured was just an angry asshole and made them genuinely happy. He's turned them into fans. In those cases, responding was the right choice. If someone is angry, and you manage to flip them, you typically flip them all the way. Flipped complainers don't become mollified and quiet. They become SuperFans who love you for life because you were a big enough person to look them in the eye and do the right thing.

I'm working on it. Until then, I guess I'm lucky to have Sean on my team.

Some Readers Will Love the Exact Same Things That Others Hate

We have a bunch of one- and two-star reviews for *Invasion* that say, "I absolutely hate these characters. They're reprehensible, and I kept rooting for them to die."

Then we have a bunch of five-star reviews that say, "I love to hate these characters! They're so flawed and damaged that they feel real to me."

About *Invasion*, critics say, "The ending feels tacked on and out of the blue."

And fans say, "The ending totally took me by surprise. Can't wait to see what's next!"

It's not only true that you can't please everyone because people have conflicting opinions. It goes deeper than that. What some people absolutely hate about your art will be *the exact same things* that others love. *Your paintings have too much red. I love how much red you use.* It's not just opposite. It's one stimulus evoking both love and hate.

This is yet another reason you should never bend to criticism without seriously thinking it out. If you change something to please one group, you may be robbing another of the very thing that drew them to you.

In the end, you can only be you. You can only have your voice. We've learned to trust ours and to deal with the inevitable criticism that comes with it. But we won't stop taking risks, knowing that some will be pleased and some will be repelled. You need to trim your tribe. At some point, you need to declare that this is who you are, and let those with an opinion — one way or the other — feel what they want to feel.

Some Negative Reviews Are Actually Positive Reviews for the Right Reader

You can't get emotional about criticism. It all comes down to *fit*. The facts are the facts in your art, and the nature of art is that it will resonate or fit with one audience while pushing a different audience away. You can't have up without down. You can't have hot without cold. And you can't make art that fits Person A like a glove without acknowledging that people have different-sized hands — and that Person B might not fit it at all.

I love it when we get bad reviews that point to fit. It happens when reviewers give criticisms about things that other readers will enjoy. Things that will attract new readers to the same book that repelled the critic, for the identical reason.

Example: a negative review of *Write. Publish. Repeat.* that says our methods take way too much work. Some readers are willing to do a lot of work and see that message as a no-bullshit manifesto.

Example: a one-star review of *Yesterday's Gone* or *Crash* or *12* that says it's "too bleak." Collective Inkwell drinks bleak like sweet elixir. Ideal readers love it.

Example: a disgusted critique of *Namaste* or *Cursed* that accuses it of being "far too bloody" or "excessively gory." Do we even need to explain this one?

We hope what's in this chapter helps when you get criticism and hate. They're seldom easy to take without emotion, and we're still iterating ourselves. But for the most part, it doesn't bother us like it used to now that we know how to categorize it and act accordingly.

Hate comes with exposure and can only be ignored.

Criticism is inevitable and can often help you, if you can get over yourself enough to listen objectively.

And lastly, your fans will always be quieter than both groups — so don't insult them by forgetting they exist and are most often in the majority.

CHAPTER EIGHTEEN:
Managing Our Workload and Knowing Our Limits

Amy would tell you that this final Part II chapter is where we still have the furthest to go. She's always yelling at us to know our limits and to stop adding new things to the pile before finishing up some of the old stuff.

We think we're making progress in terms of finding balance, but it's slow. Part of the problem is that S&S — and this may be the same as your business — is a startup. The startup growth curve requires a disproportionate amount of effort at the beginning, akin to pushing against a boulder for a long, hard shove until it finally starts to move on its own. Once the boulder is rolling, things get a bit easier. But it's never simple at the start and requires countless tasks and hours while you're working out the systems and gaining momentum.

We *do* handle a lot of stuff. We *do* have a ton on our plate. Sean is an idea machine with a loose bolt and very little filter. That makes the problem worse. We always have thoughts on how we could do this new venture or improve that existing venture, and they seem like such excellent ideas. Many times, we've changed our direction on a dime, abandoning the current plan to pivot toward something new. Some of this is squirrel behavior, but we won't apologize. Some of our best stuff (*Fiction Unboxed*, writing *Dead City* to debut the *Indie Fiction Podcast*, the *Invasion* launch that spawned the company's current best-selling series, the complete reinvention of one of our lines in a way we're not ready to disclose yet) literally came out of nowhere to temporarily claim our lives. One day there was nothing, then the next we've birthed a game changer for the company and shoved everyone in the new direction.

But when you add idea diarrhea to an already overfull list of projects, there's a genuine chance of overload (and overwhelm). This chapter is about the ways we've evolved our ability to cope. As you read it, think about your own writing and publishing practice, and about your business (and life) as a whole. Are you like we were, or like we still are? Will acknowledging any of the epiphanies we mention here help you, and if so, how can you apply what Sterling & Stone did — even if you need to start small and iterate forward over time?

Here are the takeaways we've found in our business. All are things we're working hard, day by day, to address and incrementally improve.

Admit That Resources Are Finite

We used to behave like we had a bottomless well. "Oh, we can fit that in" might as well have been our company motto. Toward the end of 2013, the Realm & Sands production queue was an already-full glass of water, but we kept pouring more atop it. *Want to finish the first four* Cursed *books even though I'm already writing eight thousand words a day? Sure, throw it on there.* It comes from being *and*-thinkers who feel that *or* belongs in a pessimist's nightmare. The only problem is that thinking that way too long will break your back.

I've never burned out, but I've sure come close. In any other career I would have for sure, but the joy in my work has kept it at bay. But I'm self-aware enough to see its approach, and having Amy on board helps because she already thinks we're more crazy than brilliant. So over and over, I keep trying to unstack the precarious production pile. "After this project, I'm producing no more than thirty thousand words per week no matter what," I'll say. It never sticks entirely, but it's now sticking far more often and longer than it ever used to.

Slowly, we've come to admit that there is a bottom to this well, and that we'd do best to avoid scraping that floor. The needs of our startup keep us hopping, but we're learning to say no more and more. We're learning to ask for help. We're learning to build systems to help us do more with less effort.

And when that can't be done — when we reach our personal limits, or our team has reached theirs — we're getting slightly better, with heel-dragging effort, at doing less.

Now, when something new moves in, we don't just pile it on top of what we're already doing. We've surrendered to the occasional *or*. Our pivot to *Dead City* is a prime example. We hadn't planned on writing that book, but we knew we had to if we wanted to properly kick off the *Indie Fiction Podcast*. Because we learn from our mistakes, Sean and I didn't just add it to our queue. Instead, we removed two books that we'd badly wanted to write. It had to be done; there are only so many hours in the day, no matter how much we might pretend otherwise.

Practice the 80/20 Rule

Sean (it's usually Sean) will say, "I had this great idea. Let's do X."

I'll respond with, "Hmm. Interesting. But it feels kind of like a 20-percent activity."

Dave might weigh in. But instead of saying "20 percent," he'll use the alternate phrasing of "stupid."

At this point, Sean will consider the matter, and more often than not admit that yes, it's a 20-percent activity — likely to require a lot of effort for only 20 percent of the benefits. Yes, it seemed like a fun and shiny idea, but in the end it wasn't vital enough to bump something more important.

But in addition to cutting 20-percent ideas off at the knees, we're increasingly applying 80/20 to the stuff in our docket.

Remember the social media chapter, and how we said we don't see return from most social media? Well, that makes it a 20-percent activity.

Or what about our day-to-day schedules? Mine is filled with activities that need doing, and I'm always overestimating what can be done in the time I have. Because I know this, I do the essential items first (those that are 80-percent vital, like writing books) and let the less important things wait. If something gets bumped, it's never vital. This may all seem obvious, but few people do it. It's simple to indulge in 20-percent crap as a break because it's easy.

Time is precious. We're turning down more and more stuff we could do and used to do (interviews on other podcasts are taking a heavy hit right now) because there's just not enough juice from the squeeze. Right now, we can spend an hour writing autoresponder emails to better engage the customers we already have or spend that same hour doing an interview that will probably be fun but ultimately subtract from our core needs. Which is more sensible? It's a case-by-case thing, but with each choice of how to spend our time, we're trying to make the one that nets the most output for our available input.

Prioritize Rest and Enforcing Work/Life Schedules

Sean works every day, including weekends. He didn't work Christmas last year, but only because Cindy would have killed him. He works at night. He works when he travels.

By contrast, I'm militant about my schedule. I stop working at 6 p.m. sharp. I don't work on weekends or holidays. And when I travel, I don't work except in incidental ways.

Dave works all hours. He'll work through the night and sleep through the day more often than not.

I'm not saying that any of these ways of handling work/life balance is right or wrong. But I am saying that you need to pay attention to whatever balance you have and the rules that you set. You can't let it happen by default. This isn't something you can tumble into without consideration then wake up to realize you haven't seen your family in days and that you're so burned out, you hate life.

I *know* work is important. But when 6 p.m. rolls around, then *Fuck you, work;* my family is important, too. There's putting in the necessary effort to succeed, and there's being a martyr. The fact that I love my work actually makes all of this more vital. Because sure, I could work all the time. But that would be selfish. My family needs me, too.

(Worth noting: Sean, who never seems to stop working, also just so happens to be Super Dad. It's embarrassing to the rest of us. So despite all that work, his mode of balance works for him.)

We've been more deliberate as we've optimized over the past years. We've paid more attention to our work/life schedules rather than just doing what seemed necessary whenever it occurred. Sometimes, stuff that comes to me simply has to wait. I'm righteous about it. If it's 6 p.m., screw it. Unless it's mission critical, it happens tomorrow or someone else can do it.

We've tried to keep in mind that life (including our health and energy/motivation levels) is a support system for art and vice-versa. If we only pay attention to one side of the equation, the other atrophies, and the system collapses. If you sacrifice your health and your outside life for your art and your business, you're screwing your art and business in the end. Because when you're wounded in one way, it bleeds into the rest.

Enlist Help

We hired a lot of help in 2014 and 2015. You might just hire one person, like a part-time virtual assistant. It's a great place to start. Because not only will bringing on people to do part of what you're handling free up your time to get more done, it'll also focus you on what you should be doing most. For us, that means creating new content and planning strategy. We want help that removes things from our to-do lists that are neither of those things. The result makes the machine run better.

Because this chapter is about managing workload (being able to do a lot of stuff without losing your mind), consider our aggressive podcasting schedule.

That's a lot of stuff. Across our nine current podcasts, we produce fourteen episodes every week, all of them featuring at least one of the three of us as the host(s). Those shows don't just need to be cut and produced and ID3 tagged and converted to MP3; they also each need a write-up describing the episode for the show notes before getting posted to the feed. Doing two episodes a month used to piss me off, with all I had going on. But now Audra and Maya handle it all. We talk then drag the raw recordings into Dropbox.

We couldn't do a tenth of what we do without our team. If you want to do more and take stress off your back, start building yours.

Build Systems

Having a team seems simple enough, but management isn't always so easy. You have to know what needs doing within your operation so you can hand the appropriate tasks off then make sure that they're all getting done. This is a problem because so many tasks seem to have a way of multiplying into ten.

Consider the task of adding the back matter to a new book. It sounds simple until you realize that the back matter calls for a CTA to add people to a mailing list that needs to be set up, and that means a form needs to be created on a web page, and the new mailing list needs to have an opt-in email and a welcome email written, and whatever enticement we're offering for people who join needs to be compiled, and uploaded, and linked, and ... *whew*. It gets exhausting.

And that's a simple one. Consider bigger-picture tasks like launching a book. I could list all that goes into it, but it would exhaust me and bore you. Oh, and also, I *can't* list all that goes into it. Because there are too many pieces to remember, and I'm bound to forget one until I go to do it and discover something that's a prerequisite for something else, or that I forgot to tell reps about the debut in time for them to feature it, or that a pre-order sample was never compiled for readers to sample (a big deal on iBooks), or that we forgot to hand out advance copies to our street team.

For the longest time, we handled all of this the way we'd play tennis: When balls flew at us, we tried our best to swat them away before they smacked us in the face. Then we iterated a bit by adding some team members to help, and everyone swatted balls as they came screaming forward. Only that's not an accurate metaphor. Our new team members kept asking *how specifically* we wanted the balls swatted. Sometimes, we tried to explain. But often, we just told them never mind, we'd swat them ourselves because it was faster. This is not something we recommend you do, by the way. It's what we did wrong before we began inching forward as we are now, and we don't recommend it. It's exhausting.

Building systems was — and, as an in-progress thing, very much still *is* — the next step in our evolution. Systems make you proactive. The right systems put checklist-style processes in place so that everyone can learn what they should be doing, well in advance. Systems are repeatable, so they improve a little each time you run through them. Systems say, "What exactly did we do, in what minute ways, for that last book launch — and what changes can we make now, in advance, so we can improve the process for the next one?"

Trust Our Systems Wrangler

Sean and I are shit at systems. We're too distractible. Dave hates systems. If life were a western, systems are the bad guy who *kilt* his pa.

So as great as the idea of building systems to give our chaotic, Muppet-like frenzy repeatable order sounds, it also makes our brains want to cry. We agreed that lists and procedures would help organize things and make us more effective. But who has time to make lists? Who would ever *want* to make lists? And once the lists are made, then what? I've heard rumors that lists don't actually do themselves — that you need to somehow follow them, whatever that means, while tennis balls are flying at your face. So what good could they really do us?

That's why we have Amy.

Amy is an organizer. Amy likes lists. Amy likes order. Amy has plans. It's all very strange. We'll look at Amy in befuddlement and say, "What now?" and she'll have an answer. I know; I wouldn't believe it either. But it's true.

In order for any of what we're building to work, we need systems and best practices. We need to record what we did last time so we can do a post-mortem afterward and figure out what we could do better. We can't iterate to our best ability without solid systems in place.

But in order to have and then implement systems, we need someone to wrangle them for us. We need someone to take notes and make sense of disorder. We need someone to tap us on the shoulder at exactly the right time (not too early, not too late) and say, "Do this now." Or, preferably, to have other members of our team do it without us needing to see the guts that make the big machine run.

Like we said at the outset, we're far from perfect in this area. We still take on a bit too much and fly by the seat of our pants. Sean works too hard, and I always feel behind. Dave yells at us to stop giving him tasks. It's a grotesque dance, like watching giraffes trying to mate.

But our ability to safely handle all that we take on with grace is improving. Little by little, bit by bit, and too slow for Amy's orderly tastes, it's improving.

PART III:
STEPS YOU CAN TAKE TO START ITERATING AND OPTIMIZING RIGHT NOW

Tired Yet?

Whew! Are you exhausted? I know I am. Sean gave me a rough outline for what you just finished reading, but it grew and multiplied like I was battling a hydra. There's a ton we've iterated and optimized over the past few years. None of us realized how much there was until it started coming out. And to think: We still have many miles to go as we grow. Then again, that's half of the fun.

But if you're feeling overwhelmed, just breathe. We said it at the outset, and we'll say it again: Part II was about what *we* did, not what you should feel *you* need to do. Not by a long shot. The preceding section is like a buffet. You can take what you want and leave the rest for later or not at all.

This section, by contrast, is all about YOU.

Most artist-entrepreneurs aren't where we are. Most, we'd bet, don't want to be. Not everyone wants to build an app. Not everyone wants to write books. Even fewer want to do both at the same time. Even if you could take the preceding section as a best-practices list for your business, it wouldn't make sense. Because your business is different from ours.

Your creative business is shaped by your needs and goals, and your needs and goals are shaped by who you are, where you are, and what you'd like to achieve.

So let's bring this full circle. Set thoughts of the chaotic Part II aside for a moment, and instead think back to Part I, when we asked you to know yourself.

You might want to flip back to that part of the book and/or consult any notes you may have made while reading before pushing on and starting to iterate and optimize your business in earnest. But in case you don't want to, at least give some mental real estate to Part I's three questions:

Who are you?

What are your strengths and weaknesses?

What do you want?

As you consider these — and especially the last one, as iterating and optimizing is results-based stuff — remember to think in terms of ends versus means. Don't consider what you want to do. Instead, try to suss out what you think that thing will give you so you can ensure that your plans are aligned.

We have a popular podcast network. That's a means, not an end unto itself. It could be, though. Some people just want to have a popular podcast, or maybe a few. Doing so *is* their art, and they long to express themselves through audio. For us, we enjoy podcasting but want our network because we believe it will ultimately offer exposure. If there were a better and more enjoyable way to get the kind of exposure we want in front of an ideal audience, we'd do that thing instead. Always consider your ultimate ends, not the means to get there. Then choose accordingly.

In the following sections, we'll take you through three main ways that you can begin moving your business forward in ways similar to what we've been doing at Sterling & Stone. They cover the spectrum of creation: ways to iterate and optimize *before* creating, *while* creating, and *after* creating, when your goal is most likely to publicize and/or sell.

Like a coach, we're about to nudge you along on your personal journey.

But like any good coach, we'd like to say a few opening words to make sure your head is in the right place before we get started.

The Future Is Up to You

Despite the fact that the title of this section will make Dave throw up a little, Sean and I refuse to change it because it's true — sunshine, unicorns, and rainbows or not.

The future really is up to you.

That didn't always used to be the case. I'm thirty-nine years old as I write this, and I know many of you are older than me. But I also know that somehow, an entire swath of the population became younger than me while I wasn't paying attention. And for you kids out there, let me tell you: you have it easy, at least as far as creating and making a living off your art.

You didn't have to put up with the bullshit that my generation had to, creative-wise. We had to walk to school. Uphill. Both ways. And now, between yelling at kids to get off our lawns, we old codgers like to look back on the *bad old days* of the creative world and recall just how hard it was to do any of the things you young whippersnappers take for granted today.

When I was trying to publish my first book back in 1999, I had to use snail mail to contact agents with a query letter begging for them to accept me as a client. Uphill. Both ways.

I was told that if I wanted to have a shot at getting an agent to look up from his cappuccino (or down from his ivory plinth) and deign to consider me, I had to publish a bunch of short stories in shitty little literary magazines to get pub credits. This process involved writing stories I didn't actually want to write then sending query letters to college graduate students who ran said magazines and begging *them* to accept me.

Again, this was done uphill, both ways.

There was no self-determination in the way, way long ago of 1999. Writers could write all the books they wanted, but they couldn't write their own ticket. It wasn't any better for musicians. Today, you might take it for granted that you can produce your own music and put your album up for sale all on your own. Or failing that (the music industry lags behind a bit, hanging back with the film industry), you could just put videos up on YouTube of yourself playing or singing. That's how Justin Bieber was discovered, after all.

But not long ago, there was none of this. There I was back in the Stone Age of 1995, turning the manual crank on my ancient computer to wake the squirrel that ran on a wheel to power its giant vacuum tubes. Furrowing my caveman brow and trying to understand this newfangled electronic mail thing. Back then, if you wanted to do something awesome and put it in front of the world, you had to ask for permission. Nothing was meritocratic. Your book would be rejected by the seventieth agency, and you'd snap, yelling on the phone (a device we used to have in the olden days; it plugged into walls, and you had to be home to use it) that your book was *good*, dammit. That if they'd just give you a chance, it would succeed. That if you sent the book out to the world yourself and let the *readers* weigh in rather than being stopped by a gatekeeper in a fancy suit and a power lunch appointment, they'd say so themselves.

And the agent would laugh and say, "Well, good luck with that, sucker."

That's how it used to be. But today, you've got your Kindle Direct Publishing. You've got your iBooks producer. You've got your NOOK Press and your Kobo Writing Life and your DIY music distribution, even if that's just on your website. You have Facebook and YouTube. Caught a celebrity's attention with a random Tweet on Twitter? The celeb reTweets it, and in the millisecond it takes for that Tweet to go out, your life changes. From off to on, just like that.

We don't believe in lightning-strike thinking or that any artist gets to the point where they're making a living (let alone getting rich) without a lot of hard work. Even then, they might never make it. But the point is, *there's a chance.* Today, it's up to you. There's no one standing in your way.

You don't have to ask permission to do your thing or distribute what you have. You don't have to get someone else's approval on a design or an okay to make changes. You don't have to run your ideas by marketing or your grand scheme by legal. That's good and bad news because sometimes those old structures acted as quality control and kept you from embarrassing yourself when you were too blind to see it. But as we've said before and Wayne Gretzky said first, you miss 100 percent of the shots you don't take.

You may just be at the beginning of your artistic entrepreneur's journey. And for that reason, you may feel daunted. It may seem like a long road — and we'll be honest: It is. But given the choice between a long, hard road of slow improvements and a road blocked by a tightass gatekeeper in wingtips, we'll always take the work. The effort. The risk, which is finally ours to accept.

For the first time in history, you have a shot at making — literally *making* — your own future. Don't screw it up.

Or, actually, go ahead, and screw it up. As long as you try, you can adjust and fix almost any mistake.

That's what iterations are for.

CHAPTER NINETEEN:
Ways to Iterate and Optimize Before Creating

In *Write. Publish. Repeat.*, we said that in order to be a successful indie today, you have to be both an artist and a businessperson — but that those two things aren't simultaneous. They're *sequential*. First, during the creation process, you're an artist, and the businessperson takes a back seat. Only once your work is finished should you switch hats (or shoes, like Mr. Rogers) and become the smart, business-minded person who can sell your product without undue emotion.

What we forgot to mention was that there's a part that comes before you create, and that it kind of calls for both hats and/or shoes.

The pre-creation period — for us, at least — is a Frankenstein's monster. Before we put metaphorical pen to paper and begin creating, we always find ourselves in a weird middle ground. We're *sorta* thinking about what the market wants and what the company needs most, but it's heavily influenced by what we want to write. Importantly, those two things need to agree. We'd never greenlight a project that was good for the business and a surefire moneymaker that we weren't excited to write. You may choose to do something for the money, but we never have.

When you think about iterating the pre-creation parts of your art/business, we'd advise you to keep a close eye on that balance. If you've just written a successful thriller, the smartest decision from a business and marketing standpoint is probably to write a sequel. But if you hate the idea of writing a sequel and would rather write historical fiction, then doing so is probably the best choice for your artistic half. The trick is finding something both halves agree with. Historical fiction might fail business-wise, and a thriller sequel might leave you feeling empty like a sellout. You can't move forward until you find a project that satisfies both.

We'll get to some ideas for blending business and art in a bit, but for now — if you want to take the spirit of this part of the book to heart and start iterating and optimizing your own stuff right now — it makes sense to start with parts of the pre-creation phase that you'll face no matter which project you choose. Again, much of what follows will read as author-centric, but you can generalize if you're not a writer.

A good place to start this Frankenstein phase is with an understanding of what you truly want to create — and for what reasons — so that you'll understand where to go once you begin.

Let's start with your purpose.

Know Your Outcome

Why are you creating this specific piece of art instead of something else?

Remember, the pre-creation process is a time when you wear both hats: businessperson and artist. We suggest you don't consider money to be your solo driver (you've got to have some enjoyment, too), but you'll want to find your own unique personal balance.

There are probably some highly commercial ideas floating around in your head. There's *absolutely, positively* no shame in going for those ideas so long as they don't fly in the face of your artistic half. We're entrepreneurs. Everyone reading this book is an entrepreneur to some degree. And entrepreneurs should think prosperously, unafraid to profit. Consider those commercial ideas, and make sure they won't conflict with your artistic intent — which they would have for early Realm & Sands when Sean and I consistently eschewed sensible profits in the interest of building a wide, cross-genre base.

Alternatively, there are probably some art-heavy ideas in your head as well. These are your passion projects. But because this phase has you wearing both hats, don't let art dominate just as you wouldn't let business reign in the paragraph above. It's as poisonous to your creative enterprise to contradict business for art as it is to contradict art in the name of business. Both must harmonize.

Assuming you've found something that hits both sides — like writing a commercial story that also excites you or doing a highly artistic but low-profit project that you're able to justify financially — let's talk about that big *why*.

Don't pay this process lip service. Ask yourself big questions, and be honest with the answers. Don't bullshit yourself, which we all (present company included) tend to do. Investigate your purpose with clarity, and without flinching.

We'll give you two of our own examples.

We wrote the first three *Invasion* books at the end of 2014 and into 2015. The idea was highly commercial and, handled correctly, stood to make us a good chunk of change. It ticked both boxes per the above arguments: *Invasion* (as a full series, not just the first book) was a story from our ideas file that colored outside the usual lines enough to be artistically interesting beyond its commercial appeal. We decided to embark on it only after we'd built our wide, multi-genre, profit-secondary base at Realm & Sands because it was time for a financial infusion that would let us give our established catalog legs.

So: with the assumption that we'd write the story we honestly wanted to tell, *Invasion's* goal was *to create a commercially appealing series that would sell a lot of copies.*

We needed to know that before the project began because it influenced our approach. *Invasion* is science fiction, so we could easily have mapped out the plot to mirror the style of our existing sci-fi titles: *The Beam,* which is layered and intellectual, or like *Robot Proletariat,* which is thoughtful and introspective.

But what was our outcome? We wanted it to be highly commercial. That meant it should hit the same tropes of highly commercial titles rather than any of the many sidetracks we could have taken. We wanted apocalypse-level panic; we wanted urgency; we wanted peril and high stakes and a nation in chaos losing its collective shit. We also wanted it to be a furious page-turning experience because that's what commercial alien invasion stories are. The books that people tear through have short, fast chapters with an aggressive, this-happens-then-that happens sort of pace. There are reflective chapters in *Invasion* (stuff we might have cut for the strictest definition of commercial appeal if we were sellouts), but it's mostly relentless. We wanted the pages to practically turn themselves, so that's how we built it from the start: as the kind of book you couldn't put down because each chapter ended on a cliffhanger, and the reader would continually justify *just one more chapter* until reaching the end.

It must have worked because that's the most consistent comment we get: *Thanks, assholes, you made me stay up until 3 a.m., and I couldn't get up for work the next day.* Even Robin, who reads all my stuff, looked up at me from *Invasion* to complain: "Dammit, you're going to force me to read it all this weekend, aren't you?"

Is it our most artistic book? Definitely not. We love *Invasion* and wouldn't have written it if the story didn't excite us, but it's unapologetically not the most literary thing in our catalog. It wasn't meant to be. Our desired outcome, when we wrote it, was to sell a lot of copies and excite people in a pulse-pounding way that our other books hadn't.

Our outcome when writing *Axis of Aaron* (our literary mind-bender) was different. We knew from the start that *Axis* would barely sell because it's not commercial at all, and we were right: At any given time, *Invasion* sells more copies over the course of a few hours than *Axis* sells in a month. But the outcome wasn't to make money. It was far more artistic: to write a book we, as the creators, would love. And we were right about that, too. To this day, *Axis* is my favorite of our books.

We continue to serve both outcomes: profit and art. The book we wrote before *Iterate and Optimize* was *Annihilation*, book 4 in the *Invasion* series and damn near a best seller in pre-order, well before launch. But our next project is *Devil May Care* — this year's spiritual successor to *Axis of Aaron*. We have no illusions about *Devil*; it will sell as poorly as *Axis*. But even so, we've booked more time for *Devil* than any other project this year simply because we very much want to write it. The project's only goal, in our minds, is to be a better book (artistically speaking) than *Axis*.

This pre-creation phase is where you need to ask yourself the same questions. Why are you creating the specific project you're about to create? What's your outcome? That outcome will have strengths in some areas and weaknesses in others. It's possible that you'll craft a stunning, selfish, screw-the-market work of breathtaking art that breaks all the rules, and it'll become an unlikely hit, but that's not something you can (or should) count on.

What do you want from this project? And here and now, before you begin, what does that mean about your approach? For us, it meant writing a fast-paced, mostly surface-level narrative for *Invasion* and delving deep and slow for *Axis*, because those suited our most desired outcomes.

What are the answers for you?

Consider Pre-Optimizing

When I outlined this section, I put one quasi-word in this document as a note to myself so I wouldn't forget it: *maaaaaaybe*.

That's right: six As worth of maybe. The kind of word you're supposed to understand is drawn out because the person saying it is hedging their bets. When I was a kid, I'd want to play at the playground but knew my mom was in a hurry. When I asked for permission, this is the *maaaaaaybe* I'd get. Because she didn't want to but was opening the possibility as an almost-for-sure-not.

That's the way I felt about this section. Because it's sort of dangerous if used incorrectly. I figured writing it might be like handing a crazy man a handgun as a tool to clean my gutters. You can get into the tight spaces with the barrel. Oh, and you can get your face shot off, too.

I decided to include it, and Sean decided during the edit to leave it in. That means we're trusting you to understand the proper use of this strategy and not to shoot yourself with it. Cool? Then let's get to it.

Pre-optimizing is a way of engineering a hit from the start.

I feel the need to repeat that you shouldn't be an idiot. If you read the sentence above and got all giddy, please calm down. We've never been the easy button guys and don't want to start now. There was never any ebook gold rush worth being a part of, and that hasn't changed. The path here is still long and hard. Hell, half of *Write. Publish. Repeat.* is a deterrent, telling you to stop right now if you expect quick money from publishing.

Yes, you can do your best to engineer a hit. But it's not simple, and you definitely can't do it every time, or maybe at all. The usual restrictions apply: don't be a sellout or a whore; don't be manipulative to your readers; don't shoehorn your work into becoming something it shouldn't be just because you think doing so will sell copies; don't assume that book buyers are stupid and that you can fool them with a title and cover then dupe those readers with a crappy book that's hardly what they expected.

But given the right circumstances, the right platform, and the right thinking and motivations, it can be done. *Of course* it can. Because it's just a matter of optimizing — something we've spent an entire book proving our faith in.

We'll give you a brief primer here because, holy crap, is this a book in itself, but here are the basics: *You take an idea you're excited about and feel you can tell well, then optimize the book as if it were finished to suit a niche market focus. Then, once you've decided what those optimizations look like, you turn around and write the book with the revised concept firmly in mind.*

Okay, that wasn't as easy button as I thought it would be. In fact, it kind of looks like common sense. You still need to write the book, and it still needs to be good — good enough, ideally, to get people to read the sequel. You still need a platform to market that book. But if you're going to write one anyway, why not write one that you know in advance fits your market best? Why not give it the highest chance to succeed *before the first word is written* — and then write those words knowing how you'll market that title ahead of time?

Invasion was the first series we pre-optimized. Here's a whirlwind tour of that pre-optimization's components:

Genre and Sub-Genre

For us, this was easy. By the time *Invasion* rolled around, we'd already written in most of the big genres out there. We'd also written a book from scratch in a month and one novel *(Axis of Aaron)* starting with nothing but a cover design. We knew we liked to do all sorts of projects, so finding something commercial that we wanted to write was a relative snap.

We had a story in our *possible ideas* vault that was simply called "Invasion." It was something Sean and Dave had pitched to Amazon publisher 47North before they ended up writing their serials *Z2134* and *Monstrous*, but Dave was lukewarm on the concept. So when we were looking for a potential hit, we grabbed it.

The trick here is to find a popular genre you genuinely enjoy and feel you can write strongly in, then narrow it down to a subgenre and certain story elements common to books that sell well in that subgenre.

For us, it was sci-fi — a category that indie writers sell especially well in. Within that, the subgenre was alien invasion. And because the best-selling stories usually have aliens out to end the world in some way, we figured a post-apocalyptic alien invasion series was something we could get excited about.

And that became the start of our framework, inside which everything else was built.

Title and Keywords

We could have called our book something less obvious, but *Invasion* tells readers what they're getting immediately. This isn't about being obvious. If you're writing a legal thriller, my guess is that a book called *Legal Thriller* won't sell all that well. *Invasion* works because it's an ominous title that strikes right at the heart of what the genre's ideal reader already wants. For other genres, you'll need to look at conventions.

But what else did well within alien invasions? Well, they made first contact and did some colonization after that. So we chose first contact and colonization as two of our series metadata key phrases and named book 2 *Contact* and book 3 *Colonization*.

But here's the part where you can't be an asshole. Titles, keywords, and descriptions (which contain keywords and key phrases) make a promise to your reader. If we name a book *Contact* and promise first contact, we'd damn well better deliver some first contact. *Invasion's* invasion is an atypical one in that the ships arrive only at the end and do some damage in the final pages (part of our insistence on telling our own story within the genre's guidelines), but *there is an invasion.*

What's key, from a pre-optimization standpoint, is that it's a back-and-forth process. Once you identify an optimized element that suits your story, isn't shoehorned in, and excites you to write, then thread that element through your outline or beats. Make it a theme. Make your story great by ensuring that your chosen element is coherent rather than slipped into the title in the hopes of grabbing eyeballs and people searching for phrases. Never fail to deliver.

Cover

We had *Invasion's* cover before we wrote the book, and the cover informed it. This is part of the back-and-forth that intelligent pre-optimizing entails.

Launch

It's not magic and is totally up to you.

We're making a point to include this last bit in the pre-optimization section because we don't want anyone believing in get-rich-quick, pushbutton-best-seller bullshit. We hedged on even including this section to avoid that misperception, but it's worth adding this capper to underscore it now.

Invasion hit because we launched it to a receptive audience (our email list and podcast listeners) and lined up some merchandising and advertising to promote it — and then, once it got its exposure, it nabbed those people's attention. But both parts were needed. If it hadn't been pre-optimized to suit the readers it would reach, they wouldn't have bought when they saw it. And if we'd pre-optimized without any way to put the book in front of people, it would have died an attractive death upon release.

Pre-optimizing is a bit like soaking a rag in gasoline. You're priming it to catch fire, but it can only blaze when exposed to a flame. Soak a rag and lay it on your driveway and watch it do nothing. But light a match and touch it to the rag then guess what you'll get. Combine the spark (broad exposure to ideal readers) with the gas-soaked rag (a book that's been engineered to convert to sales), and magic can happen.

Don't expect to craft the perfect book with the ideal cover, title, and keywords, then publish it to instant acclaim. That *can* happen (and you can accelerate its chances through KDP Select exposure, though it pains me to say it, and we didn't do that ourselves), but you shouldn't count on it.

Improve Your Pre-Planning Process

The better you plan your stories, the faster you'll be able to write them, and the better they'll turn out.

And to that end, we'd like to give you a resource. Want to help your pre-planning process iterate right now? You might want to listen to our StoryShop conversation series ... which just so happens to have the tagline of *Better Stories Faster*. It's nine episodes long and will take you through the method that we use to produce a lot of words that readers love.

The StoryShop series is free, of course. You can get it on iTunes, or if iTunes scares you and you'd rather just listen on our website or download the MP3s, you can do that at SterlingAndStone.net/series/storyshop.

Basically, you want to know your characters, your world, and at least the general direction of your plot in advance. That's how you improve your pre-planning. That's how you write better stories faster.

Here are some exercises you might want to try:

Write More In-Depth and Less Story-Focused Character Profiles

The second half of this one may seem counterintuitive, but it's been a big leap forward for us. Obviously, creating *more in-depth* character profiles will help you to better know the people who will inhabit your story. It's not as obvious why being *less story focused* in those profiles would do the same.

When Sean and I started writing together, I was coming from a position of being a pure *pantser*. I didn't do any pre-planning at all. None. Zero. Zilch. But for our first story, I rolled with the punches and wrote to Sean's story beats — a series of short, somewhat vague paragraphs detailing things that might occur in our narrative. There was no talk of characters other than in those paragraphs.

When we evolved our beats to Beats 2.0, as discussed earlier, character profiles were born. I never thought they were necessary, but having those profiles made a huge difference for me.

Now to the point. Sure, you can write more about your characters if you want to know them better. But we've found that the more we know about how the characters are *outside of the pages of our book*, the more real they feel. More importantly, they're easier and more fun to write. I might learn a character's earliest memory or a habit she used to indulge in while alone but has since broken herself of. That stuff probably won't be in our story, but you wouldn't believe how much it helps. It becomes like writing about a friend. You don't need to stop and consider what your best friend would do in a given situation because you know her so well. The same can be true of your characters.

Sean has a huge list of questions he pulls from to *ask* the characters he's creating. The list is called Character DNA and is built into the StoryShop app. In this way, he more or less interviews them then does a write-up. Today, fully iterated, these character profiles, complete with Character DNA histories, can run to five thousand words. But *man*, do I know these folks well by the end, *before* I start writing.

Questions like:

What's your most significant childhood memory?
What do you like to do in your free time?
Do you believe in true love?
What was your relationship with your parents like?

And on and on and on. We'll answer these like essay questions on a test, writing a paragraph or so for each. Most of what comes out of this faux interview doesn't even show up in the story, but it helps us to know the characters. And the better you know the characters, the better you know how they'll react, and hence the more the story has a way of driving itself.

We work collaboratively, but this is all the same if you write alone — you'd just do both planning and writing on your own.

If you don't write character profiles now, try writing them on your next project. You may like the process and might find that your stories take an appreciative leap forward. If you already write them, try going off script. See what your characters are like when no one is looking.

Cast Your Characters

There's a session in the StoryShop series on this one, and we also talked a bit about it earlier, so I won't spend a lot of your time discussing it here. The concept is simple: We treat each book as if it were a movie and cast actors who'd play the parts. This is insider stuff, and we never talk about who is cast as whom unless someone asks (my wife, Robin, is always curious), but it helps us to have yet another shortcut to understanding a character: how he or she looks, moves, speaks, and so on.

For a quick bit of experimental optimization, you might want to give this a shot. Who would play your main character in a movie? Drag a photo of him or her in a fitting role into your profile. Once a character has a face, they'll be much more familiar.

Give Serious Thought to Your Setting

Remember my example of how *Breaking Bad* wouldn't have been the same if it had been set in LA instead of Albuquerque? That's the kind of thing we'd suggest you consider as you're inching your pre-planning forward. You might be ignoring setting right now. It's easy enough to do; setting is, by definition, literally in the background. But if you want to iterate, try making setting important in your next book. Give it genuine thought; maybe location scout like we do. Then make it vital. What things might happen in that setting that couldn't happen somewhere else? Walter White wouldn't have been nearly as able to drive out into the barren desert to cook meth if he'd been in LA — and hell, that's an iconic thing for fans of *Breaking Bad*.

Try Using Story Beats

The nature of iteration is to experiment. Stick with how you're doing things now, and you're unlikely to find the small improvements that work for you. The things we chose to improve won't be exactly the same as what helps you, of course — but how will you find any of it if you never leave the box?

Many writers decide they are one thing and make it part of their artistic identity. They'll say, "I'm a plotter and want to know every detail before I start writing so I understand what has to happen." Or, "I'm a pantser; plotting too much stifles my creativity." But why not experiment? Why not see what improvements might be out there that you're missing — that could make your work better, faster, and more fun to do?

As I said, I used to be a pantser. But when I tried writing to Sean's beats, I found that my creativity swelled where it had merely settled before. I felt more freedom working to those rough outlines because I wasn't groping around in the dark, not knowing where to go next until I tripped right over it; free to articulate Sean's bones rather than gasping in open air like I was used to. I found that there's more to discover once I stop wondering what might happen next on the largest of levels. In essence, working to story beats — always looser than an outline — gives me enough guidance to know I should head from A to Z. But I don't necessarily get there by going A, B, C, D. I can go wherever I want within those skeletal fences.

Again, you're different from me and different from Sean. But consider experimenting if you want to advance. If you plot to the detail, try something looser, like beats. If you pants your work, try something slightly more stringent — again, like beats. Beats can be the roughest of concepts or almost an outline. You can obey them fully or get a quarter into your story and find yourself ignoring them. I usually do. By the 25-percent mark, Sean's original beats are a ghost. That's why we have story meetings: to see where we think the story should go after I've discovered bold new lands between the lines.

Try it. Then make it better (meaning: more facile for you, as an individual) every time.

CHAPTER TWENTY:
Ways to Iterate and Optimize Your Creation Process

Okay! So you know what you're going to write. (Or, if you're not a writer, you've given serious, outcome-based thought to what you're going to build in your own unique art.)

You know your characters well and have fleshed out their on-paper life. You know your setting. You have a great idea of the shape your narrative might take and are prepared to hit the ground running on day one of writing. You might have pre-optimized a bit to give yourself the best chance of success once you get exposure. And maybe you've done some prep that we didn't touch on but that struck you as obvious from reading Part II of this book: creating a podcast if you're a nonfiction author, for instance, to build authority in advance.

Now it's time to create. And as with anything, you want to incrementally improve the more you make so that you can achieve continuously better results. *The only way to improve the creating of your art is to do it.* To put in your ten thousand hours, as Malcolm Gladwell said.

This chapter will focus on ways you can improve the meta-level of your creative process. How you can take the heart of what you do and become better at all the stuff that surrounds it.

Let's get to it — starting with the most obvious tip, coming from us.

Create More Stuff

It's probably not shocking that the authors of a book with a name like *Write. Publish. Repeat.* advocate being prolific as a key strategy. But it's true: In our opinion, the best way to get better at storytelling is to tell more stories. The only way to improve technique is to practice more often. The best way to sell more books is usually to write more, but we'll leave that for the business chapters.

The concept is simple and requires no explanation: *Create more stuff* is sort of a *just-do-it* situation. But there are a few caveats.

The Definition of Prolific Is Up to You

My normal rough draft production rate is six thousand words per day. I can reasonably sustain eight thousand as my semi-comfortable max over an extended period of time. The most I've ever hit in a day was over sixteen thousand words — but off the top of my head I know two people who can easily top twenty thousand per day. And not long ago, as I write this, we had Chris Fox on the podcast, who spoke to us on the rather juicy topic of how to write five thousand words per hour.

I'm trying to make a point by tossing up the biggest numbers I know — ones that are surely dwarfed by plenty I'm simply unaware of. Hang in there.

When we started *SPP*, I talked a lot about my production because it was all I had. There was no Sterling & Stone; there was no sophomore Johnny B. Truant novel; there was no Platt & Truant partnership; there was *definitely* no fiction-related income. We were nuts and bolts in those days, and so I became known as our most consistently prolific writer. It became a thing.

But then we stopped talking about numbers because we kept getting emails that said things like, "I can't write as much as you, but … " or "What's a 'good enough' strategy for someone who can only put out one/two/four books a year?"

When we started to hear from people who *only* put out four books a year and felt bad admitting to such *low* production, we decided it was time to knock it off. I never reported my numbers to brag; I was simply discussing my work. Unfortunately, it was discouraging people. Even listeners who felt inspired by those numbers and wanted us to keep listing them (Garrett was one, before he joined us) admitted to being intimidated at the same time.

Today, we flip-flop now and again. Sometimes, we talk production, and sometimes we don't, but we always give caveats. Specifically, my production works for me. Garrett's production — which, asshole that he is, sometimes makes mine look low — is what works for him. Dave is much more methodical — but again, that's *his* process.

This section's lesson is to create more stuff, but that means two things: actually finishing up and shipping off what you have rather than weaseling out of it from fear, and making your time more efficient. The goal isn't to publish ten thousand words per day or week or month or year. The goal is to publish more this year than you did last year. It's all relative.

Don't ever compare yourself to someone else. Only compare yourself to *you*. To the degree that you can improve your skills and put more art out into the world, do it. But don't look at me or anyone else. Those people aren't you, and your style and situation are unique.

Never Sacrifice Quality

There was an article in the *Huffington Post* in 2015 that made us at S&S alternately laugh, rage, and throw up. It was about how indie writers should stop being so prolific. STOP WRITING A LOT OF BOOKS, came the message. The article infuriated a lot of indies because it seemed to be written from some sort of ivory tower, from a place of superiority, looking down from The Plinth of Amazing Literary Quality on The Unwashed and Untalented Masses with Their Scads of Shitty Books.

In retrospect — once I was done laughing at the absurdity, raging at the author's perceived arrogance, and throwing up — I think the author was saying something different from what everyone thought she was. She did an awful job of articulating herself, however, and came off like a pompous ass.

I think her message was supposed to be, "Don't write a ton of books if you can't write *good* books in those numbers and are only writing a lot because although your natural speed is deliberate and methodical, you feel outside pressure to ramp up."

It's a mouthful, but I *think* this was her intent. But good luck explaining that to all the people she pissed off by unintentionally implying their work was crap.

As much as we hated that article, we all agree with the corrected, missed-the-mark message she almost made: *Don't produce four books a year if you honestly don't want to, can't, or will seriously injure your quality by doing so. Don't write a ton simply because someone says you have to.*

The irony of our pointing this out in a section called "Create More Stuff" isn't lost on us. But there's not really dissonance here. You should ship more of what you make instead of weaseling out, and do more of what you're good if you want to improve. These changes should, in line with this book's title, be incremental. If you can publish a book a year now and would thoroughly shit the bed while making yourself a basket case by trying to turn that into four books next year, then by all means don't try. Don't let the market tell you how to write. Don't sacrifice quality in the name of dumping more words into the world.

And hey, if you're happy at your current production, keep it up, and don't change. But this section is about how you can iterate, and there's little chance that plodding ahead without consistently challenging your writing muscle will iterate you all that fast.

Create Faster

Since we've just spent a whole section talking about creating more art, the "create faster" stuff that's left will hit the same territory from a different angle. In general, if you create faster, you're going to make more stuff. But the mechanics and results are subtly different.

What we mean when we say write faster is to literally *write faster*. Not to put more hours in but to churn out more words in the same amount of time.

Like being prolific, the idea of being fast is usually crapped upon by the writing world's nose-in-the-air authorities. "It can't be good if it was made quickly," these people sputter while trying not to spill their old-fashioned.

But if you want to iterate your process, this is one of the obvious stops as far as we're concerned. It's quantifiable, which means you'll clearly be able to see if you're getting faster or not. It's incremental because although 1,250 words per hour is faster than 1,200 words per hour, you'll barely notice the difference. And it's achievable for the same reasons.

But why? you might be asking. Sure, more words per hour is a tidy metric, but so what?

In our experience, writing faster is the best way to outrun your doubts. The faster you work — always incrementally and within reason — the closer you'll come to your natural voice.

Without exception, the fastest stuff we write tends to be the best. We differ in the modalities of *best* (my fast rough drafts tend to be clean whereas Sean's require more edits), but the content is always the best stuff because it's coming from our deeper mind. We stop worrying about mechanics and self-censorship long enough to *tell the damned story.*

Plus, you'll also get all the benefits from the "Create More Stuff" section if you write fast. You'll produce more words in the time you have, and that's good because you might not be full-time writers like we are. Maybe you only have an hour every other day, and that's ironclad. In that case, physically writing faster is the only way you *can* create more.

One final note: For a great example of what's possible with fast writing, iterating to improve, and making use of the time you have, listen to "*SPP* Episode #177 — How To Write 5,000 Words Per Hour With Chris Fox." You probably won't learn how to literally write five thousand words per hour (I can't approach half that), but you'll learn plenty. Chris's writing time, around his full-time job and social life, is extremely limited, and yet he makes insane word counts work. The dude writes on the bus. He dictates fiction while *waiting* for his ride. He's churning out work in his life's every nook and cranny. And as we'd suggest for you, he's learned this habit one day and one small change at a time.

Tell Your Internal Critic to Piss Off

Do you know what happens when you write fast? Your internal critic gets out of the way. You know whom I'm talking about. The internal critic is that jerk who peers over your shoulder all day long, telling you how much crap you're shoveling when you create.

Dave's internal critic is the strongest among us. We're pretty sure Dave's discarded story fragments could fill a library, but he throws them out as fast as he makes them. Dave's critic is always telling him that his work is crap, that he should toss it all and start again. And he does, over and over.

Dave succeeds and publishes great work despite himself. Most writers and artists aren't as lucky; they let the critic win then never put anything out there. Do you know what's the opposite of iteration? *Stagnation.* It's all you can do when you're constantly crapping on yourself.

Writing fast is one way to outrun the critic, but there are others. Have a supportive group of peers around you. Form a solid network and/or mastermind. Learn better how to deal with criticism because external critics and haters feed the critic's confidence. Ways we'd iterate through all of those are in the last part.

Much of it comes down to practice. Every day, you learn to ignore the inner critic more. And you have to. You can't hit your potential with that much self-doubt, so keep powering on.

My favorite idea for dismissing the internal critic came from my friend Jon Morrow. I've never tried this because I'm apparently arrogant enough that my critic usually starves to death, but Jon described a funny way to murder the voice. He suggests writing a letter to your internal critic. In that letter, be ruthless. Tell that guy or gal exactly what you think of them. Cuss them out if that's your nature. Be a dick because the inner critic is a dick to you.

After you do this, apparently your internal critic will be so shocked — I picture him with his mouth open, eyes wide, hair blown back as if by a strong wind in the wake of your angry letter — that you'll be able to get past whatever blocks you may have.

If you try this, let us know how it goes. I imagine hilarious and inspiring results.

Focus on Consistency

More important than being amazing or fast is simply showing up day after day.

You want your art to be a habit. You want to trigger yourself into a creative flow as if on command so it's not as hard to find your rhythm in the time you have. You do that through consistency. Through repeated actions. Your brain likes patterns, so give it one. Do the same things every day to build a creative habit, and sooner or later your brain will catch on and make it stick.

We blew someone away with an astonishingly simple stat at a recent in-person event. This person didn't understand how writers could produce as much as some do. And so we said, "If you write five hundred words a day, that's two books a year."

Five hundred words a day is nothing. Not once you get used to it. Do the math yourself. Five hundred words times 365 days a year is 182,500. That's two full-length books. And really, most writers can do far more than five hundred words a day. Hell, if you took all of the weekends and holidays off and threw away a chunk of what you wrote as crap, you'd still end up with *one* book a year. In that scenario, you could do what needed doing in a half hour per session, even if you're ridiculously slow. And to think: most people say they can't find the time.

Tell most people they could write two books per year, and they'll protest even if they feel they have the chops to do the word making. But could they write for a half hour a day? That adds up.

Make a habit. Any habit, no matter how big or small, that supports your creation. Then simply *do it,* come hell or high water.

Finish What You Started

Here's a typical scenario:

Writer Jane begins her novel then gets a third of the way through and decides she needs to add a character. So she goes back to the beginning, noodling and editing, and maybe adding a few fresh words. Then she gets to the halfway point and realizes there's a plot twist that should have happened, so she goes back to the beginning again. Then she realizes that chapters 2 through 7 are horrid on rereading and trashes them. But now there are new holes introduced by the replacement chapters, so she starts the whole thing over. And on and on, never quite getting it right.

Guys. Gals. Seriously. *Just finish the damned rough draft.*

You need to get the story out of your head. For visual artists, you need to get the wireframe or first wash or rough sketches down. For musicians, you need a few rounds of verse-chorus-verse, all the way through. You get the idea. Stop screwing around and trying to make something perfect in the first pass. That's like expecting a single machine to roll through the countryside once, laying down a perfectly finished road with stripes, marked shoulders, guard rails, and grass neatly trimmed at the edges. That's not how things are built. Your art is no exception. You have to finish one pass so the thing is out of you, then go back to improve it. You can't keep second-guessing yourself. Create first. Improve second. But *finish what you started.*

I once wrote a post on my old blog that contained a four-step formula for success. It was the shortest post ever and basically just said *1) Start. 2) Finish. 3) Adjust. 4) Repeat.* You feel like a condescending dick bag writing something like that, but it's astonishing how many people feel stuck because they have great ideas but never work on those ideas. Or, to this section's point, start all sorts of stuff but never finish a thing.

The simplest things are usually most effective. The last little section on consistency was about starting things (and then continuing them), and this one is on finishing.

Do both. Then do it better the next time around.

Cut What Doesn't Belong

If you really want to iterate the core of your creative process, this is where we feel you can do the most good — or damage, depending on how you look at it.

You can barf out a rough draft of anything then send it on to someone (like a line editor) who will clean up the details — essentially dotting i's and crossing t's. But adding lipstick to a pig won't make it pretty. If you haven't self-edited enough before handing it over, you're making superficial changes to a mess. It's like Miss Manners coming into a hoarder's home and putting doilies under the thousand decaying cups of Mountain Dew balanced atop piles of garbage. It's using a toothbrush to excavate an artifact that requires a jackhammer.

You're the artist. Claude Debussy said, "Music is the space between the notes." We couldn't agree more. Great art is often more about what isn't included than what is. You might write an epic screenplay of five hundred pages, then trash 380 of those pages to end up with 120 remarkable ones. Hemingway was famous for saying he wasn't a great writer; he just knew his ratio of crap to good stuff and had figured out what needed to be thrown away. Our favorite example is probably Quentin Tarantino. Quentin is known for his fantastic dialogue. He does this by letting his characters talk … and talk … and talk through their scenes. He waits for the gems to surface, then discards the rest.

Our early books are too verbose. That happens when you're new because each word is precious. As you write more, you find yourself more able to cut. Some of this evolution happened for me in the dark; Sean would take a rough I'd given him and cut 20 percent, and I'd get it back and have no idea whatsoever what he'd removed because I didn't care enough to compare versions. *Robot Proletariat: Season One* is maybe the best example. He casually told me, "I cut a quarter of it." All I knew when I read it again was that it was really good.

This pattern went on for a while. Some projects turned out fairly clean (hint: they were always the projects I wrote the fastest) and didn't get a ton of cuts, but others were slashed without mercy. "I cut fifteen thousand words," Sean would tell me of a finished novella totaling forty-five thousand words. I'd read it and think it was great. What of my imagined first-draft genius had hit the cutting room floor? I didn't have a clue.

As time went on, I started seeing full sections in the projects I gave a second pass that could just go. I learned to smell them. A sentence into a paragraph, I'd know it should go. I'd keep reading just to be sure, but I was always right. A loose end section starts to clang on the ear, and you know it like instinct.

We're of course still nowhere near perfect. People still sometimes say we're too wordy, and we are. Some of that is voice, and will stay. But some will be trimmed. Some will be optimized because optimization is always possible.

See what you can cut from your work. Hire an editor to help you and enlist beta readers. Look for places where you repeat yourself (we're guilty of that often, for sure in this book, but hey, we keep slowly working on it). As you read through your draft, look for spots where your attention wanders, then consider those spots good contenders for edits. Remove things that the reader will already have figured out or doesn't need to know. Don't expect to get it right the first time. Just get *better* each time.

It may be hard to find things to excise, but if you do it right and get a little better with every book, your quality will improve, almost guaranteed.

CHAPTER TWENTY-ONE:
Ways to Iterate and Optimize after Your Creative Work Is Complete

Okay! The hard part is done. You've meticulously planned your story, which hopefully will allow you to — slowly, bit by bit — get better and quicker at writing your first draft (or the equivalent steps for non-writers). You thought about what you want from this particular work ahead of time, so now that it's complete, you have it in the right mental file folder (i.e., as a quiet passion project, as something with commercial potential, or as somewhere in between).

You're also being mindful of incrementally improving your process as you go. If you'd like to physically write faster, you're not trying to leap from a hundred words per session to ten thousand. You're trying for 105. Or 110. Or 150 and on up. And because we've suggested you be consistent, you're no doubt discovering, rediscovering, or confirming the simple and should-be-obvious magic that happens when small actions are faithfully repeated.

You're editing better. You're writing through blocks and ignoring the internal critic more than you used to. This is making you slightly more prolific every month (and year; remember, this is a long-term game) — and readers, noticing the improved quality and reliable consistency, are loving you more. Maybe you even pre-optimized. And if so, you no doubt found the story within your wireframe of an idea and are now ready to go try and light it on fire. And if it doesn't catch as much of a blaze as you'd like this time around? No worries. You'll do better with your next book.

This chapter is about what happens next — after you've taken off your artist's hat and put on the businessperson's.

First step. Let's talk framing.

We don't mean to be blunt, but let's rip one particular Band-Aid off right away: now that creation is complete and you're wearing your business hat, the soulful piece of art you painstakingly finished (possibly with much blood, sweat, tears, and beret-wearing angst) is now a *product*.

We know that's a hard switch to flip, particularly if this is your first go-round. When I finished my first book, I didn't want to give it away for free to gain readers or face the inevitable criticism. I had no funnel for the book, but that didn't matter because putting it in a funnel felt cold anyway. This was my baby. I didn't want to let her go.

Fortunately, this gets easier the more you stick with your creative business — one more reason to keep producing. The more you have, the less precious any single piece is. The less you mind thinking of it as a product because you recognize that products sell (or are sold in terms of attention, even for free), and that if you want to *keep* being a working artist, you need those sales.

This is the part where you try, perhaps with some difficulty, to see your work objectively.

What will make it attractive to people who aren't you? How can you get it enough exposure to thrive? How can you improve your business with each new release, broadening your reach and magnifying your wins?

Let's find out together.

Ship

So … you published your work. You did all the stuff we've covered in detail in *Write. Publish. Repeat.* (which you read before this book, right?), like sending your book to an editor, writing a compelling product description, commissioning a professional cover, and so on. Now that all of that is done, you *did* put your book out into the world, didn't you?

When we reach the post-creation product stage, this is equivalent to the twin commandments of *write the book* and *finish what you started* from the previous chapter. We shouldn't have to mention this one, but it's amazing how many artists get stuck right here, in analysis paralysis, endlessly tweaking what they have until it's perfect. But nothing is ever perfect. You have to ship it, as clean as is reasonable for a human being, because *perfection* is the enemy of *done*.

This subsection is a bit like when you call tech support for your washing machine, and they begin by asking you, "Is it plugged in?" So when we're talking about optimizing your post-creation process, that art *HAS* been shipped, right?

Just making sure.

Do Some of the Stuff From Part II of This Book

Part II was surely overwhelming, but the point here is to ask how what we did to iterate and optimize our admittedly complex business can be applied to ways you can iterate and optimize your likely smaller one. If you're like most readers, it's probably just you as a solo author, possibly working with a partner, maybe employing a virtual assistant, perhaps with a few (or a lot of) books under your belt. You might be brand new, or you might be a multiple *NYT* best seller. Either way, there's a level of what we've done that you can and should consider doing, too. You don't need to start nine podcasts, build a web app, or launch eight publishing imprints. So scan the index, and ask yourself: *What applies to me?*

Here are some suggestions, but be sure to scan Part II quickly for more:

- Decide whether you want to stay exclusive to Amazon or go wide, considering our arguments for our choices.
- If you don't have a professional cover and instead are using a cover that's "good enough," go hire a pro. Don't skimp. Your cover is your biggest conversion element by far — so much that for book 1, the rest comes close to barely mattering (within reason, of course).
- Write your book's description in a way that engages interest rather than merely summarizing the book. Ask: **What's in it for the reader? Why should they care enough to want what you're offering?** It's shocking how many writers believe that explaining why something is precious (to them) should make anyone else care enough to open their wallets.
- Tweak your metadata and keywords/key phrases for maximum effect.
- If the book is in a series, consider ways to optimize your funnel. Change the back matter for the previous book to, "Get the next book to see what happens next."
- Consider the pros and cons we gave about the changed role of free books, then decide what might work best for you with your catalog.

The rest is optional, and most of what remains in Part II is probably a 20-percent activity or less for most artists. You can advertise in a few limited ways, but please don't spend a bunch of money on Facebook ads for your first book or your highly uncommercial series. If you feel tempted to do that, just send the money to us. You'll get exactly the same results as you would from the ads, but this way at least someone will be happy.

Oh, and if you did any pre-optimization on your book, now's the time to look at your pre-optimization thoughts and compare them to the finished work to see how well you did in matching them up. You'll probably notice some changes (maybe your alien invasion book became sort of a space opera, thus opening a potential category), so be sure to adjust accordingly when you publish. Don't use your *pre* stuff verbatim. Make sure it most accurately fits what you ended up with versus what readers want most.

Understand the Difference Between Marketing and Advertising

About that advertising ...

Don't overspend here, but consider spending something — maybe to promote a first-in-series free book. With advertising more than anything else, *start small*. It is ridiculously easy to look at ads as an easy button, and easier than you'd think to flush a few hundred to a few thousand dollars right down the toilet. Consider $5 on some sort of free book ad. If it works, scale upward. If it doesn't, try a different approach.

Whenever you place ads, be sure to continually put yourself in the shoes of someone seeing those ads. And ask yourself: *If I were seeing this ad, would I care about what it's pitching me?*

Really? *REALLY?*

If you say yes and you're not an established name yet, you're either the exception to the rule or kidding yourself. Because it's rare that an ad, from an unknown author, merits serious interest from someone who's never heard of you.

The truth is likely that the average ad viewer won't give a shit about you. That means your ads need an incredibly low barrier to action so that taking action on what you want the prospect to do is practically brainless. You can advertise a free book as a list builder, for instance (receiving a free book in exchange for an email address is pretty low-risk for a consumer), and plan to make your money on the *next* book you send to the list. It might work because the recipient doesn't need to spend money, whereas advertising "Buy my bundle for $7.99" is a whole lot harder. But even with a free product ad like that, you still need to convince people that you're worthy of their time and attention. It takes time to read a book even if it's free, after all.

If you advertise at the start, we suggest simple things, like promotion through sites that advertise free books, where the ad itself costs little or nothing. If you're more advanced, we don't need to tell you your business. You can reread our "Advertising" chapter in Part II and follow some of what we've learned works for us.

Marketing, on the other hand, is different from advertising. Marketing is what you do *before* you consider advertising. Marketing is preparing your product for the ideal customers. Advertising is spreading the word.

Marketing is much quieter. We'd argue it's also more important because it has a longer tail and shelf life. When you pay attention to your marketing, you're asking questions about your audience: *Who are they? What do they truly want? What price will they pay for which sorts of products? What convinces them to buy or not buy — is it words on a page, word of mouth, or visuals like book covers? When they don't buy, what is it that's turned them off?* Then you're adjusting your product to put its best face forward, in light of what you've learned. Your goal is to take what you have and present it in the way that most closely mirrors that audience's triggers, wants, and turnoffs in a way that's still honest and in no way deceptive.

You need to make sure your marketing is in shape before you consider paying for ads. But to some degree, marketing will do its job without advertising. On a bookseller, algorithms will make your book visible if you give it an initial shove. How well you've done at positioning the title with proper marketing (including positioning within a product funnel or series, or in relation to similar books) will, to a large degree, determine how many sales you get sans ads.

If you can only focus on iterating and optimizing one key thing about your art during the post-creation, ship-it-to-the-world phase, we'd suggest putting intense focus on learning more about marketing and discovering ways to improve it.

Talk to Your Fans

We're being intentionally vague with this subsection's heading: "Talk to your fans" rather than "Get on Facebook," for instance.

The reason is that if we're talking about things you can improve right now to get better results, Facebook is probably not the best answer for all but a handful of artists. That might be one component, sure. But focus on ends, not means. Focus on results, not vehicles to reach them. Facebook, other social media, mailing lists, websites, blog tours, and other means of getting out there to mingle and chat with your audience are all just ways of talking to your fans. So focus on talking, not any single method.

Chances are, you already talk to your fans, even if you've never published a thing. We know this is a lame example, but the reason we say this is that everyone's social circle starts somewhere — and yours might start with family and friends. Is it a cliché that only your mother and college roommate buy your first book? Sure. But it's what happened to me at first. Clichés are clichés for a reason.

If that's you, talk to those people, then try to get them spreading word to their friends.

If you're further along, you might already have a fan base. And if *that's* you, your task is easier. You'll want to grow that group by encouraging sharing, of course. But you can also just talk to them better. Strengthen your bonds. One of the most interesting things we've found — and either frightening or encouraging, depending on how you look at it — is that attention and exposure are fickle. You might get a BookBub ad and reach tens of thousands of new readers, and your sales rank will spike to the top. But then it all goes away. In time, in most cases, booksellers mostly forget you. So do readers. This is true of just about any marketing, advertising, or simple exposure strategy you can conceive.

Because of this, we keep circling one realization that's either fantastic or terrifying: **the only surefire way to consistently sustain and magnify your sales is to be your fans' favorite artist.**

Selling books is great, but at S&S we're after hearts and minds. We want the fan who's so into our stuff, she buys hardbacks. We want fans who are so unreasonably into us that they'll listen to *SPP* even though they're not writers and only read fiction. Those fans are few and far between, and you won't get many, proportionally speaking, but they're like the haters: The more you have, the bigger your (less fervent) audience is. It's a direct correlation. If you want more casual readers, focus on getting more SuperFans. It's like buying insurance for the long haul.

Whatever you do to engage your fans now, always look for ways to make it better. Say thank you when people praise you. If you have a mailing list, occasionally offer signed copies in a raffle with no strings attached, just because you want to be nice. If you're on social media, be there a bit more (as long as you enjoy it and it doesn't compromise your creative time), and be nicer. Be cool. Be the kind of person people like.

Now, you'll notice we said, "Be the kind of *person* people like," not "Create the kind of *art* that people like." You should do both, but the former is more relevant here. Do you know how we're able to get nonfiction-only people to read our novels? Do you know how we get people who've known us since we were marketing bloggers to attend our in-person events today — like Amy, who followed me from my old blog to the *Self-Publishing Podcast*, then became a reader, then started following S&S and came to our first mastermind, and actually works with us today? Do you know how we get western readers to try our literary mind-bender, tell their friends about us, and defend us when someone starts talking shit?

It's not because they like any one of our books or podcasts or products, though they inevitably do. It's because they like *US*.

Whatever your fan communication is now, improve it.

Be your fans' favorite artist because creating their favorite art might not be enough.

Know When to Take Feedback (and When to Ignore It)

Read your reviews. Listen to what people say about you. Within limits.

Reading bad reviews sucks. I avoid it most of the time. I can afford to do this because I know I'll see some of them anyway when I check in on our books whether I want to or not and because Sean can't help sharing negativity with me, usually in our company Slack with a one-word comment like, "Fucker." So I get the flavor. Whether I want to or not, I know what people don't like about us.

Conversely — and this one is easier — I know what people like about us.

We don't recommend indulging in an overabundance of either side of this coin. If you get a bunch of terrible reviews in a row and have already absorbed the message (it might be a wave of haters or, if you admit it, you might have just written a crappy book that people don't like), then there's no point in flogging yourself. This is why I eventually learned to ignore our run of hate for *WPR* at the beginning. I saw what was happening: Some people really disliked our admittedly rambling style, and others had been waiting in the lurch for the book to come out so they could crap on its pages. I got the message and stopped watching.

That's true on the plus side, too. You'll get unadorned love for your art sometimes, and it's easy to sink in and indulge in good reviews forever. Doing too much of this wastes work time and inflates your ego. Feeling infallible isn't good for an artist. You can't think you're perfect because you're not. We all need to improve, and too much positivity can warp you.

But listen enough to know what people like and what they don't.

Then use that feedback when you go back to the lab. Don't simply bend to audience will, doing more of what got you praise and less of what drew criticism. Doing so makes you a weak-willed, bland artist. Art is risky by definition, and if you don't attract some negativity, it almost for-sure means your work is vanilla or irrelevant, and possibly both.

But as we talked about in Part II's "Dealing with Criticism" chapter, you should send both the good and the bad through your internal filters. The criticism you agree with is stuff you may choose to adjust because you always want to grow and improve.

Fire Yourself From Jobs You Shouldn't Be Doing

Okay, so that's the art itself. What about the business behind it?

Well, because you've read almost to the end of this book, you're clearly an improvement-minded creative person. You believe in the idea of iterating and optimizing, even if you're about to put a fork through someone's eye if we say iterate or optimize one more damned time. And if you are that person, you're going to keep creating. Keep getting better. Keep using what we learned to inch your creative business forward one tiny increment at a time.

That means you'll make more stuff.

That means you'll get better at marketing and selling what you make.

And as you accumulate more of a product catalogue that's selling a bit better every month or year, you'll find yourself with some funnels. Maybe you'll even decide to do some in-person networking. Build a community. Possibly start a podcast or something else nutty. Then you'll start to get the loose ends we had and continue to have here at S&S, and you'll hire admin help. Maybe you'll get lucky and nab yourself an Amy.

If you don't already have a full-on creative business as an artistpreneur, you soon will. And that means your company will have all sorts of possible jobs.

At first, because you were this company's genesis, your tendency will be to handle all those jobs yourself.

So how can you iterate and optimize [dodges to avoid fork stab] this part of your business right now?

Well, you can *fire* yourself.

Not from the company, of course. But from most of the jobs you're doing now that you really shouldn't be doing. At S&S, Dave's main focus is writing stories, which means he's been fired from most of what's not his core work. Sean and I are only partway along that journey.

Ideally, Sean and I should be creating new content (books, podcasts, screenplays, more), building new worlds, strategizing, and handling the key components of our marketing that are too intimate and/or vital to outsource (for me, that's writing all of our broadcast emails and autoresponders).

We shouldn't be compiling books from Scrivener. So we fired our lazy asses from those jobs and hired Garrett to do it. And really, Garrett shouldn't be doing it either. He's more of a creative. As soon as we find a good replacement, we'll fire his ass from that position, too.

We shouldn't be uploading files and doing admin on the back of it, either, which is why we canned ourselves and brought in Maya for those jobs and dozens more.

We shouldn't be producing audio. We should be *creating* it but never cutting it, adding bumpers, crafting the branding, or anything else. So we fired ourselves and hired Audra.

We *definitely* shouldn't be trying to manage our many projects and wrangle staff to get things done. *Fired!* Amy took our jobs there.

So consider starting small, where you can, and inch your way out of them as time, money, and growth allow. Amy pre-sifts a lot of our company email, but you don't need to hire someone right away to do this. The first step is to think about the process first, and get it ready for handing off later. So let's say you include your personal email address in the backs of your books. Maybe swap it out for a different email address so that you can hand it off later, keeping book email out of your main inbox. You can handle that mail now, then plan to have someone take it over eventually when you fire yourself from that part of your business.

You get the idea. What jobs in your business should you already be fired from? See if you can find a replacement, even if it's someone virtual who can tackle one tiny corner of your task load. Then give yourself walking papers, focus on the jobs you're right for, and move your business forward.

Know Your Outcome (Yes, Again)

We'll close this part of the book by circling back to something we mentioned in the beginning, because we're fiction authors — we like callbacks and closing open story loops.

Know the outcome of everything you do.

Yes, you went through all of this before, but this is a little different. This time, we're talking about knowing the outcomes of individual actions and strategies, not the global *why and what* that gets you up in the morning to make your art and run your business. Here, we're not talking about goals like hitting a best seller list, quitting your job, or leaving a legacy. We're being more granular as we finish Part III, and getting at the intended end results of your bigger strategy.

Because really, all tactics and strategies can work, if you do them right. But you don't want to blindly follow any of them without knowing your why, because they'll take you to places you might not want to go.

For instance, we're fierce indies. That means that for now, we're uninterested in traditional book deals with major publishers. That flavors our approach to promotion and how we'll answer emails. There have been times when we've been contacted by representatives requesting something reasonable, and we've pushed back. We don't really have an agent, but we *kind of* have one, meaning a guy we'd contact the minute certain attractive deals were presented to us. But when some people have inquired and asked to be put in touch with him, we've asked if there's a genuine offer beyond the connection. Because there are a lot of tire kickers out there, snooping around without any intentions of a serious offer. You might be different and really *want* a traditional deal. If you handled things like we did, you'd be heading down *our* path — but that's not the path you actually want.

We've also actively turned down traditional book deals — something that would've sounded like sacrilege to the younger me, who yearned for one of those coveted spots. And something that might sound like sacrilege to you if you'd rather write and sell instead of doing all this indie stuff on your own.

We told you how we've been optimizing our audiobooks by giving Podium first pick of any titles they want — the *opposite* of the strong indie bias we described having for ebooks and print. But what if you have an excellent audiobook distribution platform already and would rather make audiobooks on your own via ACX then sell them and make 40 percent instead of our lower royalties with Podium? We've chosen high quality and Podium's superior distribution and promotion systems over profit per unit, but you might not want to do that. If that's you, don't follow our optimization strategy because it'll take you where you don't want to go.

Most things *can* work. The question is whether those strategies and tactics have a place in your toolbox, given your intended outcomes.

What do you want? It's your ship, so choose those methods that will steer it best.

The final part of this book, to follow, consists of interviews with folks we consider to be our SuperFriends: smart, creative entrepreneurs who've spent the past years iterating and optimizing as we have, but with different results (because everyone has unique situations and whys). You'll meet them in a minute.

Part IV, like the interviews section of *Write. Publish. Repeat.*, is kind of an appendix in disguise. That means this, here, is the unofficial end for the authoring trio of Platt, Truant, and Wright. But before we pass the baton to our SuperFriends in the section that follows, we'd like to end Part III with a soft close.

First of all, we'd like to thank you for reading this book. Not only have you done us the obvious good turn of purchasing our work and supporting *our* creative business, you've also raised a flag for the entire family of creative entrepreneurs out there by reading it. You've declared that you're one of us. That you're not a *starving artist;* you're a *Smarter Artist.* That's a good thing. The more of us there are, the better this community is for each of us. We're creating a DIY world where nobody stands between an artist and her intended audience. That requires a groundswell, and by joining us here, you've become a part of it. So thank you.

Second, we'd like to give you a gift. Back in 2013, we wrote our bestseller *Write. Publish. Repeat.,* but by 2015 we'd learned a ton more on-the-ground, in the trenches details about how *WPR*-appropriate publishing works best. So rather than releasing another book to teach those new things, we made a comprehensive 8-hour video course called *"Write. Publish. Repeat.* Conversations." We normally sell it for $49, but we'd love to just *give* it to you for being awesome. **You can get your free copy of *WPR* Conversations here: SterlingAndStone.net/repeaters.** (You'll also be joining our list, which you will want to be on anyway. We're planning two more nonfiction books right now: a collaboration guide about how *one* writer plus *one* writer can equal *three* writers' worth of creativity and productiveness, plus a creative business parable (think *Who Moved My Cheese* with more attitude and less Dilbert) that every single creative person should read. Our list learns about new books first and gets them cheapest.)

Third, we'd like to wish you luck. A creative person's path isn't easy. It's never a small amount of work. But once things start rolling, if they aren't rolling for you already, you'll see how worth it all of this is. That's why we wrote this book: because every indie's path is always changing. You must be able to adapt as you go. To — one more time, with feeling — *iterate and optimize* all that you're doing.

Finally, as a parting shot before you move into Part IV, we'd like to ask for your help in spreading the word. You can tell people about this book or *Write. Publish. Repeat.,* of course, and doing so would be dandy. But we're not even asking for you to help our book sales. We mean *spreading the word about the movement.* About the message of freedom that comes with being one of us out here on the edge, refusing to settle, helping the community that pushes the ball forward for all of us who consider ourselves creative entrepreneurs. Forget the stuff we have that costs money. Tell people about our free stuff. It's great, it doesn't cost a dime, and we do it week after week, filling it with our best and most up-to-date advice.

The link to share with your creative entrepreneur friends (or those who wish they could be creative entrepreneurs) is **SterlingAndStone.net/fm**. That's our podcast network, chock full of tip-of-the-spear Smarter Artistry with hours of new free stuff weekly.

Thank you so much for reading. Now go out there, and conquer the world.

PART IV:
ITERATION AND OPTIMIZATION SUCCESS STORIES

Meet the SuperFriends

This part is where the rubber meets the road.

What you've just read is basically one huge case study (that of Sterling & Stone), followed by a section on how you can adapt our case study to suit your needs. We tried to distill the best of what we've learned while slowly honing and evolving our business so that the larger creative community can apply it and benefit — because when one of us wins, all of us win. Just look at Hugh Howey *(Wool)* and Andy Weir *(The Martian)*. They did and continue to do great things that are obviously of tremendous benefit to them … but because of those big personal successes, the world now takes us indies seriously. Everyone wins.

In the final part of this book, we wanted to provide you with additional case studies: nuts-and-bolts Q&As with the smartest indies we know, all about how they've iterated and optimized *their* businesses. You now know how we did it. But these folks did it differently because — surprise, surprise — they're not us. They have unique goals and outcomes, in varying situations. As a result, things that were vital to our trajectory at S&S don't mean much to them — while things we've ignored have been essential to their growth.

As you read through the following seven interviews, you'll learn new angles on what you've read in this book. It'll bring the idea of incremental evolution to brand new life.

So let's rock 'n' roll with the first of our *Self-Publishing Podcast* SuperFriends.

J.A. Huss

Johnny B. Truant: Hey, everyone. Today, we're talking to Julie Huss who writes under the name J.A. Huss. Julie is a *New York Times/USA Today* best-selling romance author, and an interesting person — one of those people who isn't just an author. Julie is a true *authorpreneur*, and we've really gotten to know and love her over these past few months. So she was a perfect fit for this because she's a constant tweaker and optimizer. So welcome, Julie; thanks for joining us.

J.A. Huss: Thanks for having me; I'm so glad to talk to you guys again.

JBT: You used to write science homeschooling books. What was the change from that to becoming a best-selling romance author?

JAH: Well, I started doing that in, like, 2007 maybe. I had just finished my master's degree in forensic toxicology, and I had hurt my knee and couldn't walk. I was stuck in bed for, like, a month and a half. And I was just kind of down, and wondering what I'm going to do with this degree because I was actually smelling hog farms for a living at that point. That was my job — to go out and, like, check on all the hog farms in Colorado and make sure they're abiding by this odor standard that we had.

David Wright: I have somebody that comes by my house and does that to me.

JBT: See now, I thought *I* had a good story. My job was to count fruit flies for a while, but I think you win.

JAH: Oh see, fruit flies, that's actually a lot more interesting than smelling hog farms.

Sean Platt: Smelling hog farms is *so unsexy*, she started writing sexy books: it's the opposite.

JAH: It didn't really pay very well because it was only part time, but I worked from home unless I was on the road, so I had a lot of free time. I started making a website about homeschooling. I decided that I had a master's degree, and could be an expert in something. I'd been homeschooling my children a really long time by then. I decided to write these little homeschool module workbooks for other homeschool parents in science, because that's kind of like what I was good at. I did that for two years, publishing one new little workbook every Monday, like, literally every week. Eventually, I started running out of topics.

SP: What was the length of those?

JAH: Some were really long; some are textbooks; like I wrote an entire anatomy and physiology textbook. And I wrote an entire physics textbook, but most of them were anywhere between twenty-four and eighty pages. And they had a lot of illustrations and stuff because I'm really good at the artwork. So I was teaching myself Photoshop, and I would make cool diagrams and stuff. And then I also learned how to do online courses, like using software to build Flash courses, so each one had a course to go with it so the kids could take them online and, like, play games and stuff. I did that for so long, I actually ran out of ideas of what to write about. Like I did bears and pine trees and seas and gardens and even a whole semester of biology.

I was in a truck driving around Colorado to these hog farms, and they were so far away. There were only, like, eight of them, but some had, like, forty barns. So I'd have to drive, like, hours and hours away, and sometimes I'd stay overnight so I could check all these farms. The actual inspections were taking me, like, ten minutes. So if there was only one farm out in Holly,

Colorado, I would drive four and a half hours to get there, do my ten-minute inspection, and drive four and a half hours back. I was in the truck *all the time*. So I started thinking maybe I could write science fiction. People were taking off in self-publishing at that point, I think it was, like, 2011.

Amanda Hocking comes to mind because I had stumbled across her book — that paranormal romance. And that's how I came up with the *Junco* series. So it was just, like, an experiment. Of course, everybody who tries to write a book hopes that people will love it, and all those great things happen to them, but the truth is it doesn't work out that way, right? Science fiction is a hard sell; it's *way different* than romance. It sells different; everything about it is different. I got laid off from my job because there was this big turnover with the government, and they were like, "We want you to come into Denver every day and work." I live an hour from Denver. So, like, that's never going to happen; I'm never going to drive an hour to work and then an hour home to work in a government office.

SP: I cannot see that happening — *at all.*

JAH: I was, like, no I'm just going to not accept the position, and I'm going to try and do something on my own. I had three science fiction books out, and they did okay, but I'm not going to be able to make a living off of that. So I decided to write a romance, a new adult romance, because that was really big at the time. And I wrote that *Tragic* book, and I think I got lucky with that book. I mean it's a good book, but lots of people write good books and never get exposure. Somehow, I had put my name out there in all these different ways, like with blog tours and Twitter and Facebook, and I mean I just did *everything*.

SP: But that's not luck. If you're *doing everything*, you are making your own luck there. You wrote a good book, but then you also did everything possible to support it, right?

JAH: I did everything I could think of, so I didn't just sit around and wait for somebody to come find me. I don't — do people do that? I don't know if people do that.

JBT: Yeah, that's the default.

SP: Yeah, a lot of people do that. They think, "If my book is awesome, the world will find it."

JAH: Yeah, I don't think that works. I think you actually have to, like, put it out there in any way you can. So that's just kind of what happened, and then it was a long progression, like no two books ever release the same way; they never perform the same way. And I think anybody who has written a lot of books and had a lot of release days, they all know this. Sometimes, they surprise you, and they do a lot better than you think they will. It's just constantly tweaking, like that idea of iterate and optimize, it's really, really kind of what you have to do to make it.

SP: You started with science fiction but ended up with romance because, I mean, we all know that's an eager, rabid, ready-to-consume-anything audience. But is that where your *heart* is? If you could write anything, would you still write romance, or are you iterating your way into being able to write something else like mysteries, or thrillers — a return to sci-fi?

JAH: I guess I would, probably. I do like the romantic part of it. Like whenever I read a sci-fi book — because that's really all I read — I'm interested in the characters' relationships, and I really like if there is a romance in there; that catches my attention. So I don't think I would ever move out of romance completely, but I would like to do something like the book I just released, *Anarchy Found*. It's a superhero romance. And that was fun because I got to do all the sci-fi stuff and have the romance in there at the same time. So yeah, I would like to do more stuff like that.

DW: How has listening to your audience helped shape the books you're writing now?

JAH: Sometimes, I listen to them, and sometimes I don't. If I listened for every book, I'd write the same thing over and over.

SP: It's a bit like that Steve Jobs quote: "People don't know what they want until you tell them."

JAH: Some of it. I think a lot of them do know what they want. And I sort of maybe deliver that in a way they don't expect. And so I think they kind of like that about my books.

SP: But for the most part, you're not afraid of disappointing a segment of your audience?

JAH: No, I'm not because I write fast enough. If they don't like this book, maybe they'll like the next one.

SP: So do you feel that even if you let down a segment of your audience, you might gather new readers, anyway?

JAH: Yes. That's absolutely right. I always find new readers, and not everybody likes every book. Even my favorite authors, I don't like all their books. I don't think it's reasonable to expect everybody to like every book.

SP: And what a way to stunt your growth if that's all you try to do.

JAH: Right. I agree. You have to take risks. I think risks are the most important thing in writing because it's easy to go out and put out a serial that's nothing but smut and release one book every two weeks. It's easy to climb the charts by doing that. And I don't begrudge anybody who wants to do that. I actually did that with social media, and that was my goal. But that's not something I want to do for, like, a year or two. That's just … *no.*

JBT: What have been the challenges to moving forward as fast as you want? The roadblocks that have stopped you from taking various steps, and how have you approached them?

JAH: Roadblocks. I don't know if I believe in roadblocks.

JBT: What about restrictions, boundaries you need to work within in terms of budget —

SP: Hurdles.

JBT: Or staffing, or your available time?

SP: Roadblocks don't stop you, but hurdles are something to jump over, right?

JAH: Time, yeah, time is always a concern, but I don't think I compromise the writing as far as the time goes. My office is always messy; that's why I'm not on-screen right now. You don't want to see my office.

DW: We *are* soul mates.

JAH: Yeah, stuff like that is, like, the stuff I just don't do — because I don't have the time. Or I let the mail stack up for a month, and then I have to take a hundred packages to the post office. Stuff like that, but I don't really know. I do have constraints on all my plots. I always use *Meet Me in the Dark* as an example because it's such a strange book. It found its audience, like, so well. I mean it didn't make any lists, but the people who found that book just sort of loved it. And it was a really out there, dark, dark, dark book. So I really wasn't expecting that. I think that's, like, when the little light bulb went off in my head: "If people liked *that* book, there's got to be an audience for *every* book. So maybe I can find a new audience each time I write."

SP: Do you feel like you get bolder by the book — willing to take chances that you wouldn't have taken before?

JAH: I guess it depends on how the last book sold. You know, you get a little gun shy if you don't have a great seller, and you think, "Wow, maybe I should go back a step. Try and find those fans who want something simpler or something less dark or something like that."

SP: Yeah, that makes sense.

JAH: You know, you change that all the time, and I think everybody is that way. If they don't have a book that does as well as they expected, then they kind of — they should reevaluate what they are doing unless they want the next one to perform the same way.

JBT: You have one assistant. Have you ever run into a capacity issue where you're thinking, *Maybe I should hire a second assistant, or I wish I had a bigger budget or a specialist to handle this or that?*

JAH: Well, I do have — like Jana Aston; everybody probably knows her by now. She had that mega best seller in October. She's been my assistant for two years, and does most of my stuff, but I do have other people who help me. I have an assistant named Nicole. She's not on a monthly payroll, but I pay her by the job. I have a book blog called *New Adult Addiction*, and we are doing thirty-one days of giveaways. She just did *all* the blogging stuff for me. Then I have a co-blogger named Kristi, and she does a bunch of stuff on the blog. So it's not like Jana does everything, but she does most of the really complicated stuff like the spreadsheets and tracking.

JBT: What about formatting and compiling, because your formatting is *spectacular*.

SP: Yeah, your books are *gorgeous*.

JAH: I used to hire a formatter, but stopped a couple of books ago. I'm doing it all myself.

SP: The chapter heads and title pages, you do all of that?

JAH: It depends which book you're talking about, but yeah.

JBT: *Anarchy Found* — you did the headings for that?

JAH: Yeah, I did that whole thing myself.

SP: Well, your work is better than most professional work I've seen. So bravo for being able to do it all, Julie Huss.

JBT: Do you feel like a control freak. I mean, like, a lot of entrepreneurs have trouble giving certain things up. Is it that you really just want it done it right, or do you enjoy it and that's part of the process for you?

SP: Do you truly enjoy it, or do you not want to let it go because you don't think anyone will do it as well as you?

JAH: I think it's a little of both. I know I'm a control freak. Every time I send a book away for formatting, I say, "I should just do this myself because then if I want to make changes, I have the file, and it's so much easier. You don't have to wait for somebody to do it for you." But I've always made the chapter headings. I don't recall; they might have done it once or twice, but I don't think so. I think I've always done it on my own because I have such an artistic background. I think with all the design stuff, I'm a 100-percent control freak because I know I can make a good design myself.

SP: Yeah, after reading *Three, Two, One*, I bought it for Johnny and said, "You need to read this." And then I bought it for Garrett and said, "You need to look at the way this is formatted." I love those chapter heads. It didn't matter that it was an ebook. It had such a professional feeling. Most authors don't go that extra mile. They know their reader will be reading on a black and white device. But your chapter heads were brightly colored, anyway. It's one of those things that made me like the book even more than I already did.

JAH: I was thinking about that while doing *Anarchy Found* because it has so many graphics inside. And I thought, *Why not?* Like, where's the rule that says it has to be boring, and it has to be black and white? *Why can't I put images in there?* I have full-on teaser images in the beginning. I hired an artist to do all these sexy drawings, and I'm like, "Yeah, I'm going to use every one of them because they are awesome." I don't think there are rules here.

SP: Yeah, the next few years are going to be really exciting because I think we are going to figure out what ebooks actually are. And we're not there yet. Right now, they're digital versions of print books, but there's so much more potential in the format. We've barely scratched the surface.

JAH: Yeah, and I think images are an easy way to do it. I read on the iPad, and it looks really awesome. It doesn't even take that long. I just did it last night for *Happily Ever After*. It took me a while to come up with what I wanted, but I came up with a really cute chapter heading for each of the points of view. I really like doing it, and then it kind of makes you smile when you open the book. Everything is pretty and colored …

SP: I have a 6+, so it has a nice-sized screen, and that's where I do most of my reading now. Your books POP! They're better than almost everything I open, including traditional stuff. That's an awesome thing to iterate towards, being able to make your books better than other people's. It makes them feel more worthy of the download.

One of the things I really admire about you is that you never seem to count pennies, and you certainly aren't tripping over dollars to pick them up. You'll spend money on Facebook, you'll spend money on ads, you'll spend money on design work to get a custom drawing for your cover because you really do care about the art and the presentation and pleasing readers and all of that. How do you feel about managing expenses, and how do you not let that get out of control?

JAH: If I have money in the bank, I figure it's there to spend. It's all a business expense. I won't go and buy myself something really expensive because how is that going to get me ahead? But when I buy a Facebook ad or a custom drawing or audiobook production, that's all feeding my business. Even if I'm not making that money back in the next month, it adds up over time, and I'll eventually get something back. I don't spend like that in my personal life, but whatever I want for the business I get. There is never a hesitation, like if I —

SP: That is *exactly* how I feel.

JAH: If I want a $2,000 drawing for a cover, that's it; I want it. You know what, that guy over in Spain who I paid to do that, he went skiing in the Alps off of what I paid him. I'm spreading the money around. He's got a job, I got a job, and it all works out. That's kind of how I look at it.

JBT: When I hear the idea of making images and spending a lot of attention on the formatting, I think that sounds awesome. I agree with it, and would like to do it, but we're limited by the fact that we can't scale if we do because, holy crap, there's so much other stuff we need to be doing. So where are you looking to scale, and where do you feel you may or may not be restricted? Are you writing as many books as you want, or are there any other places you'd like to scale your business?

JAH: By scale, do you mean growing bigger?

JBT: Whatever you would want to do in your business, yes. I know you eventually want to make films, and that's a different tool set.

JAH: I don't know what I want to do, to be honest. If I come up with an idea and it sounds fun and I'm excited about it, I think I just do it. But I do have people looking at *Three, Two, One* for production or licensing the rights or whatever. But we all know how that goes: Even if they buy the rights, your movie's probably not going to get made. I like to do things that keep me interested, and I don't think too far ahead about what those things might be. Every time I have an idea, I tell Jana, and she'll say, "Yeah okay."

Because she knows I'm going to change my mind, like, fifteen times before I settle on something. I guess I don't think too far ahead as far as that goes. I always have my books planned out a year in advance. I know what I'm going to write next year, but I might change it if I get a better idea, like this *Eighteen* book I just released. That was an idea I got over the summer, and I'm like, "I'm going to fit that in somewhere, and I'm going to use it to promo *Anarchy Found*." And that's exactly what I did. I don't know that it worked the way I thought it would, but it sure as hell sold a lot of copies. I can't complain about how it turned out, so I'm glad I took the risk and forced myself to write it.

SP: I just finished *Eighteen*. I liked it, great job.

JBT: I read it, too.

SP: For my last question, I'd like to ask about your list building because I know you do most of your audience outreach and bonding and marketing on Facebook. We always preach the importance of building a list and how it's important to not digital sharecrop on another person's platform. If Facebook changes the rules, that could ding you. I know you have Facebook reps, and that kind of changes the game a bit because you're able to stay ahead of things. But does that concern you at all long term; is building a list something you want to iterate towards, or are you content with the way that you're doing it now?

JAH: No, that is one of my goals, and I've been working on that for the past few months. I don't have a huge list. I don't personally know what everybody's lists look like, but mine — I haven't looked at it recently, but last time I did, it was somewhere in the eight to nine thousand range. I've been doing bits of it here and there, but I'm pretty careful with how I ask for people to get on my list because I'm trying to make sure that the people who aren't interested in my books aren't on my list. I try to be careful. I've probably got a lot of people on there now from the last few giveaways who might not be fans, but I try not to do that.

JBT: All right, I guess that's just about all of our questions. Thanks for joining us, Julie.

JAH: Thanks you guys!

Joanna Penn

Johnny B. Truant: Today our guest is Joanna Penn. We've interviewed Joanna a bunch of times; she is a *Self-Publishing Podcast* semi-regular.

Sean Platt: I think three times now.

JBT: Yeah, we're regular buds with Joanna, but today we are going to talk specifically about how she has iterated and optimized her business forward. Joanna has two main branches or her business, much like Sterling & Stone: fiction and nonfiction. Her nonfiction is at thecreativepenn.com, and her fiction is at jfpenn.com. So welcome, Joanna, to *Iterate and Optimize*.

JP: Thanks for having me again; it's always lovely to talk to you boys.

JBT: So you've been at this a long time in what we call indie publishing years, which are kind of like dog years: They stretch out. What are the biggest changes you've seen during your time in the industry?

JP: Well, one is probably the whole perception of indie. I started in 2008 before Kindle, before print on demand really happened. I was in Australia,; I remember really just being treated like a pariah, and, in fact, in Britain I was still treated pretty badly in 2008-2009, and then even in 2011. I think what's so funny with my own trajectory, and we've seen it with the way the indies have behaved, is that at first people really wanted to get traditional publishing deals off the back of their indie success.

There was this original movement where it was, like, if you do really well as an indie, you'll get a traditional publishing deal. But there's been this real shift where there are indies like us who, let's face it, have never really wanted a traditional deal. But we've seen people now actively coming into the indie world not wanting a deal, and now traditionally published authors wanting to go indie.

And equally, I agree with Joe Konrath's idea of the shadow industry, which is they are not reporting on sales with no ISBNs. And I have been to a lot of publishing conferences, and I feel like we exist in this parallel world now, where we are just doing our thing, and I don't even want to listen to stuff they are doing anymore. There is a maturity in behavior and attitude and empowerment.

That shift has probably permeated everything in terms of the culture. And what you guys are aimed to do, which is to kind of become an indie story studio — and I have my global media empire — these are kind of mature business goals, not hobbyist self-publishing. So I think that's probably the biggest overall shift, and that's reflected in the opportunities we now have in terms of worldwide reach, with multiple platforms and formats. It's a very exciting time.

SP: It's impossible to disagree with any of that. Self-publishing seemed like an exciting opportunity maybe a few a years ago, but now I think it's established as a serious business. We all know there's opportunity; now it's about how to articulate the best possible opportunity for yourself and build a business based on what you have to offer any given audience.

As Johnny was saying, you have both a fiction and the nonfiction side to what you do. You seem to be a born teacher and a terrific leader in the community; people really respect what you have to say. But you also have the fiction bug, and love telling stories. You want to travel the world and use those experiences to tell your stories. So how do you decide what's next?

JP: Well, I think like you guys said, the nonfiction can sometimes be a bit of a palate cleanser. And I think nonfiction can be easier to write in a way, especially when it's something you've been doing for a while ...

JBT: It uses a different part of your brain, and when you spend as much time in fiction, it's like, "Oh I get to use this other part of me, for me."

JP: Yeah, and also obviously knowing you guys in previous iterations as business people, I think we all feel that there are a lot of lessons we've learned in other ways that we can bring to the author community. Like last year, 2015, I did *How to Make a Living with Your Writing*, which was a kind of slightly smaller version for business authors similar to your *Iterate and Optimize*.

And these are things we've all brought from outside the self-publishing industry. I think that's where I feel most passionate about sharing — the things I can bring from my thirteen years as a business consultant in my previous life. I have a background in psychology, so I'm looking at writing — and my next nonfiction book on the author mind-set — with all the psychology that goes into it.

Nonfiction for me is also about writing what I need to learn more about — that's probably where I am now; I have to learn more about the mind-set. The business: I'm sorted. I'm growing, but happy. Yet with the mind-set, I struggle a lot, as we all do. So I write nonfiction about what I need to learn; teach what you want you want to learn, etc.

Fiction for me is more of a fun kind of crazy escapism. This morning I've been in Goa, on the beaches of western India, exploring the Portuguese Inquisition back in the sixteenth century, so that's been fun. But it's more exciting, and I often think of fiction as more selfish in a way, because I'm spending time doing what I love, whereas with nonfiction books and courses and speaking, I'm helping other people.

Although one of the biggest things I've noticed is how fast people will overtake you if they only focus on one damned thing.

SP: Oh, that's so true; we've been lapped many, many times, and we keep telling ourselves it's okay because we're building a very specific thing. And that takes layers and time and years, and we can't worry about what anybody else is doing because they're not building the same thing that we are.

JP: Yeah, exactly, and I think that's the thing with this *Iterate and Optimize* idea, is look at the people who are living the life you want to lead. Looking at what you guys want for your story studio — you're all moving to the same place, and you've got staff, and you are going to have buildings, and I'm just like — that's sounds like hell to me; I don't want people or buildings — my number one word is *freedom*. I want this laptop and a beach in Goa.

Once you decide on your goal, you have to iterate and optimize towards what you want, not what somebody else wants. Like *getting your systems sorted*. I have my bookkeeper, my accountant, and a VA. I have designers, editors — none of whom are in my any physical location anywhere near me and never will be. And that's cool; that's the way I work. So yeah, that's a big difference, I think, to what some people want.

JBT: I think it's interesting that freedom is also my primary value, but you just mentioned that we're very different in the way we interpret it.

JP: How do *you* interpret it then?

JBT: Freedom to do what I want when I want, whereas I think yours is more of a physical freedom, like you want to be able to pick up and go, literally, where you want, whereas mine is more of a definition of possibilities.

JP: I feel the same way in terms of this freedom of possibility, but it's also just how you like spending your time. Everyone who listens to your podcast knows how much time you guys spend talking to each other in between shows. I mean you guys are, like, together ...

David Wright: She doesn't need that.

SP: Yeah, we're definitely a hive mind; it can be a problem.

JP: It's lovely.

SP: You spent a long time with a business that was anchored in one place, and that business kind of shaped what you wanted for your future business, right?

JP: Yeah, I ran a scuba diving business briefly in New Zealand. That only lasted a couple of months, before I just went "Aaaah!"

SP: Long enough to let you know exactly what you *don't* want, right?

JP: Yeah, but I think it's important that people consider that when looking at their optimizing. Let's look at affiliate marketing, for example. Now, we all like affiliate marketing: making a commission on selling other people's stuff. This is normal Internet business, and most people do it in some way. I know Dave hates it — and the $97 product — but these are things people do.

Anyway, I had a situation this week where something didn't feel right, and I decided to say, "I don't want any part of this." It doesn't matter how many thousands of dollars; I'm not interested. And I'm sure you guys have been offered money by some companies that might not be good for authors.

DW: Yes.

JP: Yeah, for leads, and again lots and lots of money involved. But saying, "No, that's not what I want" is so important because if your goal is just the financial figure, you'll struggle. You have to know what lifestyle you want, then choose the things that make you feel good along the way.

DW: Well, on that subject, what do you think about the trend of successful authors making courses — and sometimes unsuccessful authors? Do you think this is good or bad for the industry?

JP: I've done courses for years and have taken Johnny's courses in the past. This same thing has been going on inside the marketing niche and in other industries for years. What's happened in 2015 is that online courses hit the author niche. I think this is a maturity in the space. Same as self-publishing: It can be very good; it can be very bad. And the quality will differ along the way, but my husband, for example, spends a lot of time taking coding courses and things on Coursera. People are taking my courses, and partly yes, some people are making loads and loads of cash.

If the course is of good value, which a lot of times it is, and those people who are not doing great courses, then I think you have to come down on the side of good quality will win out, which is what we have in the self-publishing book space. There is a bit of glut, but if you deliver a quality product that helps people, it will do well.

DW: Yeah, word of mouth spreads on the good people and the good stuff, I think.

JP: Yeah.

SP: You could release a crappy product one time, maybe, but you're not likely to have repeat customers, and you'll burn your name, which is the most valuable asset you have.

JP: I have learned this one thing: I'm British, you might have noticed; you guys are Americans.

DW: Wait, what? You are? We're talking to a British person? Nobody told me that.

JP: You guys, I feel, fit quite well with British people, but you're not American, hardcore American like some will be — you know what I mean by that, not in an offensive way …

DW: We don't have guns all around us, is that what you're saying, Joanna, are you anti-American?

SP: I'm packing right now, just so you know; I have a rifle on my lap.

DW: Just one? I've got five.

JP: I'm a little worried about coming to Texas; apparently, you can hold your gun in a supermarket or something.

SP: You can, but Austin isn't quite Texas.

DW: Yeah, Austin is liberal, hippie Texas.

JP: Well, you know how we say that there are lots of *bad* books, like often people use *Fifty Shades of Grey* as an example. But if six million people buy your bad book, how bad is it?

DW: I want to write a book that bad.

JP: Exactly, don't we all? So I think the definition of bad is different per person, with books and courses. I have learned this recently that some things I just say, "Oh my goodness, how can people want this?" But actually, lots of people do. I think we have to be more open minded about online courses as much as we are about books, and defend the openness of the creator movement.

JBT: Yeah, for sure. So shifting to your business particularly, Joanna, how have you handled the incremental growth, and hiring people to help you do more of what you're great at?

JP: I started my business in 2008, right? So a seven-year business should be mature enough to support a number of people. So my husband had the opportunity to leave his job and join the company. But let's say it's not necessarily the best thing for your relationship if you are both working in the same house on the same business.

DW: *Amen.* I'm never hiring my wife.

JP: He's doing his own thing, and I have hired lots of people. I have eleven people working with me. They all contract work, so a designer, editors, accounting, all the usual people. But in terms of growth, although the business is growing, the income is growing, the reach is growing, the expansion has been in the number of products.

That's number of books, obviously, but multiplied by formats, so audiobooks, print books and then multiplied by platform and multiplied by country and then multiplied by language. Even though I have around seventeen books, I think, I've got over a hundred products. Take the number of products, and multiply that by the number of customers, that's how you run a business; you guys know this.

You don't need to be any more than one person with a load of contractors to run a massive business, and of course we all know some authors who are making millions per year in the same model that I am, which is just multiply the number of books by the number of products by the number of customers, and you have a scalable business. That's why this is attractive, because every book you write adds to your backlist. So pretty much, my scale — I was just looking at what I've done in terms of my scaling — has been expanding the formats, so in 2015 doing a lot of audio books, writing more.

Just recently, I've got dictation sorted, so I'm super-pleased about that, which means my products will grow, and then I've got my publishing process really slick now, and we could all use help with marketing, but I pretty much know what I'm doing is just a case of products and customers; that's it.

SP: That makes a lot of sense, and I will say that working with your spouse is very difficult.

JP: Oh, you've done it.

SP: Cindy isn't a part of the day-to-day with Sterling & Stone for that reason. She does a lot to support me so I can do whatever I can with the business, but I don't want the potential conflict of having her in the day-to-day. My parents are good friends now, but they're divorced, and got divorced because they were in a business together, and always at each other; it's hard.

DW: It's also why Sean and I got divorced.

SP: How have your list-building efforts changed over time, along with your ad spends, for both Facebook and Amazon?

JP: I've always felt like content marketing is my strongest thing because I like to give rather than to say "Buy my book." I still focus on content marketing, so for me the podcast and the Author 2.0 imprint. I now have more free books on Amazon, so the permafree side absolutely to me is a hardcore part of my list building.

I'm loving Patrion for the direct relationship with people who really, really care, so that's fantastic. I have different lists, obviously for fiction and nonfiction.

With Facebook advertising, I'm using the lead-gen ads, which are the ones that are only on mobile, which are great, because they are easy to do — much easier than trying to get conversions to paid sales, which I have not had much luck with. I just don't have the patience to work it out. I know J. Thorn has been on the *Sell More Books* show, and it was his thirty-seventh advert that started making him money. I just can't be bothered.

SP: Yeah, and the decay rate on those ads is …

JP: Yes, they work for ten days or whatever, but lead-gen ads, I find, are great, so I am doing those with my fiction, targeting Stephen King around some stuff, maybe for a longer-term growth, because my nonfiction list has been growing for years, and I regularly clean it, and I try to keep that really responsive. But my fiction list is quite small and has been growing this year. Probably the biggest thing with fiction was changing my free giveaway from a short story to a novella. Nobody wants a short story, apparently.

SP: Yeah, that makes a lot of sense. I'm not surprised by that at all.

JP: But isn't that weird? I mean you can do a cover that looks the same and all that. I'm not in KDP Select because I've always gone wide — I believe you should be on multiple platforms if you're serious about this for the long term.

I have developed relationships; what I would say is that relationship marketing and networking is a really big deal. I've used my podcast for that as you guys do, invite people on who you can help, but you're also developing relationships with them in some way, and meeting people at events, so even though I am introverted, I force myself to go to events — with alcohol — so that I can actually talk to people. Otherwise, I'd just stay in my cave.

I think those are the main things. I've still really relied on content marketing, to be honest, but when you have a blog that's been going seven years with twelve hundred blog posts and hundreds of audios and videos, a lot of my traffic is organic.

DW: So what have been the biggest roadblocks to your growth?

JP: *I* am my biggest roadblock to growth. It's so funny, this dictation thing. I've been talking about this for, like, three years, and I've tried it twice. I just gave my husband a couple of the other microphones I bought over the years because I would say this microphone doesn't work properly.

SP: It's always the microphones' fault.

JP: Of course the microphone, and it's just, like, seriously? I think — and this — I now share my honest side. I've got, like, it's tennis elbow, which is really weird, but it's just so painful. And I cannot be a writer if writing is painful. My goal this year — and I'm really good at goal setting and doing goals — was *healthy author*. Johnny will like this since he's so super-healthy, so I'm into it and fasting.

JBT: Yes, I do that.

JP: I know you do, and I like that. I put myself on a ultra marathon, for July. It's walking — 100K — Dave, so you know if you want to come over, join me in July.

SP: I would do 100K walking; that sounds *awesome*.

DW: Have you got a NutriBullet?

JP: I don't.

DW: I know where you can get one, secondhand. Un-opened.

JP: Then in order to do this goal, in order to train for that, I have to walk a lot more per day. So I have to master dictation, or I'm screwed with my production goals, so in two weeks I've gone from zero to dictation, and it's amazing. My roadblocks have been *me*. Like Facebook advertising, I should have just jumped it straightaway, but I'm like "Oh ... "

I think when you run your own business, you can be in danger of relying on the old stuff. Another example: I resisted doing images on my podcast and my graphics on the blog posts, and for months and months and months, and then eventually someone emailed me and said, "I can't share your stuff on Pinterest because it's not easily pinnable. Please put a pinnable graphic on your blog."

I was, like, "Oh my goodness." And then I just went and got *Social Media Warfare* and immediately got my VA started on doing those, but I take too long to change things. Like in one way, I am very forward thinking in doing stuff; in another way I stop myself because we all suffer from overwhelm, and we just want to write. So I definitely feel that *I* am a roadblock.

DW: I'm the same way.

JBT: Speaking of social media, how has that changed? How have you managed social media? How have you sort of optimized that, managing it with your business?

JP: I am checking social media *less* in the last six months. I did love Twitter; I am starting to find it's less so now. To be honest, I'm probably producing as much as I ever did or more, and I'm consuming less social media, listening to more podcasts and audiobooks. I got one of the Great Courses after Sean mentioned it. But I'm doing the Apocalypse — Revelation, the book of Revelation, which is super-fun.

SP: Dave reads that before bed.

JP: Exactly. I did it in Greek a long time ago. So to be honest, social media is one of those things I haven't changed. Like I still do the same thing on Twitter; I still do the same thing on Facebook; I just share a few things, one thing a day. I don't think I really do anything different; I've just done the same things for years. And the thing is, if you do the same thing for years, you do build up some kind of momentum, but, like, I've not joined Instagram or Snapchat or anything like that.

SP: You're not periscoping?

JP: No periscoping or grabbing or whatever thinging. I am doing more images, and focusing on that more. I am doing Facebook advertising, but that's not really social; that's advertising. I do use Pinterest for fiction, so I have Pinterest boards for my fiction books. Per book, I do a Pinterest board, and my readers really love that because they get to see the research behind the book, but essentially I ...

SP: That's a really smart idea by the way. I love that.

JP: Well, I know you guys do audio behind the book, and I've written that down. I was, like, "Should I do that?" But to be honest, while I'm writing, the images are the things that ...

SP: No, your method is *way* better. That doesn't work with our flow, but I think it's a much better idea than what we do.

JP: I would say just on the writing, like, you guys have been collaborative for years, but I did my first co-writing with J. Thorn last year, *Risen Gods*, and I did that because of James Patterson. You guys didn't convince me. James Patterson convinced me. His master class.

DW: That hack? I'm kidding.

JP: His master class is brilliant, absolutely brilliant.

SP: I loved it.

JP: I thought it was great.

SP: I think you are actually the one who sent me the link.

JP: But his co-writer was the one who convinced me to co-write. I just went, "Do you know what? He's totally right!" And I love the result of that. So I will probably do more of that. Are you guys — are you guys still in love with social media?

SP: No. Basically we had Tara. Tara is another one of the *Iterate and Optimize* interviews, and we talk a lot about this in that interview, but basically we had her come in and kind of overhaul our social media. But her way wasn't native to how we think or work, and that's the key to all of this. You can't do anything that you're not genuinely excited about or that doesn't work with you. So our main takeaway was that you have to do what works for you — so we started the podcast network because *that does* resonate with us.

Now we need our hub taken care of — SterlingAndStone. net, at this point, is terrible —but once we fix that, it will be much easier to integrate other things. But the podcast network is our *answer* to social media, essentially.

JP: Yeah, and I listen to a lot more audio, and I like producing the audio, and I've thought about it with my fiction. I think the thing is, like, I really feel I *am* two people. Like J.F. Penn doesn't come out to play. I put stuff on the blog sometimes, and Pinterest, and I have my Facebook page where I put weird links on that about skulls and things. So I don't actually do much on that side of it, so to me, you can have a fully functional business just putting content on the book sites.

SP: Yeah, agreed. Wrapping this up with our final question: You've always been wonderfully focused on the future. What do you see for the future of the indie publishing industry and creative entrepreneurship in general?

JP: Well, it's funny because I'll just keep talking about it for years, but we haven't seen the global shift yet. They're talking about getting a streaming Internet to the whole world through mobile devices by 2020, and now I've seen it change to 2018.

That is a big deal. The fact that they now believe that every person on the planet will have a mobile device with streaming Internet within three years — that means this kind of global shift is much closer. When you hear most people talking about the global shift in online sales, they are mainly talking about like Germany or Brazil, countries that are already quite mature.

I listened to a podcast on the BBC World Service on India, and they interviewed Amazon India, and this was the January 2016 podcast, and he said we are on minute one, day one of ecommerce in India. And that, to me, is stunning. I mean when was that for America; was that 2006? I'm not saying that in any way that India is behind, but if you consider where indies were in 2006 and where we're going to be in, what, ten years, this is why I am super-excited about ...

SP: Yeah, that's *so* much potential.

JP: Isn't that incredible? And I think we are so gung-ho about everything we have, the fact that we are all talking across the world on Skype. Now with Skype Translate, what's going to happen, we could do this with people in India, people in Nigeria, just going for it.

For me, the biggest excitement is if you take that basic equation of number of products multiplied by number of customers, and we all keep working on the product side, and as the world expands, the number of customers expand ... I've actually sold books in seventy-one countries now, in English.

SP: So, so awesome.

JP: It's amazing, and that's without marketing to people in Cameroon, or Colombia. It's incredible to me that this is happening already, but if you fast forward a couple of years, that, to me, is the most exciting thing, so I would say to people who are, like, "Ah, there's so much to do," just focus on getting your baseline creation sorted, and the customers are going to be there. The great thing for indies is we can be there early because the publishers are not caring about people in Cameroon or even Nigeria or India, and there's so many places where we are selling books just because we are *there*. So that, to me, is what I am very excited about.

JBT: All right, so we'll bring this to a close. Thank you, Joanna, for joining us.

JP: Thank you for having me!

SP: Thanks, as always.

Danny Iny

Johnny B. Truant: Today our guest is Danny Iny, entrepreneur and business educator. Danny has stated his long-term goal, which I'm chuckling because it's such a wonderfully audacious goal, is to "fix business education." Danny has a long history with Sean, and I feel like I've had a remote kinship with Danny even though we've only met recently. Welcome, Danny!

Danny Iny: Thank you. I'm very excited to be here.

JBT: All right, you got in a few words, and now it's my turn again.

David Wright: Shut up!

JBT: How has your company handled the incremental growth going from a lone-man operation to a thirty-man team? What are the logistics and difficulty when you go from controlling everything and knowing where all the pieces are to working with others? I can just imagine the logistical nightmare if you botched that.

Sean Platt: Or even just letting go, because when you are that lone operator, it's difficult to start defining jobs and delegating when you go from doing everything to operating at the highest level. That takes a lot of time and patience and mistakes.

DI: It is something that happens gradually, and we've grown, I think, pretty fast. We went from me to thirty people in about five years. But still, it's five years. It's not like it was overnight. I don't think going from me to a few more people was ever a challenge because — and you guys know how this goes — when you have you, the entrepreneur, and you bring a few more people on, everyone's job description is *miscellaneous*, and they do a bit of everything, basically expanding your bandwidth.

Nothing is really changed. It gets tricky when you're looking at somewhere between four and eight people. It's not just a bunch of generalists expanding your bandwidth; you start hiring people who are supposed to be better at something than you are. Then you've got to let go and be willing to trust someone. There's a mental shift that happens somewhere along that scale, because when you're hiring your first few assistants you're still the solo player with a bunch of help in your head. There is a mental shift that has to happen from, "This is something I'm doing with some help expanding my bandwidth to I'm building an organization." Even if you're six-seven people, that's an organization; that's different from you with a bunch of virtual assistants. You've got to make that mental leap, and that's the first big hurdle.

The second big hurdle, I think, is around somewhere between eight and twelve people because it tends to grow very ad hoc; you don't have, like, an org chart you have an org bush. The lines are all going in different directions. That's about the point where you cannot effectively stay on top of eight-twelve people's work. You're going to miss things; things aren't going to be done properly, and that's when you need to start empowering other people to not just run with something, but be in charge of something and report to you.

I'm sure there have been other thresholds like that along the way, but those were the big ones. If you've got three people under you managing everyone else, or six people under you managing everyone else, it's more of the same. The transition to having people under you managing everyone else: That's a big transition, and now we're starting to get to the point where we are not there yet, but at some points relatively soon in the next year or two, we'll probably reach a point where there's a layer of management. I don't know how it's going to work out, I don't know how I'm going to deal with it, but I imagine that will be another hurdle as well.

SP: In *Iterate and Optimize*, there's a section that says, "You need to hire an Amy," because our Amy is a layer between us. If X job needs to get done, we don't assign that job; Amy does. It's so much more efficient than worrying about this and that getting done; it's Amy making sure that all the i's are dotted. We can make sure our conversations with Amy are fluid, but we're not in the weeds with fifteen little things when we should be focused on one or two big ones.

DI: The next hurdle is probably when Amy reaches the scale limit?

SP: Right.

DI: What if you need two Amys, and how do the two Amys talk to each other or divide responsibilities. There will always be threshold limits, but a lot of it comes down to having the right people in place. Try to build this with the wrong people, and it's like, "Oh my God, that's so bad."

SP: Right, because if you have the wrong person in the Amy spot, then those fifteen decisions could amount to twelve bad decisions all of a sudden, and …

DI: Well, not just that there are twelve bad decisions, but you're not getting the updates. You don't even know that a bad decision was made until six months later, when you're, like, "You did what? And this has been going on with all our customers for how long?"

SP: Right. So, how have your products evolved, and how were the funnels changed?

DI: Our way of doing things is exactly what we teach our students. It's about piloting something, then iterating and optimizing much like you guys are talking about. We put something out there, and it's going to start out as the minimum viable offer. The minimum thing we can put out there that's valuable enough to someone else for them to pay for it. That's going to be a big, giant mess because we're not automating or optimizing anything. We're delivering it, so we can see what happens and how it goes.

We want to make sure that through that process people get a great experience, but then we want to take notes and see what went well so that we can do more of that. We need to see, what didn't work well? What kind of work that was really inefficient and could be improved, and sometimes at the end of that process we're like, "You know what? That was fun, but we're not doing it again." Or, "That was not fun at all, and so we're not doing it again." But often, we'll say, "Okay, there is a lot that worked well; there is a lot we can do better; let's iterate, let's improve, let's make it better." Pretty much everything we do follows that process. We don't expect a new launch to be a home run.

SP: But that *was* the case in the early days, right? You'd build a product and assume people would like it, because you *thought* it was what they wanted?

DI: Once upon a time, before I knew what I was doing. I wish this was more ancient history than it is. The first big product I built when starting out was this massive course — six months long, a lesson every week. I spent thousands — I'm not exaggerating, thousands of hours — building this thing. It's what I knew the market needed, but I hadn't validated that they wanted. I think my ROI and the time I spent on that was, like, 11 cents per hour or something like that.

SP: (Chuckling) Awesome.

DI: I learned a lot from those lessons, and that's how we came to be doing things properly today.

SP: The pilot program just … It makes so much more sense because you're saying, "What do you want? Oh great because now I can go take care of that."

JBT: How have your list-building efforts in ad dollars evolved over the last few years?

DI: They actually haven't evolved all that much. I don't use the language of building a list. I talk about building an audience because you can have a giant list of names and email addresses, but if they don't like you or listen to you, who cares? It's really about the relationship that you build with people, and the process I've always followed pretty much from day one, I call it "the warm traffic pyramid."

It distinguishes from a lot of what marketers teach about cold or paid traffic where through whatever mechanism, someone is basically being referred to you by a computer. Whether it's a search algorithm or Facebook's ad-serving system, it's a computer sending them to you. There's no real endorsement or trust, and that's never been my approach. The warm traffic pyramid is all about getting people to come to you already warm, because you've been endorsed in some way. There are three layers:

You start at the bottom with participating communities, where the people you want to reach aggregate. You become a part of that community, and you participate. Most of my experience is in the blogging world, so let's say we're talking about blog communities, where you could start leaving worthwhile, valuable, substantive comments. You're more likely to get noticed if you have something worthwhile to say, so it must be substantive. It has to add a perspective, ask or answer a question, that sort of thing. Become a part of the conversation, and members of the community will notice you — so will community leaders. You'll get some people subscribing to your list or joining your audience, but not a lot. If you go to, let's say, one or two hundred subscribers in that way, you can do that if you take it seriously for a month or two. Then you will have become known in the community in a short span of time.

That's when you're ready for the second stage: contribute to communities. Go to the owner or leader of the community and say, "I have an idea for a post that I think your audience would really like. How about if I write it for you?" And if they know you, and you've interacted with them, and you're kind of a known quantity to them, they'll say, "Yeah, let's try that." You get dramatically more exposure and credibility for doing that, and a lot more people will discover you. Again, you're not going to go from zero — there are flukes where you happen to get lucky and it goes viral on BuzzFeed or whatever, but that's not how it usually …

SP: But you can't plan on that.

DI: You can't plan it, but you will probably — if you spend a few months working at this really hard — go from a couple of hundred to a couple of thousand subscribers. Most importantly, it's not just about the subscriber count; these are all people who came to you because they really like your stuff. There is an opportunity to build a real relationship, and if you grow that subscriber base by doing this, you will have also built a lot of relationships with the owners of the blogs enough so that once you kind of reach that scale, you can say, "Hey, I've got this training I want to present. I've got this webinar I want to deliver; do you think your audience would be into that?" And that's kind of the third rung in the ladder, the third stage in the pyramid. That's where things can accelerate a lot.

That's pretty much what I did. The commenting brought me from zero to a couple of hundred, guest posting from a couple hundred to a couple thousand, and then webinars and other promotions with people I've built relationships with to many tens of thousands.

DW: How have you optimized your ad spends over the past few years?

DI: We haven't spent money on ads in most of our company's history. It's something we've started playing with in the last year, and we have spent an awful lot of money and not gotten a lot of return. We're finally starting to get better, but in the last year I've probably spent 30, 40, $50,000 and not gotten much for it, which we're at a scale of business where I can afford to do that now, thankfully. I'm happy to share how we've optimized our ad spend, but ask me again in a year, and I'll tell you.

SP: So you're still iterating there. You've yet to optimize, right?

DI: Yeah, exactly.

JBT: Danny, how has your networking and in-person stuff changed? How have you iterated forward, and you handled that sort of thing with masterminds and events you've put on?

DI: It hasn't changed a lot. I am actually surprised. Before we started recording, Sean said I'm really good at this thing. I never would have thought that was the case. I'm not sure what the answer is, but my approach has always been the same: If I get in a room with a bunch of people, I am not looking for what I can get from them because they have no reason to want to help me. I want to look for opportunities to create or contribute value, and help people. If there is ever an opportunity, then I'll follow up with people later, and things organically happen. If you help people, it leads to good places.

SP: Okay, you are crazy; I'm going to correct Danny on this. I am going to give you the real answer here. Danny is great at this. One of the masterminds I'm in now I'm *only* in because Danny invited me, and he invited me to *another* mastermind, like, five years ago. I didn't have the bandwidth and said no, but then a couple of years ago he asked again.

He's always sending very nice, considerate intro emails. "Hey, you're a smart person, and you're a smart person; you two should have a conversation. Danny is always looking to help and learn. You're an infovore, and work hard to be around other smart people, and get smarter, faster. I do think you are very good at that. But aren't you also starting to put on events and form your own mastermind? That's an iteration because before you were only attending, and now you're architecting them?

DI: Well, so first of all, thank you, and apparently yes, that is my strategy. Yeah, so I decided several years ago that this was something I want to get into. I wanted to lead a mastermind because I was really excited about the strategic byproducts. Yes, it's a revenue opportunity, but not a significant one in the scale of what we're doing as a business. I like the idea of building a group of people that I help to achieve really great things. I like that strategic byproduct. I like what that will support me to do in the future, and so I did my first pilot version of a mastermind, and frankly it kind of stank, but you learn ...

SP: That's what pilots are for.

DI: Right. I got my lessons learned, and joined a bunch of groups. I spend about $70,000 a year in my organization on groups that I belong to, and it's partially because I get a lot of value, but partially because I'm always looking for how are things running, what is working, and when something doesn't work I want to know what the problem was so I can pull the best practices for myself. Now I run a mastermind group that is awesome. I'm super-proud of my group and the work they do. Yeah, I guess that is the product of a lot of iteration.

SP: Give yourself some credit, man. So, you changed the name of your company this year, which could not have been easy. You knew you were going to do it in the future, and that it would only get harder and harder. Can you explain why you wanted to do that, and what the process was like?

DI: My company used to be called Firepole Marketing, which yes, it was a stupid name, and the new name is Mirasee, which is a play on Mira. In Latin, it means vision and wonder, and see in English is to see, so it's kind of about implicitly or connoting — without needing to know this — it's about wondering and what could be. That's what we do; we are about reimagining what business could be. Firepole Marketing is a name we came up with — me and my then-business partner who wasn't involved in the business for much longer after that — because after an hour and a half of *the dot com is taken*, we were getting pretty desperate.

We came upon this name that was *close enough* given what we thought we would be doing at the time, and we've evolved a lot as a company, and I know where we are now, and I know where we want to go. I don't know if we we'll make it, but ten years from now I want us to be a billion-dollar company that's a major player in the world of business education. Firepole Marketing is never going to be — it's not a shell that could ever do that, so the change had to happen. Now, was it perfectly executed? It *so absolutely was not*, and my website is still ... it's a freaking disaster, but whatever.

Cost of doing business, and I wish it had been smoother and better done, but there's a quote that I like very much. I don't know who said it, but anything that has to be done eventually should be done immediately, because it gets more painful and more costly and more expensive and more difficult the longer you wait. This applies to anything that will be difficult, right? Ending a relationship, letting somebody go, moving in an important big, new direction, or changing a name. It had to happen, so better to get it over with so that as rough as the transition is on some levels, next year can be about bigger and better things.

JBT: Thanks so much, Danny, for taking us through the iterations and optimizations of your business. Where can people find you?

DI: At Mirasee.com. And I have a podcast, so look for *Business Reimagined* on iTunes.

JBT: Thanks, Danny!

DI: Thanks, guys; this was great.

C.J. Lyons

Johnny B. Truant: Our guest today calls her approach agile publishing, which is sort of the very definition of iterating and optimizing forward. So I would like to welcome to the podcast our good friend C.J. Lyons, a hybrid author, multiple *New York Times* best seller, and somebody who understands a lot about what it means to be adaptable in publishing and business. Welcome, C.J.

C.J. Lyons: Thanks, and I'm glad to be here. I'm still leery of the title "hybrid author" because it makes me feel like I just climbed out of a petri dish from some lab experiment gone awry.

Sean Platt: Dave wants to write that story: *Authors in Petri Dishes.*

David Wright: Only if they're in a basement.

JBT: You started down the indie road before most of us. Certainly before those of on this call, but also before a lot of the people we know in indie publishing.

CJL: November 2009 …

SP: Which is the Stone Age of indie publishing.

JBT: Right. So what are the biggest challenges?

CJL: I didn't even think of it as self-publishing. I did it as a marketing movement to keep my readers satisfied. I was published by Penguin Putnam, and they were putting out one book a year. Readers kept emailing me saying, "We want more, and more often." The book's already written, so there was no reason beyond *that was the way they always did it* — the opposite of agile publishing. So I had several manuscripts that had been under contract that for a variety of reasons never went to press; they had already been fully copyedited, page proofed, the whole nine yards of New York City publishing.

I had the rights to move other manuscripts; why not offer them to my readers, and hopefully it will keep them remembering my name during this vast gulf of time, from one year to the next between my traditionally published books. I didn't see it as this big revolution until my New York City publisher saw how well I was doing, and they were just aghast at the idea. But contractually, I was able to do it; I was actually bringing in new readers to my traditionally published books. To me it was a win-win. I didn't understand their problem. We were even raising money for charity; the first month that I had all the manuscripts available to me up was January 2010, when the Haiti earthquake hit.

I donated all my proceeds to Doctors Without Borders, and we moved close to two thousand books that month, which at the time was a huge number because Kindle was the only game out there, and few people owned a Kindle. We gave all our money to Doctors Without Borders, so I was kind of like, *How can people say there is anything wrong with this?* We should be creating synergy; it should be a tool that both authors and publishers are using together —

SP: But they saw it as a threat?

CJL: They saw it as a threat. Yeah, I could not sell that point to them at all.

JBT: What are the biggest changes you've seen throughout the industry between then and now, which is late 2015 as we're recording?

CJL: Oh my gosh. Well, first of all, just the attitude has come a total 180. Like I said, they still see it as a threat, but now they also see it as an audience that they can maybe capture and manipulate by buying out some people that are experienced at self-publishing and know …

SP: Such genuine terms.

CJL: Well, I mean I'm trying to be as honest as possible. Remember, I just finished a contract where they bought me when I was sitting at number two on the *New York Times* list, and I ended up being there for seven weeks straight. I did an auction, and went with the second-highest bidder, but they had the most enthusiastic plan as far as growing my audience. Because I told them that I had already moved a quarter-million copies of this book. They weren't going to find a lot of people who would want to also buy it in print unless we were consciously moving to a different audience. The *second* book would be the one with crossover.

In initial discussions, that was all great, and we are all on the same page. But by the time the book actually came out, their attitude had totally changed: *Well, why don't we just cannibalize the audience that she has and instead of the hardcover editions?* Their goal was to basically only market to my current audience. But those readers were like, "Why should we pay so much for a C.J. book?" They knew they were being used.

SP: It's double dipping, and they know it.

CJL: Yeah, exactly, and I think a lot of traditional publishers don't put the audience first. Independent publishers can focus on our audience. We have the agility to shift, as the audience shifts, to grow our audience beyond genres and age groups and demographics in different ways than the New York City publisher can — now there are a lot of things New York City publishing can do that we can't. And one of the things I've been focusing on in these last couple of years is trying to develop ways where I can fill in those gaps.

Because every person, whether you are self-published or New York City-published — and when I say New York I mean any traditional publisher around the world; it's just easier shorthand — you are still CEO of your own global media empire, and have to decide for yourself what your business plan is and how to best not just reach your audience but keep them happy and excited so you can keep going back to them, and they *want* to see your name; they *want* to click that *BUY NOW!* button. Traditional publishing plays a role in that, especially in my global marketplaces. Other times, it's things I'm trying on my own, so I have more control over the end product.

SP: What value does traditional still have over indie and vice-versa — how do you see those values changing?

CJL: One of the things that New York City publishing can do well — and this is what they've been doing well for hundreds of years — is the ability to build a franchise that can break someone out. Because they have the power and the relationships with the booksellers. They can do the marketing. If you don't have that universal marketing plan in place, it's very difficult to break out of the crowd.

I like to use the example of Dan Brown's *Da Vinci Code* because of what they did for that book. First of all, there were thousands of advance readers' copies sent to booksellers and to reviewers. That happens to one or two titles a year. They also purposely oversold that initial print run to the point where there were literally mountains of this single title facing each customer as they walked through the doors of every major bookstore.

They were inundated; this book was everywhere, so of course people started to pick it up and talk about it. That is part of what New York does, and they do this wonderfully. Of course, one of the things that small presses are striving to understand is if they can do the same thing — perhaps not on the big scale of overprinting by a hundred thousand copies, but reaching their audience and really giving them what they want. A great example of that is Algonquin Books. That's probably the only publisher on the face of the planet that if I see the name on a book, whether it's fiction or nonfiction or YA or adult, I'll pick it up and at least take a good hard look. I usually end up buying it because, editorially, their catalogue is aligned with my tastes and what I like to read.

I am one of the target audience members, and they know that. They have this wonderful, vibrant newsletter that goes out. They have websites, they're very dynamic and are always updated. They're very, very good at keeping their customer foremost, and that's probably why when you look at their titles compared to many equal-sized smaller/medium publishers, they have a significantly higher rate of award-winning *New York Times* best-selling titles — *because they don't just try to take anything that might make them money*. Instead, they publish books that their current customers will jump with joy over and be excited by. I think New York has a lot of room where if they were more agile in their philosophies, and not so constricted in their ways of thinking, they could really be taking advantage of the current market.

It's probably good for us that they aren't, though, because if they don't do well, then they aren't agile and won't think out of the box. During my last publishing contract, I sat down with the publisher — not assistants, not sales reps — *the publisher*. The head of marketing, the head of sales, the editorial executive director, my editor, you name it. The big people were there at this table. We were talking about marketing plans. The marketing guys came up with something, and I said, "No, that's really not going to work; it's not targeting my demographics. What about this?" And the publisher had been, like, checking his email, Facebook, and stuff. He finally looked up, invested in the conversation, and said, "How do you know who your reader or your target audience is? We don't even know that."

I ripped out a piece of paper, slid it across the conference table to him, and said, "Here's my target audience. They skew 65 percent women, 35 percent men, they're 35 and older. There're just those with income, they make between 100 to $150,000 a year, the vast majority are college graduates and graduate students or have graduate degrees."

I was going on and on and on, and I thought his head was going to explode. He said, "Where did you get this data because we don't have it?" It's just not in their thinking to dig down that deep.

SP: Is that because they're selling to the booksellers and not to the actual readers?

CJL: Absolutely, they have literally half a dozen people they sell to. The buyer for Costco, the buyer for Walmart, the buyer for …

SP: So they know *those* demographics.

CJL: They know what those guys like, they know what they want to hear, they know how to present to them, but they have no clue what goes beyond that. My thinking — and this has been the big thing that's taken up a lot of my time during 2015 — was could I do that because 50 to 60 percent of my audience are still wanting print books. A lot of them are coming from libraries that would like hardcover rather than the trade paperbacks I was previously doing with CreateSpace. Although the CreateSpace model is really great, I mean I loved working with those guys. To be able to get the distribution and that kind of mental real estate, even if a bookseller only had one or two of my titles on their bookcase. If someone said, "I want a book that's kind of like Lisa Gardner or Tess Gerritsen," then they could say, "Have you tried C.J. Lyons? We only have this one, but she has twenty-nine other titles. I can order any of them in for you."

In 2015, I started working with Ingram's Publishing Services and created my own publishing company at GReads — very similar to what Barbara Freethy was doing with them for romance — and became a publisher. I've always been a content creator and an ebook publisher, but this time I'm in print. I am in Barnes & Noble, I am in Chapters and Indigos in Canada. I'm in libraries and Baker & Taylor. I'm in indie book stores — *you name it*. Our eighth title will be in January, and then we have titles coming in February, March, May, and September of 2016.

We've done most of my backlist and are going forward with the frontlist. It's been quite an experience, and I totally understand now a lot more of the risk that publishers take, but I am also understanding on the things they could be doing better to create higher profit margins for themselves and authors. A lot of things are just done because of tradition.

SP: They have a lot of fat, and they don't know how to trim it because they're used to doing things a certain way?

CJL: Yeah, and unfortunately in this economic climate and with readers having more and more options, that fat has gotten really, really lean. They haven't figured out how to increase the efficiency of the publishing process on the wider New York City scale. When you walk through Ingram's distribution center and see pallets and pallets of books that you know are just going to be pulped because they've been oversold so dramatically, it's really kind of heartbreaking. I see booksellers of the future, and don't see bookstores going away. My mother was an independent bookseller for twenty-five years before she retired, so I adore bookstores, and don't want them to go away. I see them becoming what Amazon has always wanted to become online: *the every bookstore.*

In other words, they would hand curate. Barnes & Noble, and the other big chains could do this as well. Hand curate towards their local target audience the titles they want to carry, and if they can sell the best, get rid of all the chaff, but in each aisle for each different section there would be, like, an iPad or a tablet or a NOOK or — whatever they want to use. Then they could have a little message that would say, "Ask your sales representative, and we can order this and have it delivered directly to your home." Because you want to get that instant gratification convenience, but without the customer clicking on their smartphone and going to Amazon. You want that partnership and that relationship between bookseller, author, and reader to exist and to flourish. I see that as a wave of the future, and that's why I've spent so much time and energy on setting up at GReads.

Then my next thing — I shouldn't say next thing; I've actually been working on it since 2012 in various iterations, trying to find that perfect piece of the pie — and what solves the puzzle is direct-to-consumer sales for ebooks. I think we now, finally — in fact, it just came out in the last couple of weeks — have some of the technology problem solved where we can send books directly to Kindles and epub devices. Also, the ability to create a more vibrant store where it's not just my books. I could say, "Hey, if you like this book, you're going to like this title from Lisa Gardner or this title from Tess Gerritsen, and have those for sale side by side, all on my website. I want to get my readers a one-stop shopping experience just like they'd find at any other online store like Amazon or Barnes & Noble.

DW: What is agile publishing, and how does it influence where you create and sell your creations?

CJL: Agile publishing is for authors able to see opportunities in the marketplace and change with them to find those partners that can help them grow their audience and their business. I'm working right now on audiobooks. I was taking much too long to produce them myself, and I had all these new print versions coming out, plus my frontlist books needed audio. I had to partner with someone.

I sold the rights to several books to Audible, to take that off my plate. They have a wider audience than I do, so what I'm giving up in the royalty rate — because of course it's a different contract than what I could do myself with ACX — I'm making up for it in that they have the highest quality production standards, and a much higher reach as far as audience.

A lot of my overseas publishing partnerships are coming not for translations I've made on my own but rather selling to foreign publishers and having them translate products for me. Agile publishing is being able to see those opportunities and go for them, to grow the business based on what you have the time and energy and money to do and also what will best serve your readers. I think that's the thing a lot of people don't understand: it's not just about making money.

There are so many indie publishers who are all about the hustle. *How can we get more money, how can we hire for five dollars co-writers that will basically make up stories for us, or plagiarize, God forbid, from other books?* That's becoming the big thing — to farm out work to these poor people overseas and have them create plagiarized copies of books that you publish under different names, all in the name of ripping off the audience and making money. I am like, "No, no, no, it's not about the hustle; it's about finding that balance between creativity, time, energy, and money … "

SP: No one is ever going to buy one of those books like that and become a reader. They're not going to become your fan; that's never ever going to happen.

CJL: No — yes, actually, it has. Have you seen what's gone on with the romance writing community?

SP: No, but I can tell you're about to break my heart.

CJL: Yeah, this made national headlines, the *Washington Post* and you name it — they were reporting on this. An astute reader found what were basically plagiarized copies of romance titles from best-selling authors, but they had been converted a little bit. Like, instead of a male-female romance, they were male-male or other things like that. Very little was changed, and it was a new kind of plagiarism; it's called "mosaic plagiarism."

There are actually people out there that email me to take their class where for $300 they'll teach me how to be a best-selling author without ever having to write my own story. They tell you right up front on the website: It's perfectly legal because their interpretation of copyright law in the US is, well, if we steal from several books and combine them, it's not more than 30 percent of any one title; therefore, it's not the same as the initial copywritten material. There is this huge industry that is just totally ripping off the audience, ripping off the content creators who own copyright, and they are doing it just to make a quick buck.

SP: And they're getting repeat reader fans?

JBT: Let's face it: those people are going to get hit by a bus.

CJL: Well, let's hope, but it's the type of thing that the industry needs to figure out ways to deal with and move on from, which kind of got me off my point; sorry about that. Agile publishing means taking control of who you decide to partner with, and what the best use of your time and energy and creativity are so you can get the stories out to your readers.

JBT: Speaking of your readers: You've been building a list for a long time, and I know that's evolved a lot, so how has your list building and list usage changed over the past few years?

CJL: It's funny, right now a lot of authors are really focused on doing anything they can to get people's email addresses to build their list, while I've been pruning mine. If you add it up over the years, I've probably had well over thirty thousand people on my list, and I'm constantly pruning that back because I want the people on my list to be the readers who get excited when they see my email. They want to open it. I don't want the people that are just there because they feel like it would be rude to unsubscribe, then go years between opening an email from me.

SP: Yeah, that just decays your list.

CJL: Exactly. So I constantly prune my list. It's at about twelve thousand now. The highest I ever let it get was close to twenty thousand, and then I pruned it back to fourteen, then it started climbing again to, like, seventeen-something, and then I pruned it back to, like, nine and now we're back up to twelve. I've probably been between twelve and fifteen thousand; that's going to be my most effective kind of target level. I typically get about 45 percent to 50 percent open rate, and my click-through rates are really, really good.

SP: Yeah, that's excellent with your volume; that's great.

CJL: I totally credit my fans that have been willing to sign up for my email newsletters as what keeps me going, what keeps me afloat financially. Because let's face it, we're in a very gloated and overpopulated market right now. I'm a voracious reader. I have two Kindles — one for fiction and one for research, and I have more books on either of them than I could read in a lifetime. We're in a position where the reader is in the driver's seat, so anything we can do to help make it easier for them to hit that buy button, and make them remember us between titles ...

I don't know about you guys, but for me discoverability has become the uphill battle in finding those new readers. That's one of the reasons why I expanded into print — because the people finding me in Barnes & Noble and Chapters and Indigos and indie sellers hand-selling my books are not the people that would have found me online with ebooks or on Amazon or any other websites where it's difficult to get any traction or visibility right now.

SP: What is your team like? I know you've had to write, add team members, get help from assistants and people who are helping you compile and getting your print versions to market. What does the C.J. Lyons team look like?

CJL: It's me and one person. Seriously, I don't know what's wrong with me. I keep looking for assistants; I'm very good to work for.

SP: Is that because you like to have your hands in everything, and it's part of the process for you?

CJL: That's actually what it's boiled down to: that I am okay with having only one person, but I have to tell you, it's really cutting into my productivity as far as the writing.

SP: Yeah, I can imagine.

CJL: I've actually written two more books this year, but the time of setting up the publishing company was overwhelming. Now we have that up and running, so I don't perceive that as a problem for next year. The problem is, I won't hire anyone until I have a couple of phone calls with them and have made certain that we're all on the same page, and that it won't be overwhelming.

I don't micromanage. I like to get passionate, creative people involved and let their ingenuity spark some ideas. I'm good about hiring people like that, but eventually so many have just vanished. Like a couple of them before they even got started or paid, they'd just disappear from the face of the earth. At first, I was taking it personally, but then I learned from a couple of writers groups that a lot of people get into these jobs without realizing how much time it takes, or that they aren't suited to it. They talk a good game, but they actually can't get the job done.

I found one assistant who I adore, and she is wonderful. She's actually a grad student going for her master's and library degree. She loves Excel sheets and …

SP: And now you are working to clone her?

CJL: Yeah, actually, she just started her own virtual assistants business, where she is training others do what she does. I'm not certain if they are taking new clients yet, but she's wonderful. Her name is Jade Eby. She's great, and enjoys all the stuff that I hate.

SP: Oh, that's a great partnership, then.

CJL: I do have more people on my team, but they aren't full-time players like Jade. I have a whole stable of copyeditors, proofreaders, and developmental editors, when I need them. My big problem is that sometimes I write too fast, and these guys can't fit me into their schedule. So I end up having my deadlines based on when I can schedule the vendors I want for certain projects. I'm actually doing my own cover art.

I had a professional set up the template, but since I write in series, once you have that initial template set up, it's pretty easy to play with Photoshop and get the look you want. So that has helped because the best copyeditors and cover artists I've worked with are also really overbooked. So that's my team — I think of it more as partnerships. Like my go-to partner for copyediting one series, or my go-to audio person for another because

I want to develop long-term relationships, not just one-off do this, and I'll-never-talk-to-you-again type of thing.

I've also learned that there is a lot of stuff I could be doing, or could maybe hire someone to do. But I'm just kind of like, "You know what? No, it's just too much." I'm almost never on Twitter anymore, and even in the past my Tweets were pretty much just reTweeting industry news to writers. I don't have any readers on my Twitter stream. Facebook, I'm there once or twice a week maybe, and it's usually just sharing a photo or a quote. It's not that I don't want to interact with readers. I love that, and I still do a lot of interactions through messaging and emails and things. But this constant feed-me, feed-me social media model …

SP: No, it's smart. You're keeping your relationship in the books, and I actually like that. We're similar for the most part.

CJL: Even when you pay money for a Facebook ad, your audience reach is so limited. I just don't see the return on investment. Jade is playing around with some Facebook ads for some of our newer books, but other than that I only do it if it's something I want to do and it's fun, which sounds really entitled, and I don't mean it to sound that way. It's just that I have found that's the best way to keep my creativity focused on story rather than letting my attention be diverted by all this other stuff hammering at us all day long.

JBT: So what do you see for the future of indie publishing and creative entrepreneurs in general?

CJL: Unfortunately, I'm probably not the person that's going to do this — it's going to be people, well, like you guys at Sterling & Stone or my friend Joanna Penn, or people that are very good at putting the moving pieces together and handling the logistics, which I'm not. I'm a big-idea person, and I can see the ideas, but I never know how to make them happen. So what I see for the future is transmedia franchise building.

The idea of taking a story like *Unicorn Western*. Let's say there's a Saturday morning cartoon for kids, websites with animation, and — I don't know — webcasts or web episodes, or whatever you want to call it — kind of like they did with the *Star Wars* animated feature. So it started out as, like, little three-minute features that were just kind of slipped in here and there where they had a bit of free programming time, then they were on the website, then all of a sudden they became full twenty-two-minute episodes, and they kind of tapped the transmedia idea.

But not just visual, also thinking graphic novels, so Dave, right up your ally there, and looking at ways to produce content that once set up, it can come out automatically on a daily basis, kind of like what Hugh MacLeod does with his cartoons. They come to your phone or your email every day, and you can buy a physical copy or just enjoy the email and its little commentary. So things that are creating synergy and feeding on each other and are doing it in multiple ways, then reaching the consumer where they are, and when they want it. So it's consumer driven; it's not Random House printing a million copies of *Da Vinci Code* and shoving them onto the consumer and forcing them to pay attention.

Instead, it's the consumer saying, "Oh, I stumbled across this really cool website, and look, there's a link to an ebook. I'm going to go buy that. And I don't have time to read it right now, so I'm going to listen to the audio version, or I'm going to look at the graphic novel. Or gee, while I'm going to go watch TV — oh, they are carrying on an independent channel, and I can watch the video versions."

DW: It's a puppet show at the local theatre.

CJL: There you go.

SP: I really agree with this. I know they were ahead of their time, but the Wachowskis did this with the *Matrix* sequels. They had the two movies, and the *Animamatrix* series of animated shorts. And they had the video game, and some comics, and the story line all sort of blended together. And you didn't need to experience them all to enjoy them.

CJL: Yeah, so I think the total visual would be any screen, any device, any time you can reach out and immerse yourself in the universe. Like I get frustrated, I'm a *Dr. Who* fan, and I go back and rewatch the same episodes over and over because they are so limited; that's it. And now, finally, they're starting to have more of the *Dr. Who* books and things like that, so I can do different things. And of course don't forget the merchandising. You can have your TARDIS teapot or coffee mug.

You can really go whole hog with this. I've been creating Zazzle and CafePress stores for mugs and T-shirts and things like that, and I'm going to integrate them more into my direct-to-consumer feed. Because again, it's just another way if someone wants to identify with the C.J. Lyons brands, I'm not going to stop them; I want to make it easy.

JBT: We'll get on that and let you know how the transmedia stuff gets going.

CJL: I'm going to be watching you guys, and I'm in the rearview mirror, waiting, because as one person I can only do so much. And I have had this idea for, like, three or four years, figuring out a way to tackle transmedia, and I just have not figured out the logistics. Because those partnerships are very different than what we usually have in a publishing world.

JBT: Thanks for joining us, C.J., and for telling us how you optimize your business. And the best place to find you is Cjlyons.net.

CJL: That's right. And thanks, guys — that was great!

Tucker Max

Johnny B. Truant: Today, our guest is Tucker Max. You may know Tucker as a multiple *New York Times* best-selling author, who has sold millions of books. Since retiring from writing, his full-time income has come from a different business with Book in a Box. And that's what we want to talk about today: evolving from the old business into the new one. So thanks for joining us, Tucker.

Tucker Max: Good. Thanks for having me, guys.

JBT: What was that transition like? Can you kind of paint the big picture for us?

TM: To go from writer to business person?

JBT: Yeah, and how did you sort of parlay that, because you had notoriety as Tucker Max the author and …

TM: Yeah, all right, so there is a couple of things. First, I had to decide: My sort of original writing career was writing essentially short stories about the stupid things I did when I was drunk and young and single. So once I kind of — once you're not young and drunk anymore, then you run out of stories to tell, which I did. I think a lot of people find something successful, then they beat that horse until it's not only dead but it's just smothered, and there's nothing left. And then it's like, "Oh, remember when they used to be good?"

David Wright: Like Arby's.

TM: Right, yeah, although I'm not old enough to remember when Arby's used to be good.

Sean Platt: I don't think Methuselah is old enough.

TM: Right, exactly, so I basically just retired from that, and then I made enough money on my books, and kind of took a little while. And I had a lot of opportunities and a lot of random things come up, and then one kind of fell into my lap that really made sense, and I decided to sort of cut everything else and focus on that. Like I wish I had a clearer answer, but to me it's sort of like — everyone says sort of investigate or whatever, follow your passion, which is total nonsense advice. I think maybe the best thing I did was to follow my interests, and my curiosity.

Following my curiosity and interests, I found something that overlapped with a problem that a lot of other people had, that I had an ability to help them solve and they would pay a lot of money for: *That's a business.* And it was distinct from writing and selling content, which is a totally different type of business.

SP: Did you feel like there were a lot of false starts along the way?

TM: I did. I actually just wrote a piece for the Hustle about all these sort of little mini projects or smaller one-off-type companies I did on the way to where I am now. The company I'm now talking about, Book in a Box, is very successful. We did $2 million in our first year. I think we are going to do about $6 or $10 million next year. And I had a lot of little things, smaller things, almost like tests, basically, along the way.

Writing is a business because you are asking people to pay for what you wrote. If it's nonfiction, then it's generally something they think they'll get an ROI for. Or if it's fiction, it's something they think will entertain or distract them, or in some way be worth reading.

It's the same thing with a business. You are asking people to give you money, and so in return you have to give them something they want. A lot of times, it takes a while to find something you enjoy doing, that there is a market for, and that you are good at, right? So, like, a lot of people want to be writers, but the reality is they suck at writing, and no one will pay them for their work. So they can't do it, and there are a lot of different reasons as to why they suck. They haven't worked hard enough with their skills, they aren't writing about the right things, they aren't writing things that are interesting to other people, etc. I mean you guys go over that a lot in the podcast and your books. But business is no different; a lot of people have a lot of ideas for business that are really stupid.

And if it's a new idea and it's stupid, you have to test it. If it's new and if no one wants it, then it's not a good idea. If you are going into an established field — like you are opening up a burger chain — there is a huge demand for burgers, but there is also huge competition. So then if you're going into an established market, you have to think, *How am I going to differentiate; how am I going to be better?* If you're going into a new market, you have to know if there is even a market. You have false starts because there is uncertainty involved. If it's an established market, maybe your product isn't any better than anyone else's, and you've got to figure out why, and if you can get it there and if it's a new market, you've got to figure out if anyone cares.

SP: But do you find a lot of value in the false starts?

TM: Oh my goodness, yeah, of course; that's the only way to learn. The only way — if you could learn without experimentation and trial and error and failure, then why the fuck would anyone fail? Failure is not fun; no one is like, "Oh man, I had so many great failures this week; it was wonderful." No one's *ever* said that. The *only* reason that failure is good is because it is one step closer to success; it gets you get a piece of information that can potentially get you one step closer to where you want to be. It doesn't automatically mean you'll succeed. There's nothing worse than those people who are like, "Fail more, fail fast." And I'm like, "Motherfucker, failure is *not* the goal; that's stupid."

Failure is this sign post along the road. It is a piece of information, and it is an incomplete piece of information, and it oftentimes doesn't even tell you what you need to know to find the right road and find the right path; it's just telling you that that's the wrong way to go. So yeah, failure can be instructive, but you've got to recognize that it is what it is, and you've got to understand what it means and then use it the right way. Most people aren't willing to actually do that because most failures are due to a problem someone has that they don't want to recognize about themselves, but that's the hard truth of business.

DW: Do you ever find that your notoriety in your former existence gets in the way; do you wish you had created a pen name for that? Does that hold you back?

TM: It's one of those things where it's both the positive and the negative, right? So everything in life is a trade-off, make no mistake. If you ever want to find a perfect solution that has no downside, then I'll be happy to kill you because you are going to have to go to Heaven; that's the only place you are going to fucking find it. The upside of having written books that were very famous and sold millions of copies is that everybody knows who I am, or at least they've vaguely heard of me. And having any sort of fame, it helps in business; it just does. If people know who you are, that's almost always a good thing; it gets you meetings and whatever. But your question is a good one because my fame was in many ways infamy.

There are a lot of people who associate negative things with me, and so yeah, it absolutely does hurt in certain ways. There are people who won't work with our company because they hear I'm involved; there are certain, like, associations we're doing a partnership with where they're basically dealing with my co-founder and not me because of various issues. There's a price you pay for everything, man, and on balance it's helped us a lot, and accelerated our growth, but no, it's not all been positive.

JBT: But the net effect is positive. You would rather have notoriety than nothing?

TM: In America, there is very little currency that's more valuable than fame.

DW: Like the Kardashians.

TM: Yeah, seriously, I mean it's true. Like you can get famous for sucking a dick if you play it right in this country. America is a weird place. If you were talking about — I don't know, a lot of honor cultures or like fourteenth-century England, then being famous for something that was shameful doesn't work because you are essentially ostracized. America doesn't have that sort of culture anymore. I'm not going to say anything is helpful because obviously then the counterexample is like, oh go shoot up a school — that's not going to help, right?

DW: Jared from Subway probably isn't getting a lot of these offers.

TM: No, he is not. Fame helps, but within reason.

JBT: Well, I was going to say we heard you on the *Self-Publishing Podcast* talk about criticism and haters, which you are sort of uniquely good at because of the trial by fire you had as classic Tucker Max. So has any of that come into play with your new business because, inevitably, any entrepreneur is going to face criticism?

TM: Yeah, you know what's funny? It's actually been an advantage for me. So that aspect of it — because a lot of the people who hated me or whatever — they didn't really have an opinion about me; they had an opinion about what they heard secondhand. So it's just like an impression. I don't follow politics, right, but I have an impression of Ben Carson just vaguely secondhand. I don't know him, I haven't read any of his books, I haven't seen one of his goddamned speeches. I don't really know anything about him, but my impression is that he is the world's first stupid neurosurgeon.

DW: He'd fit in Florida.

TM: Right, exactly, so, and that's — quite honestly, like, I'm self-aware enough to understand that this is a second- or thirdhand impression, I don't know, right? So if I met him, I would probably be expecting, like, a typical stupid doctor. There are actually a lot of stupid doctors. One of those weird things when you know a lot of doctors is, like, wow, they are just as stupid as everybody else. I would know what to expect, but then it might turn out to be a media impression and he's actually a really smart guy. I had the same thing happen to me. A lot of people think that if you drink and hook up and party, you must be a flamboyant moron.

But then they meet me and talk to me, and at first they're like, "Wow, you are not stupid." And then after thirty minutes it's, "Oh man, you are actually really smart." I'm so used to this, I'm not even offended by it, but the first couple of times it happened, I'm like, "How do you think I sold millions of books? Did I just shit on a page, and for some reason people bought it?"

SP: Look what I did, Daddy!

TM: Yeah, right, exactly. But they were, like, "No I don't know. I hadn't thought about it, and blah blah blah." Because the general impression of me with a lot of people is very low, it actually sets me up to blow expectations out of the water. Then everyone thinks, "Oh my god, he's so smart." When, if they were expecting Malcolm Gladwell they would be like, "Yeah, he was all right, I guess." The curse of infamy also brings the benefit of lowered expectations.

DW: I'm rewriting my goals right now.

SP: Okay, so your current business is really smart because, like you said, everybody wants to write a book; not everybody can write one. But everybody is a specialist at *something* …

TM: Well, they have some knowledge that's valuable, right?

SP: Right, so you captured a way where anybody can capture their knowledge, and you've systemized it so that it's kind of assembly line, and you get a book on the other end. But your previous business was really dependent on you and your personality.

TM: One hundred percent.

SP: And this business is not. Even if it's accelerated growth, that's certainly not what drives it. You don't have a list or anything like that, right? I know if you publish something to your wordpress.com account, I'll get a notification, but you don't actually have a list, right — does that matter at all? You always hear how important it is to build a list, build a list, build a list ...

TM: Yeah, that's a good question. I think for most consumer-facing businesses, having a permission asset is very important. Having an audience that wants to hear you talk, or wants you to sell for them, I think is very important. For us, it's less important, because we structured our business so we could essentially be a platform for other companies and other people to make money. And if you do that, then you don't have to do the marketing; other people will. I'll give you a great example. I think we're about to do a deal with a guy who is essentially like the big coach and instructor for estate lawyers, right? Huge numbers of estate lawyers pay him a lot of money to get his newsletter.

And pretty much every estate lawyer should have a book for client lead gen. And he did his own sort of thing, *here's how to write a book about estate law*, and, like, all of them bought it, and, like, 10 percent of them actually finished the course. So he's been trying to figure out a way to actually do the book for them because estate lawyers have a lot of money, and when he met me, he was like, "Oh my god, this is exactly what I want." So we did a deal where he's going to offer added-on services, things that only estate lawyers would care about. He is going to charge $25,000 to his people, and they are going to pay it. And he'll tell them it's in conjunction with us; it's not like some secret, but we are going to — our fee is 18. And we are actually going to do fulfillment on the other things that he is doing for them.

So he is going to make $7,000 a client and do nothing, and we are going to do all of it, and our marketing costs are essentially zero. Now, you could argue that we could charge 25 and pocket it all, but I think it'll probably cost us a lot more than $7,000 per client in that niche, to build that trust and that audience within that tiny little space. There's just no way — it would be very difficult; it would cost more than seven grand a client. So we're essentially subcontracting our marketing to him, then giving him all the profits, and it's a win-win for all parties involved.

There are a lot of companies like that. A great example is Postmates. Like, they are building a logistics thing, and there are all these delivery services, all these different types, they all use Postmates, including Amazon Prime. We're kind of the same thing; we are building a platform. Now long term. We are going to build our own audience, we have a lot of content we're doing, and we'll figure that out, but for short-time, especially for high-dollar, high-value sorts of products, it's a lot easier to partner with and leverage existing channels, but if you help them make money, then they are super-eager to do it.

JBT: So how important is networking, because I mean this is all very much a people business and who you know, so how do you handle that?

TM: That's an excellent question; that's where being famous really, really helps. It's like, I'm not just some fucking schmuck, right? I'm a dude who sold three million books and actually started his own publishing company then got his own distribution deal for his last books. So, like, I have a lot of credibility. Even though it's a slightly different field, it's close enough to the realm of books and authors and publishing that it makes sense. I'm an authority.

Networking is easy — this sort of thing is. You can email anybody and say, "Hey let's do this deal." But so much of that is based on trust and getting to know somebody. I don't really think of it as networking because networking is just one of those terms that's been used so much that it's really *overused*. I think even more is relationship building, because, like, we have — honestly, man there are probably fifty thousand people we could do partnerships with. And I don't want to do partnerships with shitheads and people I don't like, and there is just — life's too short to waste your time on that.

I already have a set of friends, and people I know and like, and I go to conferences or events where I think I'm going to meet more people like that. Then I meet them, and build a relationship with the ones I like and get along with, where I think our interests align. If the relationship make sense to do business, then we do. For a lot of those people, it doesn't. But those people are friends with someone that it does make sense for me to do business with. So they introduce us, and it works great, and that doesn't happen when you network, but when you relationship build, it does.

DW: What's been the biggest challenge as far as changing a brand and identity from who you were to who you are, and who you want to be in the future?

TM: Part of the problem with my old stuff is that I never thought of myself as a brand. Like, I'm not. I'm a human. If you are Kim Kardashian, the worst thing she can do is say, "I am a human. I am not a brand." Of course she's a fucking brand. Good or bad, she is a symbol of many things to a lot of girls in America. I always resisted that, which in reality was a stupid business decision. It was probably a very good human decision for me personally, but if I decided that I was going to turn my stuff into a brand, I could have been like theCHIVE, or College Humor, or what's that idiot on Instagram, has a little picture with guns, I can't remember his name: Dan Bilzerian, someone like that, right?

Or like a male Kim Kardashian, whatever, I could have easily done those things. I just hated the idea of being a brand, and I resisted it for a lot of reasons. It's not hard for me to, like, shift from one thing to another, and I just don't ever think of myself as a brand. The only people who ask those questions tend to be either media people or people who think in those terms. But most of our clients and people we do partnerships with and stuff, they don't really care. And the people who do care about my brand just don't do business with me.

SP: Right, those are people you probably wouldn't want to do business with anyway, right?

TM: Right, exactly.

SP: Has becoming a father influenced your business at all in the way you think, the way you approach things?

TM: Well, it's definitely reducing my sleep hours. You know what's funny? It almost feels like being a father and leading a company are really actually very similar. It's funny, man. Like, you can't bullshit a kid; you can't really bullshit your employees forever. Part of being a leader is taking responsibility for, like, everything and putting other people first. It's one of those things where you can kind of bullshit that as a CEO; you can't really bullshit that at all as a father, at least not for any extended period of time. Either you are going to be a great leader, or you are not. And either your kids are going to be happy and healthy, or they won't. Either your company is going to be happy and healthy and your employees will be happy and healthy, or they won't.

If I'm going to build a company and have a family, then I have to fully commit to putting those people and their interests first. And understanding that I have a certain set of jobs, and that there is no one standing behind me to get that shit done. If I don't get it done, it doesn't get done, and if I don't do it right, it doesn't get done right.

I'm glad, man. I'm forty now, and I'm glad that fatherhood and CEO both came far later in my life because I was poorly, poorly equipped to do this before. Even, like, six, seven years ago I would have been a disaster. I'm only just now ready to do even a solid job. And I'm not great at all at either one yet, but I think I'm doing well enough. I'm growing, but yeah, but the two things are very similar, man; they really are.

SP: One of the things that I've always really appreciated about you is how self-aware you are, like you know who you are, and you know what you are good at, you know what you need to work on, and that's a really admirable quality. Have you become more self-aware in your business lately?

TM: You have to, man. When you're a writer — I'm sure you guys understand this very acutely — it's so easy to tell yourself a story about who and what you are because you are the only one responsible for the output and for the work and whatever. It's a what-you-kill mentality, and that's great, but it's a very different mentality than being a leader. You can't lie to yourself about results because either you finish the chapter, or you don't. You finish the book, or you don't. It sells, or it doesn't, right?

In some ways, you can't fool yourself, but there are a lot of other things about yourself and how you interact with other people in the world that you can definitely lie to yourself about; you can't do that as a CEO or as a father. Like, I can tell myself that I don't have an anger problem and that I deal with people fine, and if I get frustrated and scream and my son starts crying, my lies to myself don't hold any fucking water. I have had to become a lot more self-aware, but in a totally different way. I've had to become acutely aware of how I impact other people, which was, like, the antithesis of how I was, both as a person and as a writer. It's just a self-contained entity; it's totally different, yeah.

JBT: All right, I think that's actually all we had to discuss, so bookinabox.com, what else? Anything else, Tucker, that people need to know about you?

TM: No.

JBT: All right, good.

TM: That's good enough.

SP: Don't eat at Arby's.

TM: Yeah, right. Don't eat at Arby's.

Tara Jacobsen

Johnny B. Truant: Today's guest is Tara Jacobsen from Marketing Artfully. And Tara is a social media marketing expert. She did a bunch of stuff with us, and of course for other clients. So we are going to talk to her about iterating and optimizing her own business. So welcome, Tara.

Sean Platt: Tara is sort of ninja, and she's *so* ninja that she thought she could chop-sockey *our* social media performance, but clearly we got in our own way. She gave us all the right advice. And while we ignored a lot of stuff she had told us to do in the first half of last year, we ended up launching a podcast network in the second half, which does follow her ultimate advice, which is to *find the space that you love, and do a lot of that.* Podcasting is native to the three of us, and seemed like a natural place to spend our social energy. So that's what we've done.

It's great to have Tara here because there's no one I'd rather talk to about social media. I guess I'd like to start by asking, what are the biggest changes that you've gone through as social has changed over the last few years? What are the big changes you've gone through when iterating and optimizing your own social platform?

Tara Jacobsen: The easiest one to call out and say it works really well is Twitter. I have a big old account that covers all of social media, or all of marketing. It's a mishmash of everything.

It's my TARAdactyl account. I think I have nine others that are for ebook nerds, for my authors. And I have one geared towards realtors, and another towards startups. So to succeed on Twitter with your message, you want to have tight channels for each of your accounts. And it's easy to do on that platform. It's not the same as having multiple accounts on other networks, or having tons of Facebook pages to manage.

SP: Where you feel schizophrenic just trying to keep up with it.

TJ: Exactly, so that is really awesome. I think Pinterest is an amazing tool. One of the reasons being that those pins stay there forever. And so it's nice that time spent there feels like it's going to have legs beyond just today.

SP: It's also the most aesthetically pleasing, which I think helps its longevity, too.

TJ: It's beautiful, so those two are great. I think it's still very, very easy to grow your following on Instagram. It's much like Twitter in 2008. So if you're thinking about starting your first social network and growing something, I would suggest Instagram. I mean there's a lot of users there, but it's still very natural and native. And they've done an awful lot of things to make sure it stays that way. Like, you can't put links in your posts, so it's harder for marketers to hurt it.

SP: And you can't do it from desktop either. It's only mobile.

TJ: Right. You can't post from desktop, though you can like stuff from the desktop. There's a program called Iconosquare that's really nice for that if you are looking for a tool. It doesn't let you post, but it does let you do a lot of other things, like putting people in groups. For example, I have a bunch of realtors in a realtor group. So if I'm trying to make connections with people in the real estate industry, I would just look at their information. So that's a really neat tool to have.

Facebook, I will tell you that unless you're willing to kind of start a private group in your industry that people will be interested in, you might be wasting your time. And it can't be a private, "Hey, like my company group." It has to be "all Etsy sellers" or "all people who are doing journaling" or "all people who like cats." Everybody likes cats, but you have to put in a ton of time because the organic reach of Facebook is zero to three right now. And we manage a lot of Facebook pages.

SP: Wow. That's terrible.

TJ: And a lot of it is zero. You know, you may get one or two posts. There's a lot of opportunity there if you're willing to work it. Now, the difference is that I'm paying somebody to do paid advertising on Facebook and am totally fine with that. They have all the demographic data. You can drill down really far. Say you are writing, I don't know, superhero romance; you could literally find people on there who like Iron Man and Nora Roberts or Danielle Steele and Marvel Comics.

SP: So before, you would have tried to figure that all out yourself, but now you say, "I already know Facebook isn't worth my personal time, but I can outsource that and have somebody juggle that ball for me because I don't want to miss out on Facebook's opportunities, but I also don't want to lose all my time there."

TJ: Well, especially because how would you grow a following of people who like superheroes *and* love stories? You would have to convince them of the velocity of that niche before you could pay to have a group of people that do that. I just wouldn't. Now, if you adore Facebook, then rock your little Facebook heart out because the people who adore it tend to do really well. And LinkedIn. If you're a business writer, there's a lot of opportunities on LinkedIn. I don't know that there is a huge opportunity for fiction writers.

SP: LinkedIn is a great place for nonfiction.

TJ: It's a really great place. And so for the nonfiction writers, you're going to make money on your authority and speaking and developing products. So that's even a little different than looking at book sales or trying to dominate a genre. You're doing authority marketing as opposed to book sales.

David Wright: What are some of the biggest mistakes you see creative entrepreneurs making with social media?

TJ: Oh my goodness. So nobody wants to see forty posts in a row of "Buy my book," right?

SP: No, nobody has ever wanted that in the history of ever.

TJ: Nobody's ever said, "Please spam me over and over again with your book." Authors should not be selling their books on social media; they should be selling themselves. The purpose of *The Walking Dave* isn't to sell books; it's to get us to like you even more than we already did. And you may not be doing it to sell books, but you're showing us your humanity. We are starting to like you more as a person, which makes us like you more as an author.

I love Hugh Howey. I've bought a couple of his books. I think I read the big one, *Wool*. But I did that because he was so involved in author marketing. I thought, "Oh my gosh, I just adore this guy, and so I want to read his book. I want to see his writing process and where he works." And that helps you sell more books because people are buying into the author as opposed to buying your book from a post on Twitter.

JBT: How have your list-building efforts changed over time as you are trying to evolve your business?

TJ: If you want the Rambo ninja things, right now I'm using RoboLikes for one of my Twitters and one of my Instagrams. RoboLikes doesn't follow anybody, or make any sort of permanent connection; it just likes items that are hashtagged a certain way. So if you were a romance author and trying to grow your Instagram or your Twitter account, you could say, "I want to know whenever somebody says #amreading, or #readingromance or whatever the hashtags are."

I found a really good horror hashtag today. And so if you are a horror writer, you would like things posted with this hashtag. This makes it easy to granularly grow your Twitter. Johnny, you know this. Functionally, anybody who talks to you, you follow. They've already said, "Hey, I like you enough to talk to you," so you follow them; they are going to follow you. Twitter is very much a back-and-forth — you follow me, I follow you. You can comment on somebody's post, and they will follow you.

On Instagram, same thing. You can like their posts. You can talk to them; you can do searches for hashtags because as an author you want to be following your readers. If you're writing a book about people dying in a diner, you don't necessarily want to be following people who like kittens; you want to be following people that like horror stories.

DW: And murdering people in diners.

JBT: What if you like kittens that are in diners, specifically?

TJ: Well, you know, I think that probably that would be a hard niche to find.

SP: You might be surprised.

TJ: You might be surprised, yeah. Sean did a whole series on defining your avatar. And I think this is more important on social than for finding potential readers. You can get people to read your book if they like your genre, whether or not you know exactly who you are writing for, right?

SP: Yeah, that's true.

TJ: Okay, on social media, if you are randomly following people, you'll have no luck whatsoever and no any kind of sales or any kind of email list or street team or anything like that. You have to find followers who already like people like you.

SP: Yeah, that makes perfect sense. And in that vein, there's a difference between online and offline marketing, so how important is networking and knowing other people in person? You're speaking next month in Florida. How important are events like that in general, and how have you integrated that into your business? How have you iterated the amount of networking you do over time? Do you do more or less than you used to?

TJ: I have done less than I used to because we adopted three kids, and the opportunity isn't as big anymore. But when I'm going to speak, I have business cards, and the only two social accounts on that card are Twitter and Instagram. Why would I drive people to Facebook if I'm not going to engage with them there?

So I think — and you and I were talking about this, Sean — I think do 90/10 on this. You know, it's tempting to want to be on every social network. It's tempting to see the glamor of Facebook and think, *Oh, there's billions of people, and they'll share your stuff.* But unless you are willing to spend time there, nobody will pay attention to you. An inch deep and a mile wide won't do you any good. You need to go really deep into something and really be present. That includes speaking — make sure the audience knows your Twitter handle.

JBT: What are the biggest challenges you've faced while moving your business forward?

TJ: Staying away from shiny objects. My keyword this year — actually, yours from last year — is *optimize*. I'm only allowed to do *more of what I already do*. I'm doubling down on my blogs, and writing almost every day. I'm doubling down on Instagram and trying to post daily. I am doing more webinars, interviews, and podcasts. That's it. Have you guys heard of Blab and Periscope?

JBT: Heard of Periscope.

SP: I've heard of Periscope, not Blab.

TJ: Snapchat and ...

JBT: Snapchat is where we send naked pictures to each other, right?

TJ: You and Dave?

JBT: Yes, of course.

TJ: It's really easy to say, "Oh, everybody is talking about Periscope. I should be doing Periscope. I have to build up a following in Periscope." Or your friends may try to peer pressure you into doing Instagram, and you are just not going to do it. I think it's super-important to optimize whatever you have, and I think that a lot of us have assets that we don't really use. Like, I have huge social networks that I wasn't necessarily taking advantage of. I've been using Meet Edgar, which is a paid website, but not expensive. It allows you to load a library of everything you've ever made. And because I'm a prolific content producer, I have hundreds of blog posts. I have twenty-plus books and courses. You load it in, then it spits it out forever. So that's a handy tool I've been using. It only works on Facebook, Twitter, and LinkedIn.

DW: So how do you deal with trolls?

TJ: I'm oblivious to people. I don't really care what they think. But that's a valid question because there are an awful lot of people out there who aren't feeling like they can broadcast their message because they're worried that trolls will get them. And trolls — just in case you don't know — are aggressively mean. So there's a really big thing about women programmers that some have gotten death threats, and there are gangs of people that will come and just be mean to them.

There's a saying, "Don't feed the trolls." If somebody leaves you a horrible review, don't talk to them. If somebody says something nasty or doesn't agree with you on a Facebook post, you can ignore them. That's your prerogative. If it's inappropriate and nasty, delete it or block them. At the end of the day, it truly is your world, and if they are unhappy about it, then just ignore them. Do trolls get you, Dave?

DW: I starve the trolls, then I hunt them down and murder them.

TJ: I think it's a valid concern. Do you get lots of trolls, or are you worried about getting trolls?

DW: Generally speaking, we don't get a lot. We have in the past, and I think we don't feed into it, and typically we know the score. I've dealt with bullies all of my life, so I know that. But I know a lot of people that do find it difficult, especially a lot of artists who are sensitive types, and they take it very personally. Sometimes, they are afraid, and it's easy to be in that area. I think the more you ignore or eliminate it at the very beginning, the less likely it will be to escalate because trolls are usually looking for attention.

SP: Yeah, I don't think we get more than our share of trolls, and I'm not worried about it. But I do think that's something that artists in general have to worry about because they *are* sensitive, and are putting themselves out there by nature of what they do.

TJ: If you are sensitive, and you care about what other people think, and you are already getting negative reviews on Amazon that feel like a personal attack, you might think, "Why would I go on social media and open myself up for that kind of thing, too?"

SP: Yeah, I think it's something that artists want to be aware of. We've iterated through a little of that, and we talk in the book about how we used to deal with criticism, because there's a difference between legitimate criticism and trolls. You've *criticized* us before, but it always comes from such a loving place: "Hey, you guys are awesome, but you could really be doing this thing better." And that breed of criticism helps you to grow and improve your business, versus a troll, who is always just hating.

DW: It's about them, not you.

TJ: Yeah.

SP: If you're afraid of trolls, then it's difficult to be yourself online. So how can an artist relax enough to truly be themselves? Is that something that you've had to work through at all? Have you had to learn to be a different version of Tara or the best possible version of Tara, or has there been any kind of a learning curve there?

TJ: Well, when I was married and we didn't have kids, I didn't think about it at all. I don't live an exciting, you know, fabulous life. I go and speak, I talk about marketing, I have marketing friends. If I go to a bar, it's because I'm meeting marketing people. It's really — it's not that kind of eccentric life. But then I got my kids, and I didn't want to put pictures of them out. But I've never tried to censor my life or change what I put out there.

SP: So you're not redacted like Dave.

TJ: Yeah, I'm not ▮▮▮▮▮. You can look at my address. I have a mother-in-law, three kids, two dogs, two cats, a six-foot-six husband. God bless you, come, and take some of them — just not the little one. But I do know that people struggle with feeling disingenuous by only showing the good parts. I see that a lot. People are like, "Oh well, but you only show the good parts of your life. You are only saying the good things that are happening." Well, I'm a private person for being such a public figure. If I was going to say something mean about Sean, I would say it to my girlfriend. I would never in a million years dream of going in public and saying anything bad about anyone. I assume that anything I do online is public, including my email. Do I have a kind of best life? Yeah, I only take pictures when my daughter and I are looking at the cute bunnies because bunnies sell. If I put bunnies in an Instagram hashtag, I'm going to get more followers.

SP: But if you saw a dead bunny while on a walk, you wouldn't take a picture of that.

TJ: Dave could post a dead bunny on a walk, and it might appeal to his readership, right?

DW: That might be pushing it.

SP: Right, nobody likes a dead bunny.

JBT: Tara, what's the best piece of advice you would give to an author trying to optimize her social media profiles?

TJ: I was thinking about this a lot. You guys talk about not being exclusive to Amazon. It's hard to generate true fans and connections on Facebook if you're sending all your traffic to a black hole. I started sending traffic to my website and/or to Shopify. I have a Shopify site where I only have a couple of my titles. But I *have* sold books to those people, and now have their contact information, which I wouldn't have in Amazon. So I guess one of my key tips is to find a way to have something between a Facebook post and just sending them to Amazon where all that competition is.

JBT: All right, fantastic. I think that's the last question we had about iterating and optimizing. Thanks so much for joining us, Tara. What's the best place to find you? Is it marketingart-fully.com?

TJ: Yeah, marketing the pretty way, or they can email me at Tara@marketingartfully.com.

JBT: And I'm going to guess, based on what you were telling us about your own social media presence, that you want them to follow you on twitter @TARAdactyl.

TJ: TARAdactyl, or Tara Jacobsen on Instagram.

JBT: All right, excellent. Thanks so much for joining us!

SP: Thank you, Tara!

Steve Kamb

Johnny B. Truant: Today's guest is Steve Kamb, founder of Nerd Fitness. Before we get started can you describe what that is, then we'll start talking about the ways you've iterated and optimized.

Steve Kamb: Sure, Nerd Fitness is a worldwide community of nerds, average Joes and Jills who are supportive and helpful of each other, and their quests to live a healthier life.

JBT: Originally, it was just you, and now you have a team. How have you handled the incremental growth moving from then to where you are now?

SK: I started Nerd Fitness after stumbling across Tim Ferriss's *4-Hour Work Week*. A big component of his book was that everything kind of happens without you. It's a kind of a one-man business where you don't have to deal with employees and team building and things of that nature. For quite a while — I'm going to say two, maybe three years — I didn't have anybody else on my team. It was just me. I was answering all the emails — I tried to automate as many things as I could, but eventually it got to the point that I just couldn't do it anymore.

This was right around that time I found Richard Branson's *Losing My Virginity* book, which was absolutely phenomenal. He talks about how he structured his company and how he prioritizes happiness and adventure while still building hundreds of companies throughout the world. My perspective changed, and I was, like, "I think I'm ready to start building something now." I brought people on part time for as much as I could afford to pay them, and that sustained me for another few years, and just recently over the past two years it's gone from myself and one part-timer to one full-timer, myself, and another full-timer. Now we have eight or nine full-time people, in addition to a dozen other contractors and lawyers, accountants, etc.

It's become something way bigger than I ever would have expected or anticipated, or probably considered getting excited about. It has its challenges and things I'm struggling with, like trying to become a better leader, but it's also really fun. It's cool to watch other people that are as excited about what I'm trying to do with Nerd Fitness, and they're oftentimes far better at what they're doing than I was, and more excited. That means they can do a much better job.

Sean Platt: How has listening to your audience needs helped to define the overall direction that Nerd Fitness takes?

SK: Chris Guillebeau runs a fantastic website — Art of Non-Conformity — and has written multiple books, but I found him six or seven years ago, after he'd written a free ebook called *279 Days to Overnight Success*. He talks about writing and building an audience, asking them what they want, and creating those things. *Then* you have a business. I started by writing articles at Nerd Fitness, then eventually I asked the audience what they wanted. The most memorable one was asking our community what they wanted to be called.

The word community wasn't nerdy enough. We're not just a community; what are we? I posted a poll on Facebook and went through the blog. I said, "Hey, guys, what are we? Do you want to be part of building an empire, or do you want to help me start a rebellion? Which are you more excited about?" And I think it was like 70/30 in favor of starting a rebellion.

From that moment on, any time there's been a co-opportunity to ask the community what they're interested in — be it how the message boards are organized, what our contests should be, what our next product might look like, what we name something, or what's important to us — we've asked the community. We have fifty volunteer moderators, we can send out surveys, I can ask people in person during meet-ups. We consistently poll them: "What are you guys working on, what's your biggest struggle, what are you most excited about, how can we serve you, and how else can we best help to improve your life?"

SP: But that wasn't like an immediate thing, right? Wasn't it a year and a half before you got to that point? You suffered the blogging grind for a while building that audience, right?

SK: Oh yeah, I grinded, I think it was a solid eighteen months, and I remember the first nine months of writing I was publishing five articles a week, and then …

SP: What's an article; how long was that?

SK: They were about five hundred words at the time. I had read that everything needed to be short, because nobody has an attention span, so I was writing short, quick articles every day. I was getting very little traction, but then I stumbled across a gentleman by the name of Adam Baker, who had, at the time, run a website called Man Versus Debt. He wrote an article called "How to Not Suck at Blogging." I read it and realized, "Oh man, I suck at blogging." I went through his list of ten things, and I was, like, "Yup, yup, yup. I'm pretty terrible at this; I need to make some changes."

After nine months, I completely changed my writing style. I went from five short articles a week to two long ones. These days, Nerd Fitness articles are generally between two and three thousand words. They are full of Lego photos, and personally backed by published medical research and studies. I try to fill them with nerdy metaphors and as much of my personality as possible. Once I made that change, I think our subscriber number, like, doubled overnight. From that point on, it's been a much faster growth trajectory as a result of me finally finding my voice and writing in a way that I was actually exited about.

JBT: What have been the biggest roadbloc__
faster than you intended?

SK: Hiring more people. Sometimes, you have
before you're ready. Most of what we offer is free on__
ness. There are no ads on the website, so a lot of our h__
sions were a result of the rapidly expanding communit__
not a venture-backed company.

It started with just me and my initial $100 investm__
whatever that was eight years ago — to buy a domain and
ing space. I've grown it organically from there, so it's reall__
the past two years that's required a big personal investment
where this can go, what kind of team we need to build that ou__
and how we can use the team we have to turn this into a qual__
ity company even if the revenues might not line up with that,
just due to the fact that everything else is growing so quickly. I
think it sets us up in a way to capitalize on what this thing can
become.

David Wright: How have you dealt with managing expenses? Is there a story about a $2,500 domain you want to tell?

SK: You guys are all going to laugh at me. But yeah, the domain is *Level Up Your Life* aka the name of the book that I have coming out and also the tagline for Nerd Fitness since I started it. I remember looking years ago when I started Nerd Fitness and seeing that it was unavailable. Back then, I had no money. I didn't even bother checking again until four, five months ago. I saw that it was available for 2,500 bucks. I figured if the guy found out that I have a book, he'd probably say, "Never mind. I meant ten grand or whatever."

I emailed a collective group of friends, and I was, like, "Guys, should I spend the money on this?" And they were, like, "What are you, an idiot? Do you spend the $2,500 on the name of the book that you just wrote? *Of course you do.* Are you stupid?" Fortunately, it ended up being a domain for sale website, so it wasn't like I had to negotiate one on one. I guess the remnants of scrappy Internet blogger are tough to get rid of even though I'm now running a team scattered across the country.

SP: Your perspective changes, and it's so hard when you're robbing from Peter to pay Paul like we all are in the beginning. *Of course* that domain is worth $2,500 today, but it wouldn't have been worth $2,500 a couple of years earlier when you were still trying to build the business. Just because it's your tagline, that doesn't make it worth $2,500. Now, it's a core part of your brand and all of these other things — *that's* what makes it worth $2,500. Plus, you now have the revenue to support the purchase.

SK: Sure.

SP: But it's interesting because your perspective had to catch up with your reality.

SK: Yeah, that's a great way to put it. Well said, Sean.

SP: How have your list-building efforts changed — I know you had eighteen months where you were stuck in the blogging grind, and then a couple of years where you weren't really doing what you should have been doing. Do you want to talk about that a little bit?

SK: Yeah, so after nine months I'm working a full-time day job and writing five articles a week on Nerd Fitness. After nine months, I had ninety email and RSS subscribers, so I think I calculated that it was, like, half a person per blog post. For whatever reason, I was dumb enough to stick with it — ignorant or naive enough to think, "Hey, ninety! That's a pretty big number." Little did I know about demand of effort versus time involved.

Fortunately, I stumbled across Adam, and his article kind of galvanized me into rethinking how I was creating content. Eighteen months in, I finally plunked down the twenty-five bucks for a three-month contract with AWeber so I could start collecting email addresses. I spent eighteen months running the website and *not* collecting email, then another two and a half full years before I finally created a compelling reason to sign up for the list. Before then, it was just, "Sign up for my list, and you will get blog posts sent to your inbox."

SP: Which is what a lot of people do though, right?

SK: Sure, so I wrote an article on the paleo diet, then turned that article into a PDF. The bottom of the article said, "If you'd like this article in a redesigned PDF form, sign up for the email list." That one change pushed us from a hundred email sign-ups a day to maybe two hundred. Then six months after that, I finally redesigned the website, put a big call to action where it says, "Get these free ebooks when you join The Rebellion, blah blah blah," and overnight we went to from two hundred a day to seven hundred a day. That was all done organically; I was like, "Yup, OK. I guess I had been doing this wrong for four and a half years and trying not to … "

SP: Better late than never.

SK: Better late than never, exactly.

SP: That's a great example of iterating and optimizing right there. You realized, okay, RSS isn't the future: I need to get an opt-in, find out why people aren't signing up for my newsletter, figure out ways to improve that bribe, and on and on …

SK: Sure.

SP: It takes time; that's great.

SK: Yeah, and we've done that with the free ebooks and the ability to sign up for the email list. Our flagship course, the Nerd Fitness Academy, has been redone three or four times. When we initially launched, it was like, "Hey, we're thinking about creating an online course. Do you guys want to check it out?" We opened for four days then put on a full version six months later. A year after that, we added this whole questing feature and rebuilt it so that somebody could create a character and level up. From business to book to, I guess, content creation, everything has been to follow your path, and as you said: *iterate and optimize to slowly improve.*

JBT: How much is your current business dependent on you? Are you able to separate from your business much, or is it still *you*, and you've got to be there?

SK: It's much better now than a year ago. It's still pretty dependent on me from a content perspective, because I truly enjoy writing, but I'm learning more and more that I can't keep up with it all. If I'm the bottleneck, and that bottleneck is content creation, and content creation is what drives new readers, I need to be able to step away from that. We lost a good mutual friend earlier this year in a tragic accident — a large portion of his business was dependent on him, and he had other team members and things like that.

It certainly made me reevaluate my value and how I can best serve my team and my community. We just brought in a writer to provide a perspective for moms and dads to write about ways their children can stay healthy. I was trying to identify other writers that I think can help bridge the gap between relying on Steve and still providing fun, creative content that's well done and thoroughly researched.

If it's anything like everything else I've done with team building up to this point, I'll probably discover that once I find the right person, they are way better at it than me, and that I shouldn't have waited nearly as long as I did to give up the reins. So I'm excited to learn that lesson in the next six months.

SP: It's really hard to surrender control, but how often do you do it then think, "Well, that was a mistake"? It's part of the iterating process, right, because people don't know what you know, and they have to adjust. But *not* doing it is always more expensive.

SK: I didn't want to give up control of answering emails. I was so proud of the fact that I answered every email that came in the Nerd Fitness inbox. I thought, *These emails are addressed to me, and there's nobody that could ever answer them the way that I blah blah blah.* I finally admitted, "I need help on some of these." Then I saw some of the responses from one of my team members, and I was like, "This is way better than the email I was going to write." Not only that, but it got done on time, where I was, like, three four weeks behind on responses. I mean it was bad. I had disclaimers all over the contact page warning that you will not be contacted or responded to in a long time. That's a horrible way to run a business, so …

DW: You may as well write your email, put it in a bottle, and throw it in the ocean.

SK: That might have gotten there faster. From then on, I thought, *Okay, what are some other things I can get off my plate? And how can I spend my time educating, teaching, promoting, and supporting other team members, and giving them what they need to get their jobs done?*

DW: How have you dealt with copycats in the industry?

SK: I like to think imitation is the serious form of flattery. I try not to waste too much time with it. Unless it's like website scraping or copyright infringement, I let them do what they're doing. When I started Nerd Fitness eight years ago, being nerdy wasn't a marketing decision. It was, like, this is who I am, and this is who I want to help; let's help nerds get fit.

Now thanks to Marvel and the success of *Star Wars* and what Disney has done with both franchises, being nerdy is in, and thanks to those comic characters, the actors that play those characters like being fit and nerdy at the same time — that's also in. It's led to a significant amount of people jumping into this industry and getting behind it. Overall, I think it's a net positive. If it's helping more people get fit, that's cool. If people want to steal aspects of Nerd Fitness that work for them, or can help their particular businesses grow, that's cool. I have no problem with that, and any time I spend on that is less time I'm spending on building my team, taking care of myself.

People have created copycat products or kind of piggybacked on what we've done, and I initially got — not pissed off about it, but I wondered if I should spend my time and energy trying to fight it. People said, "Dude, life is way too short; you have a community of people that need your help and a team of people that want your support. Spend your time there; everybody else will still be playing one step behind if you can continually move forward and work on what's next rather than worry about what just got done."

DW: Typically, jocks and nerds were enemies back in the day …

SK: *Revenge of the Nerds*, that's the entire plot.

DW: You've got the dumb jock mentality versus these nerds getting fit — is there any sort of resentment between the communities, or are they getting together now?

SK: Thanks to the power of the Internet and the ability to connect people, there's a home for everybody. Be they a vegan marathon runner or a paleo power lifting sports fanatic or a mixed martial artist who happens to love collecting stamps or whatever. I think everybody kind of hangs out with their group of people, and also through the Internet people might not pick fights but poke fun at another group that doesn't line up with their particular philosophy.

If we do it on Nerd Fitness, it's all done in good fun. Our community is segmented by video gaming types, depending on how they like to train. There is always some intercommunity competition between like the warriors of the power lifters and the scouts of the runners, and the druids are the yoga practitioners and things like that. There might be some fun, inner competition between them. I think now, like, the whole nerds versus jocks thing, I don't know. *Ninja Warrior* has kind of bridged the gap — it's this phenomenal show with these incredible athletes who also tend to be very, very nerdy people.

Once you get out of high school, you'll find that even a lot of jocks have nerdy tendencies, and someone just getting started with training can probably still look to that person for inspiration and education. I think it's much less of an issue now than it was back in the day, and certainly less of an issue once you're an adult compared to when you were in junior high or high school.

DW: Breaking down the walls, all right.

SP: How do you see the next few years of Nerd Fitness unfolding?

SK: Geez, I don't know. World domination, interplanetary colonization? Just really ridiculously smart, well-trained nerds traveling all over the place. I hope to see the *Level Up Your Life* book inspiring a new group of people that would have otherwise never found Nerd Fitness. There is a component in the book in which you can visit levelupyourlife.com, create a completely free character, write your own backstory, create quest submissions to complete in exchange for earning experience points and leveling up.

I'm excited to truly explore this concept of life being a game, having a Nerd Fitness avatar that carries over to every aspect of the Nerd Fitness universe, and seeing what we can do with that. That will be the perfect example of iterating and optimizing because it's something I've had in my head for years and years and years and years and years, and only now do I finally have the resources and the ability to hire the right people to build this thing out. I'm very excited to launch that. I'm hopeful that people get excited about it as well and jump on this idea that they can complete quest submissions in real life, level up avatar versions of themselves, and get off the couch.

Then, after that, I think there's going to be some amazing opportunities for us to get together in person. We have *Camp Nerd Fitness* — an event that takes place once a year. Every year, it's the coolest thing ever, and so much fun to see all these people get together in the same place and know that they're not alone. I want to bring that to individual cities in some way on a much more regular basis so that people can take this concept of the Rebellion, and have other like-minded individuals where they can talk about deadlifting and Harry Porter or World of Warcraft, and running their first marathon in the same conversation.

SP: There's something that I really like about you, that I think harmonizes with the way we think at Sterling & Stone. We rarely ever go for the easy button because …

DW: No, we hit the hard button — over and over.

SP: We really do; we slam it like we're playing Whack-a-Mole, like it's …

DW: The hard button, by the way, isn't just one button; it's, like, fifteen different buttons you have to hit all at once.

SP: Yeah, we're great at hitting the hard button, and so for us that would be marketing to a nonfiction audience. Building a big how-to-be-a-successful-published-author course would be our easy button. We'll get into education at some point, when we're ready to do it and can execute it really, really well, but we don't want to be the guys who make a living talking about writing; we want to be the guys who are making a living writing. There's enough of that in our industry. So that's our easy button, and we've never pushed it.

Your easy button is selling supplements, which you adamantly will never do. You know you can make ten times the amount on your investment, but you're not willing to do that. Do you want to talk about that and how that influences your business, because that's a great revenue stream that you've basically closed the door on.

SK: When you play any video game, there's the opportunity to change the difficulty setting from very easy to very hard. There are certain types of people that like to play the games on very easy and fight through it and look for cheats and codes and whatever. Then other people want to beat this on the toughest difficulty and see what they're capable of. Unfortunately, when I play video games I pick just above normal; I don't pick the excruciatingly difficult one. I don't have time to do that, but I think how I've chosen to build Nerd Fitness, very much trying to think in terms of what's best for my community and more importantly what's going to be best for my community and my company ten years from now.

There have been so many opportunities to take quick fixes and scores, to make a bunch of fast money that didn't line up with what I wanted Nerd Fitness to be. There's never been an ad on Nerd Fitness, which I'm proud of. We get emails every day telling us that we should be selling supplements and hearing from many people in the Internet marketing space, especially in the Internet fitness marketing space. They are like, "Why don't you just white label protein and sell supplements, slap a nerdy name on it — *you'll make a bazillion dollars!*

I'm, like, "That's not what I believe in. That's crap, and that is not what I want to do, and you don't need those things, therefore why would I promote that? That's terrible." Somebody approached me a few years ago and wanted to create, like, the next P90X or whatever. They wanted to make Nerd Fitness infomercials. They were going to fly me up to New York because they wanted to create The Nerd Fitness Workout. You get your eighteen DVDs at this low-low price, and blah blah blah.

SP: This company had built some really big names, right?

SK: Yeah, built many names that you guys and everyone else would be familiar with. I thought about it, and even talked to my dad. He was like, "What is your gut saying?" I said, "This isn't us. I don't see myself doing that; it doesn't feel right." So ultimately, I turned it down, and I don't regret that decision for a second because this doesn't line up with what we're doing.

The *Level Up Your Life* book could have been called *Nerd Fitness*, and I could have repurposed content from all the workouts I'd already created, the seven hundred-plus articles on the site. Everybody said, "Why don't you just write the Nerd Fitness book; are you an idiot? Do that, and you can have it done in two months." But I didn't want to write that book. They were like, "It's already written; just put it together." But that's not exciting to me. I want to write a whole new book and torture myself and go through the process while trying to have some fun with it.

JBT: It all sounds so familiar.

SP: When you first told me about the book, you said, "And it's actually really good."

SK: It's funny. I've had multiple people, somebody at the publisher, and a few people on my team that have read the book then said, "Steve, this is actually really good." And I was like, "What were you expecting?"

JBT: Thanks?

SK: Yeah, thanks, I guess. Like is that a backhanded compliment? But I am proud that it is actually really good, and I do feel very happy with how it turned out and what it became. It definitely wasn't an easy process. I think there are plenty of other decisions that I'll have to make in the next few years that will pit easy against hard. We've actually put together a Nerd Fitness ethos as a team. These are our rules as a company, and if it doesn't check all these boxes, it doesn't matter how lucrative that decision might be. We'll probably turn it down if it doesn't line up with what we're trying to create.

I feel confident and comfortable that I've made all those decisions the right way up until now and am hopeful that regardless of how big Nerd Fitness may become, that I continue to make decisions that way. Because at the end of the day, I want to go to bed happy and proud of what I've done, then wake up excited about what we can do. So I try to keep it on that path.

DW: If you change your mind and decide to create some sort of protein thing, just call it up-up, down-down, left-right, left-right, B-A, B-A, Select, Start.

SP: Dave's been waiting ten minutes to say that.

DW: Yes I have.

JBT: Steve's book is *Level Up Your Life*, which I've heard is actually pretty good. His website is at levelupyourlife.com and of course nerdfitness.com, so thank you for joining us, Steve.

SP: I heard he paid a premium for that domain.

JBT: I did hear that. All right, thanks, everybody.

SK: Good opportunity, guys.

**"Write. Publish. Repeat"
Conversations**

The Smarter Artist, #1 Amazon
Bestselling Authors, Podcasters, ...

★ ★ ★ ★ ★ (12)

Write. Publish. Repeat. **Conversations** is a 30+-part instructional video series (retail price $49) in which the authors elaborate on the cutting-edge things learned in self-publishing since releasing the book version of their #1 bestselling guide *Write. Publish. Repeat.* in 2013.

Visit the link below to get the *Write. Publish. Repeat.* Conversations course for FREE!
SterlingAndStone.net/repeaters

How would you like to learn in your spare time with hundreds of hours of FREE CONTENT that will help you get smarter faster? Hear us answer our most frequently asked questions, discuss the latest ins and outs of our business, offer secret peeks at our creative and entrepreneurial process, conduct interviews with authors, artists, and industry leaders, and give you FREE audio versions of our books and stories.

Visit the link below to discover your new favorite (FREE) audio addiction NOW!
SterlingAndStone.net/fm

About the Authors

JOHNNY B. TRUANT is a speaker, co-host of the top-rated Self Publishing Podcast, and the author of over 5 million words of popular fiction.

Johnny, along with partners Sean Platt and David Wright, also launched the *Fiction Unboxed* project in 2014 -- a record-setting Kickstarter after which Johnny and Sean wrote a full-length novel in 30 days, starting without any ideas or genre, in front of a live audience, sharing every detail of the process including story meetings, emails, and raw story drafts. The novel birthed through *Fiction Unboxed (The Dream Engine,* first in the Blunderbuss/Alterra series) went on to spawn what the Sterling & Stone team calls "open-source fiction": an open story world in which any author may write and publish without requiring permission and without paying royalties to the world's creators.

Johnny's fiction works (mostly co-authored with Sean Platt) include the political sci-fi serial *The Beam*, the fantasy/western mash-up *Unicorn Western* books, the satirical *Fat Vampire* series, the literary mindbender *Axis of Aaron*, and too many others to count.

Johnny, Sean, and David host their trendsetting, boundary-pushing podcasts every week on the YouTube, iTunes, Stitcher, and their cornerstone independent author website at SterlingAndStone.net.

SEAN PLATT is a speaker, founder of Sterling & Stone, and author of more than five million words of published fiction. Together with co-authors David Wright and Johnny B. Truant, Sean has written the series *Yesterdays Gone, WhiteSpace, ForNevermore, Available Darkness, Dark Crossings, Unicorn Western, The Beam, Namaste, Robot Proletariat, Cursed, The Dream Engine, Invasion, Greens, Space Shuttle,* and *Everyone Gets Divorced,* the traditionally published titles *Z2134* and *Monstrous,* and the standalone novels, *Axis of Aaron, Crash, 12,* and *Threshold.* Sean also writes for children under the name Guy Incognito and has more of his share of nose.

Sean lives with his wife and children in Austin, Texas, and has more than his share of nose. Follow him on Twitter at @ seanplatt.

DAVID WRIGHT is one half of Collective Inkwell, a publishing company specializing in dark fiction and serialized fiction. Inspired by Stephen King's serialized story "The Green Mile" Wright and co-author Sean Platt set out to bring serials back into fashion in summer 2011 with their post-apocalyptic serial, *Yesterday's Gone,* which has since been followed by dozens of other books, serials, and series.

When he's not writing books, David can be found writing about writing and pop culture at his blog at DavidwWright. com. In his "off-time" he can be found chasing his five year old around the house, cleaning up a cat whose sole talent is producing prolific amounts of hair and poop, or ranting about stuff as his wife rolls her eyes.

In September 2012, the writing duo signed a deal with Amazon Publishing's 47North to write two Kindle Serials, *Z2134* and *Monstrous.*

Sean, Johnny and Dave, also hosts several podcasts on the Sterling & Stone podcast network. You can see the full lineup of shows at at SterlingAndStone.net/podcasts, and easily subscribe on iTunes, Stitcher, or wherever you prefer to get your podcasts.

What We've Written

OTHER BOOKS BY THE SMARTER ARTIST SUPER FRIENDS

Our publishing company Sterling & Stone has six imprints, each with its own style, voice, and extensive catalog. They are:

The Smarter Artist (nonfiction)
Collective Inkwell (dark fantasy, horror, and sci-fi)
Realm & Sands (inquisitive fiction)
Guy Incognito (intelligent kid lit)
LOL (stupid comedy)

To see all our books across all six S&S imprints, please visit:
http://sterlingandstone.net/books